RED STAR OVER IRAQ

JOHAN FRANZÉN

RED STAR OVER IRAQ

Iraqi Communism Before Saddam

Columbia University Press
New York

Columbia University Press
Publishers Since 1893
New York
cup.columbia.edu

Library of Congress Cataloging-in-Publication Data

Franzén, Johan.
Red star over Iraq : Iraqi communism before Saddam / Johan Franzén.
p. cm.
Includes bibliographical references and index.
ISBN 978-0-231-70230-0 (cloth: alk. paper)
ISBN 978-0-231-80013-6 (ebook)
1. Communism—Iraq—History. 2. Hizb al-Shuyu'i al-'Iraqi—History.
3. Iraq—Politics and government—20th century. I. Title.

HX385.A6F73 2011
324.2567'07509045—dc22

2011003654

∞

Columbia University Press books are printed on permanent and durable acid-free paper. This book is printed on paper with recycled content.
Printed in India

c 10 9 8 7 6 5 4 3 2 1

کی لا ننسی

CONTENTS

LIST OF ILLUSTRATIONS

ABBREVIATIONS

BRC	Baghdad Regional Committee (mid-level ICP organisation)
CC	Central Committee
COA	Committee for the Organisation Abroad (ICP organisation for exiled members in Eastern Europe)
Comintern	The Communist International
CPC	Communist Party of China
CPSU	Communist Party of the Soviet Union
ICP	Iraqi Communist Party
IRC	Iraqi Regional Command (Iraqi section of the Ba'th Party)
KDP	Kurdistan Democratic Party
KUTV	Communist University for the Toilers of the East
NDP	National Democratic Party
PLO	Palestine Liberation Organisation
RAF	Royal Air Force (Britain)
RCC	Revolution Command Council (main Ba'thist governing institution)
SCIRI	Supreme Council for the Islamic Revolution in Iraq

A NOTE ON TRANSLITERATION AND STYLE

This study utilises a simplified version of the transliteration system used by the *International Journal of Middle East Studies*. Full transliteration of personal names, place names and names of organisations in Arabic has been avoided in order to enhance readability. For this reason, diacritics have been omitted. Only the Arabic letters ʿAyn and Hamzah have been indicated through the symbols (') and ('), respectively. For Arabic place names with well-known spelling in English, the latter have been used (e.g. Mosul instead of al-Mawsil, Basra rather than al-Basrah, Cairo in lieu of al-Qahirah, and so on). For less well-known places, or smaller towns and villages, the original name has been kept (e.g. al-Hillah, al-Sulaymaniyyah, etc.). Personal names in Arabic have all been retained in their original form, even when an English usage is available (e.g. Jamal 'Abd al-Nasir rather than Gamal Abdel Nasser and 'Abd al-Karim Qasim instead of Abdel Karim Qassem). The only exceptions to this rule are Christian Arab names, where their English equivalents rather than their Arabic forms have been employed (e.g. George instead of 'Jurj' and Peter as opposed to 'Butrus'). Some personal names have been spelt in accordance with how they are pronounced rather than their correct Modern Standard Arabic transliteration (e.g. Fahad instead of Fahd). For some personal names formed on the Arabic active participle (ism fāʿil), the letter 'e' have been used instead of the normal 'i' to avoid the name being read on the faʿīl pattern. Thus, for instance the name 'Ṣāliḥ' has been transliterated as 'Saleh', "Ārif" as "Aref", and 'Shākir' as 'Shaker'. Qasim, however, has been kept with an 'i'.

GLOSSARY

agha (*pl. aghawat*)	Kurdish tribal chief/landlord
'alim (*pl. 'ulama'*)	religious scholar; plural form used to denote religious classes
'asabiyyah	tribal solidarity; national consciousness; clannishness; bigotry; zealous partisanship; racialism
chalabi	title of merchants with high social status; also a common surname
dunum	Ottoman area unit, which continued to be used in independent Iraq (from Ottoman Turkish *dönüm*, deriving from the verb *dönmek*, meaning to turn); 1 *dunum* ≈ 0.618 acre
effendi (*pl. effendiyyah*)	Ottoman bureaucrat or member of ruling elite; later came to denote educated or semi-educated population in general (from Turkish *efendi*; originally from medieval Greek *aphentes*, an alteration of Greek *authentes*, a lord or master)
fallah	peasant
halqah	study circle (ICP)
hirafi	professional, i.e. a worker with vocational skills
hikimdar	governor; commandant
intifadah	uprising, rebellion (lit. 'shaking off')
jahiliyyah	pre-Islamic period; lit. 'ignorance of divine guidance', referring to the condition of Arab society before the revelation of the Qur'an

jihad	holy war
kasib (*pl. kasabah*)	earner; lowly people without regular employment earning their livelihood from odd jobs
kuttab	Islamic elementary school, usually attached to a mosque
liwa'	administrative unit, smaller than a *muhafazah*
mallak	landowner
mas'ul	comrade-in-charge within the ICP (lit. 'responsible')
mihni	professional, i.e. a worker with vocational skills
mu'adhdhin	muezzin, announcer of the hour of prayer
muhafazah	governorate
mukhabarat	security service
mulla (*Persian*)	mullah; male religious teacher or leader (from Arabic mawlan, pl. mawalin)
nahdah	Arabic literary renaissance in the nineteenth century
peshmergah (*Kurdish*)	Kurdish guerrilla unit (lit. 'those who face death')
qutr (*pl. aqtar*)	region; country; term used for Arab states by pan-Arabists to denote separate constituent parts of the 'Arab nation' (e.g. *al-qutr al-misri*—Egypt, *al-qutr al-suri*—Syria, and so on)
rafiq (*pl. rifaq*)	comrade (in communist terminology)
sayyid (*pl. sadah*)	person claiming descent from the Prophet Muhammad; honorific title
sharif (pl. *ashraf*)	person claiming descent from the Prophet Muhammad, i.e. a nobleman
Sharifians	followers of Sharif Husayn bin 'Ali, the Emir of Mecca, in his British-sponsored Arab revolt against the Ottoman Empire during World War I; later, in Iraq, those military men who followed the Sharif's son, Faysal, from Syria to Iraq, where he became king and they came to constitute the new political elite
shaykh (*pl. shuyukh*)	tribal chief; elderly man; title of religious scholar; master of Sufi order

sirkal	foreman supervising agricultural production at the behest of landlords
wali	governor (of a *wilayah*)
wilayah	Ottoman administrative unit (Turkish: *vilayet*)

ACKNOWLEDGEMENTS

Sources on clandestine, illegal organisations are never easy to come by, and when one's chosen subject of study on top of that deals with an organisation operating in a country known for political repression and lack of freedom of press, it makes it even harder to find the necessary material. Thus, without the willing assistance of senior Iraqi communists in exile and back in Iraq it would have been virtually impossible to write a meaningful historical account of the Iraqi Communist Party.

I am therefore hugely indebted to Salam Ali, Ghanem Hamdoun, 'Adel Haba and Ibrahim Tahir, who unselfishly assisted me in finding the necessary material and answering questions without ever interfering with my interpretation. I am also grateful to Jasem al-Halwa'i and Dr. Kazem Habib for having agreed to be interviewed for this study, and I am especially thankful to Jasem who kindly sent me his meticulously detailed unpublished memoirs. A similar thank you is extended to Shawkat Khaznadar who cordially sent me a copy of his hard-to-come-by memoirs. Appreciation is also due to ICP-critique Hesqil Kojaman who I interviewed in London. He generously gave me a copy of his unpublished memoirs, as did 'Adel Haba.

I would like to thank Professor Peter Sluglett, who read the manuscript and offered valuable comments. Professor Charles Tripp at SOAS has been helpful and has read drafts of my writings on Iraqi history and politics. Michael Dwyer of C. Hurst & Co. Publishers deserves my gratitude for believing in me and for calmly guiding me through the publication process.

On a personal level, I am much obliged to my parents who patiently supported me during the writing of this book. The greatest debt, however, I owe to Sada who always stood by my side and selflessly supported me through thick and thin.

INTRODUCTION

This study analyses the ideological and political development of the Iraqi Communist Party (ICP) before Saddam Husayn's usurpation of power in 1979. Prior to the Husaynian era (1979–2003), the ICP was one of the most prominent and influential political parties in Iraq. At certain moments during this period, the ICP attracted a mass following making it arguably the largest and most important communist party in the Arab world at the time. This book seeks to answer the question of how the ICP came to play such a notable and instrumental role in Iraqi politics. How could a party with a rigorous ideology steeped in the political traditions of Europe become not only a political factor in Iraqi politics, but, crucially, an ideological influence shaping culture and other social aspects of Iraqi society during the period under study?

The book aims to show how the ICP went from being an 'internationalist' communist party, established with the help of the Communist International in Moscow and ultimately intended to pursue revolutionary policies aimed at advancing the 'world revolution' in Iraq, to becoming a largely 'Iraqi' political party. Unlike communist parties elsewhere in the Third World, and in particular in Eastern Europe, the ICP never developed into a satellite of the Communist Party of the Soviet Union (CPSU). While ideologically constrained by the ideational framework laid down by its rigorous Marxist-Leninist ideology, invented and reinvented over time by Moscow, the ICP constantly stretched the limit of this framework, and at times arguably transgressed what could reasonably be considered orthodox Marxism-Leninism. It is primarily this aspect of the ideological development of the ICP that this study addresses. Analysing the intersections of communist internationalism and local nationalisms, the study demonstrates how the ICP was instrumental in shaping not only Iraqi territorial nationalism (*Wataniyyah*) but also how it was influential in the development of local pan-Arabism and Kurdish nationalism (*Qawmiyyah*). In taking part in the intellectual and political production and formulation of these nationalist ideologies, reacting to and interacting with local and regional developments, the ICP arguably developed into a leftist nationalist party during the period in question.

The foundation of the ICP in 1934 marked the beginning of a new era in Iraqi politics. Gradually, over the course of the 1940s and 1950s, political mobilisation along lines of ethnicity, tribe and sect began to give way to modern forms of political mobilisation based on ideologies and carried out by political parties. The ICP epitomised this development; it drew support from all sections of Iraqi society, from Kurds, Sunnis, Shi'is, Jews, Christians and so on. Indeed, one of its founding members and its legendary leader in the 1940s—Yusuf Salman Yusuf (Comrade Fahad)—was an Arab Chaldean Christian. He was later followed by Husayn Ahmad al-Radi (Salam 'Adel), who was a Shi'i. He, in turn, was succeeded by 'Aziz Muhammad—a Sunni Kurd. Likewise, in the rank-and-file membership the party counted supporters among Iraq's various sects and ethnic groups.

In fact, in the make-up of both its leadership and wider membership, the ICP was a genuinely 'Iraqi' party inasmuch as it, better than any other political party operating in Iraq before or after, represented the population as a whole rather than sectarian interests. Yet, this development occurred more by default than by design. The ICP was neither set up to represent the interests of the various ethnic and sectarian groups in Iraq, nor did it pursue everyday policies that were particularly catered for any group. The question is thus, why did the ICP attract such a large following from so diverse sections of Iraqi society? The key to answering this question lies in the transformation that the ICP underwent from its foundation as a Marxist-Leninist organisation in 1934, until the 1958 Revolution when it had turned into a true 'Iraqi' mass party.

However, this development came at a price; the ICP's turning into an 'Iraqi' political party meant that it went against many of the ideological principles upon which it had been founded. Ultimately this led to an ambiguity among party leaders and members as to what the ICP's role in Iraqi politics should be. Was the purpose of the party to work for a revolution and the establishment of the 'dictatorship of the proletariat' or was it to support local 'progressive' regimes against the evils of 'imperialism'? These quandaries were constantly at the forefront of the party's ideological struggles. Before the 1958 Revolution, when the country was run by an unscrupulous monarch, put in place and ultimately protected by Britain, whose local government 'advisors' ensured that British interests were guarded in Iraq, the ICP's main political policy of anti-imperialism and opposition to the regime worked well. Its staunch ideology of anti-monarchism, anti-Britishism and anti-imperialism, coupled with its championing of democracy and social justice in domestic politics rendered the party much of its popular support. Ironically, it was the successful overthrow of the monarchical regime and ousting of British influence with the 1958 Revolution that proved to be the real litmus test for the ICP.

From having been a clandestine oppositional party, operating under unfavourable conditions, hunted down and executed by the political police of the monarchical regime, the members of the ICP now found themselves in the midst of the new politics of the Iraqi state. Caught in the political and ideological struggles of local and regional *watani* and *qawmi* nationalists, as well as seeing the country drawn into the global politics of the Cold War, the party now had to take a practical stand on many of the issues that it before had only commented on in principle. Thus, the period from the 1958 Revolution until the rise of Saddam Husayn in 1979 was the crucial period for the party, both politically and ideologically.

Saddam's rise to power marked the end of the period of ideological politics in Iraq and equally meant the end of the ICP as a major political player on the Iraqi political scene. As such, it constitutes a natural cut-off point for this book.

1

THE MAKING OF A NATION

Creating a New State and Political Elites, 1918–1932

The modern Iraqi state was constructed in 1920 out of the three Ottoman provinces (*wilayahs*) of Mosul, Baghdad and Basra, which were combined into a new entity called Iraq following the Allied defeat of the Ottoman Empire in World War I.

Initially, British administrators were intent on setting up direct colonial rule in Iraq based on the model of its Indian Crown Colony. However, indigenous protests soon challenged their plans, as evidenced by the outbreak of the 1920 revolt, popularly known as the 'Revolution of 1920' (*Thawrat al-'Ishrin*). Though this 'revolution' was more a tribal uprising than a coherent nationalist response to foreign domination, it can still be seen as a first step toward 'national cohesiveness' as it brought together previously separated Sunni and Shi'i communities in joint political action.[1] While ultimately defeated, the revolt had a traumatic effect on the British. The death toll on the British side (mostly Ghurkha and Sikh soldiers) has been calculated to have been approximately 500 and on the Iraqi side to some 6,000, while the cost of subduing the revolt amounted to a staggering £40 million—twice the annual budget intended by the British exchequer for the Iraqi Mandate.[2] Despite its military defeat, the 1920 Revolt forced the British to rethink their whole policy toward Iraq.

[1] For a discussion of the interpretations of the 1920 Revolution, see Amal Vinogradov, 'The 1920 Revolt in Iraq Reconsidered: The Role of Tribes in National Politics', *International Journal of Middle East Studies* 3, no. 2, Apr. 1972.

[2] Ibid., pp. 137–139.

The cost of suppressing the revolt and increasing domestic British criticism of the high expenditure of direct rule, eventually obliged the British government to introduce indirect rule through the establishment of an Iraqi monarchy, a government and a civil service, controlled by a small but authoritative corps of British advisers.[3] Faysal bin Husayn, the son of the Meccan *Sharif*, was appointed king of Iraq in 1921. During the short-lived Iraqi mandate, which lasted until 1932, Iraqi elites for the most part accepted British rule. Faysal, however, was more refractory. Despite owing his position to the British, at times he espoused a moderate anti-British and Arab nationalist stand. This rendered him and the fragile new state some nationalist legitimacy in the views of its people.[4]

The inclusion of the northern Mosul *wilayah* proved more difficult. In accordance with the October 1918 armistice of Mudros, Ottoman forces withdrew from the city of Mosul, which was then occupied by the British.[5] During secret Anglo-French negotiations in 1916 outlining the spoils of war, Britain had expressed no interest in the Kurdish areas, but after effectively having captured the whole *wilayah*, they realised the economic benefits of incorporating it into the future Iraqi state given its vast oil reserves.[6] Following the war, British policy toward the Kurdish areas (roughly corresponding to the Mosul *wilayah*), as with the rest of Iraq, was anything but straightforward. Colonel Arnold Wilson, the Acting Civil Commissioner for Mesopotamia[7] and an imperialist of the old stock, firmly believed in putting the occupied territories, including Kurdistan, under direct colonial administration. Yet, between the end of the war in October 1918 until the summer of 1919, a Kurdish autonomous entity was briefly allowed to function under British supervision. This was mainly due to British military exhaustion, its desire to consolidate the whole of Mesopotamia which required a peaceful Kurdistan, the fear that neglecting Kurdish aspirations might open the scene for Turkish and

[3] See Toby Dodge, *Inventing Iraq: The Failure of Nation Building and a History Denied*, London: C. Hurst & Co, 2003, pp. 18–19.

[4] For a description of the tensional nature of the relationship between King Faysal and the British, see ibid., 19–21.

[5] David McDowall, *A Modern History of the Kurds*, 2nd ed., London: I.B. Tauris, 2000, pp. 107–109.

[6] Ibid., p. 117.

[7] 'Mesopotamia' was the term used for the new polity before 'Iraq' was adopted as its name.

Bolshevik anti-British propaganda, and that Kurdish autonomy could be used against the Arab nationalists' attempts to establish a state incorporating all three *wilayahs* of Basra, Baghdad and Mosul.[8] Nevertheless, the Kurdish autonomous entity was eventually incorporated into Iraq following Wilson's wish.[9]

Yet, the status of the Mosul province and the fate of its largely Kurdish population continued to be challenged until 1925. At the San Remo Conference in 1920, the three victors of World War I—Britain, France and the United States[10]—agreed on a local autonomy scheme for the area. Later the same year at Sèvres, another treaty was forced upon the remnants of the Ottoman Empire stipulating Kurdish autonomy.[11] Meanwhile, however, Turkish troops under Mustafa Kemal (Atatürk) had launched an armed resistance in Anatolia, and set up an independent government at Ankara. It targeted British control in Mosul by stirring up tribal unrest, prompting the British to employ the RAF to bomb areas that were nominally under their own control. In October 1921, the Kemalists signed a treaty with the French, from whom they managed to wrest much of Cilicia, with the exemption of Alexandretta. In 1922, the Kemalists managed to drive out the Greek forces from the Straits Zone, forcing the British to agree to an armistice. Allying with important Kurdish tribes, Turkish forces had meanwhile managed to seize parts of the Mosul *wilayah*. On 24 July 1923, a formal peace agreement was eventually signed stipulating that the province's future was to be decided by League of Nations arbitration. As oil had become increasingly important to the British, they had now taken the view that the state of Iraq would not be viable without the inclusion of the *wilayah*. In fact, when Britain signed its Treaty of Alliance with the Iraqi government, an important proviso was included invalidating the whole treaty should the attempt at including the Mosul *wilayah* fail. In January 1925, the status of the Mosul *wilayah* was finally settled by a League commission who ruled in favour of its inclusion into the Iraqi state on the condition that it remained

[8] Saad Eskander, 'Britain's Policy in Southern Kurdistan: The Formation and the Termination of the First Kurdish Government, 1918–1919', *British Journal of Middle Eastern Studies* 27, no. 2, Nov. 2000, pp. 140–145.

[9] Ibid., p. 160.

[10] Though formally among the Allies and hence one of the victors, Russia had renounced any 'spoils of war' after the October 1917 Bolshevik Revolution.

[11] McDowall, *History of the Kurds*, pp. 136–137.

under a League of Nations mandate for twenty-five years and that Kurdish officials were appointed to govern the area. On 5 June 1926, Turkey and Britain finally signed a treaty agreeing to abide by the League of Nations' decision.[12] Thus, nearly eight years after its creation, the Iraqi state had attained its final form. However, the struggle over Mosul and other border disputes in the south with Saudi Arabia had imprinted on the minds of the Iraqi elites the vulnerability of the new state and its fundamental dependency on Britain for survival.

At any rate, local Iraqi elites, such as members of the old Ottoman bureaucracy that had ruled Iraqi prior to the British arrival, the so-called *effendiyyah*, and the ex-*Sharifian* soldiers that accompanied Faysal when he arrived in Iraq, had by now become accustomed to the parliamentary system created in Iraq by the British. They began using the medium of parliament to launch increasingly vociferous demands for independence, something that eventually forced the British to oblige. A series of negotiations resulted in the gradual devolution of power to the indigenous administration, and culminated in 1929 with the British decision to terminate the mandate,[13] promising support for Iraq to enter the League of Nations in 1932. An Anglo-Iraqi treaty signed in 1930 paved the way for the end of the mandate, which formally ceased in 1932 when Iraq was granted formal independence and League membership. To maintain its imperial interests, however, Britain ensured that the new treaty dictated the establishment of a 'close alliance' between the two countries. The treaty effectively laid the foundations for the system of dual control that characterised the post-independence years: Britain was to remain in charge of foreign affairs and Iraq's military security, with the right to retain military bases in the country in order to protect her imperial interests, while the Iraqi government became nominally sovereign.

The British mandate also significantly altered power relations in Iraq. In Ottoman times, each of the *wilayahs* of Baghdad, Mosul and Basra had been ruled by a *wali* (governor) appointed centrally from Istanbul. Since his tenancy usually was short,[14] and because he therefore had little

[12] Ibid., pp. 138–146.

[13] Majid Khadduri, *Independent Iraq 1932–1958: A Study in Iraqi Politics*, 2nd ed., London: Oxford University Press, 1960, p. 310.

[14] Hanna Batatu, *The Old Social Classes and the Revolutionary Movements of Iraq: A Study of Iraq's Old Landed and Commercial Classes and of its Communists, Ba'thists and*

time to develop firm links with local elites, real power in the territory was vested in the top echelons of the Ottoman bureaucratic elite who while in the majority were ethnic Turks or Caucasians, usually had been living in Iraq for centuries.[15] This segment of the population was known as the *effendiyyah*.[16] Together with commercial and religious groups, this bureaucratic elite by and large constituted the ruling stratum in Ottoman Iraq. However, with the establishment of the mandate, and the setting up of a new British administration, little attention was paid to the wishes of the traditional elites. Thus, in the first administration in 1920 only twenty out of 507 senior bureaucrats were Iraqi[17]—a situation fundamentally challenging the power base of the old *effendiyyah*.

Yet, the most important political actors under the monarchy were the *Sharifians*. As mostly low-ranking Ottoman soldiers, they had joined *Sharif* Husayn of Mecca in the Arab revolt against the Ottoman Empire during World War I, with the expectation of being granted independence for an 'Arab nation' by the British as a reward. As is well known, Britain had been pursuing mutually contradictory plans for the post-war division of the Middle East, as enshrined in the Husayn-McMahon correspondence in 1915–6 and the Sykes-Picot agreement of 1916. While the outcome of the Husayn-McMahon correspondence concerning areas to be included in a future Arab state had been inconclusive, to the Arabs there was no doubt about the wider promise of an independent 'Arab nation'.[18]

Free Officers, Princeton: Princeton University Press, 1978; reprint, *n.p.*: Saqi Books, 2004, (page citations are to the reprint edition), p. 219.

[15] Ibid., pp. 212–213.

[16] In this study, *effendiyyah* is understood as corresponding to this old Ottoman bureaucratic elite and families from this background that remained influential during the monarchy, using the definition offered in David Pool, 'The Politics of Patronage: Elites and Social Structure in Iraq', Princeton University, Ph.D. diss., Ann Arbor: U.M.I. Dissertation Services, 1972. A clear distinction is thus made with the rise of new educated groups, which some have called the *effendiyyah*, see Michael Eppel, 'The Elite, the Effendiyya, and the Growth of Nationalism and Pan-Arabism in Hashemite Iraq, 1921–1958', *International Journal of Middle East Studies* 30, no. 2, May 1998, pp. 228–230. See also discussion elsewhere in this chapter.

[17] Batatu, *Old Social Classes*, p. 220.

[18] For extracts from the Husayn-McMahon correspondence, see Charles D. Smith, *Palestine and the Arab-Israeli Conflict*, 4th ed., Boston: Bedford/St. Martin's, 2001, pp. 95–100.

The so-called Sykes-Picot agreement of 1916, however, negotiated between the British and the French, divided the region into areas of British, French, Russian and Italian direct rule and areas of influence, with little room for any independent Arab state north of the Arab peninsula.[19] Nevertheless, in the political stalemate briefly following the war, the *Sharifians* were temporarily able to set up an Arab state in Syria, but were within two years ousted by France in accordance with the stipulations of the 1916 agreement.[20]

After the short-lived Faysal government in Syria (1918–20), some *Sharifians* returned to Iraq and joined the 1920 revolt. Following Faysal's coronation, they became part of his entourage and employed as high-ranking officials in the bureaucracy of the new state. While *effendis* to some extent were able to reclaim some of their former prominence, it was the *Sharifians* who became a new political elite. Lacking socio-economic ties with the population and traditional elites, however, they were initially wholly dependent on the state and the British for their position. The dependency was reciprocal as Britain exercised its main political influence through them and the monarch. Over time, however, some *Sharifians* managed to build clienteles by distributing state resources, which they now controlled. They thus managed to create their own followings and considerable independent wealth. Though some members of the old bureaucratic elite managed to reconcile the new situation and gradually work their way back into the corridors of power, ultimate authority remained in the hands of the *Sharifians* by virtue of the 'British connection'. Thus, gradually, most *Sharifians* overcame the problem of lacking wealth through alliances with rural landowners and through taking over large tracts of tribal lands. For instance, while being Minister for Communication and Works in the early 1920s, Yasin al-Hashemi granted a concession for a land and irrigation scheme to a group of his followers. He later invested in it himself, and in 1926 while Minister of Finance he granted tax remissions and grants for people investing in pumps, effectively exempting large landowners from taxation. By investing in pumps for uncultivated tribal lands, al-Hashemi and his fellow *Sharifians* thus converted these lands into agricultural lands, thereby increasing their value manifold. This way, by the mid-1930s, he had become a wealthy landowner, possessing no less than sixteen large estates.[21]

[19] See Smith, *Palestine*, pp. 67–70.

[20] Ibid., pp. 83–86.

[21] Pool, 'Politics of Patronage', pp. 138–139.

The main difference between the *Sharifians* and the *effendis* during the mandate, as pointed out by Pool, was that the *effendis* because of their longstanding positions and their independent wealth could maintain independent political careers while the *Sharifians* had to 'live off politics'. Since wealth generation in Iraq was dependent on having access to the circles of power and state patronage, that process was never stable and reliable since political office could not be guaranteed at any given moment.[22] But as the *Sharifians*' power base gradually was transformed from state to land, by the end of the monarchical period the distinction between the political and the bureaucratic elites had become blurred as they to some extent fused. Although in some sense remaining overshadowed by the *Sharifians*, during the period 1921–1958 the *effendis* managed to receive 110 ministerial appointments out of a total of 575, and six premierships out of fifty-eight.[23] This way, *Sharifians* and *effendis* came to constitute a heterogeneous social group—a politico-bureaucratic elite, which dominated Iraqi politics.

Initially, the most serious challenge to British authority came from the tribes, who at the inception of the Mandate constituted the majority of the population, controlled vast areas of land, and thousands of armed men.[24] Since the mid-nineteenth century, the integration of southern Iraq into the world market had set decisive historical forces in motion. Increasingly tribes became sedentarised, and a shift toward agricultural production occurred in the countryside. This inevitably resulted in a move from the mostly subsistence economy that had characterised the tribal areas for centuries to a system more and more centred around the notion of private ownership of the land. Shaykhs, whose leadership before had largely been symbolic, were now transformed into landlords, while tribesmen found themselves having to till the land as landless peasants in order to sustain themselves. Some landlord-shaykhs moved to the cities where they as absentee landowners lived well from the land rent. Meanwhile the peasants had to remain and work for their foremen—the *sirkals*.[25]

[22] Ibid., pp. 122–123.

[23] Batatu, *Old Social Classes*, p. 221.

[24] For an extensive treatment of the tribes, and the development of tribal shaykhs and *aghas* into large landowning elites, see ibid., Chapter 6, pp. 63–152.

[25] Eric Davis, *Memories of State: Politics, History, and Collective Identity in Modern Iraq*, Berkeley: University of California Press, 2005, pp. 29–30.

When Britain occupied Iraq, these developments were reversed. Already in 1916, Britain introduced the so-called 'Tribal Criminal and Civil Disputes Regulation', which in effect created two separate legal systems for the country—one for the tribes and another for the rest of the population. This regulation was integrated into the Iraqi Constitution in 1925. The reason for this separation was the British lack of military and financial resources, which eventually forced the British to co-opt belligerent tribes rather than subduing them militarily, clearly a more costly option. Exclusive judicial authority was thus vested in shaykhs, effectively creating autonomous tribal regions throughout the country. Not only did this arrest the de-tribalisation process that had started during the nineteenth century but it also solidified the divisions between tribes and cities and officially recognised age-old tribal customary law. In their attempt to pacify and settle the nomadic tribes Britain handed out feudal property rights to the shaykhs, granting them 'ownership' over land that customarily belonged to the whole tribe, thus creating internal divisions between 'landowner' (*mallak*) and peasant (*fallah*).[26]

The tribal shaykhs functioned as intermediaries between the political centre and their tribal populations. They were integrated into the Parliament and thus tied into the state administration. Their allegiance to the new state was further advanced by using them as entrepreneurs for tribal labour, commanders for tribal expeditionary forces, and by granting them financial subsidies.[27] This was particularly the case of Shi'i tribal landlord-shaykhs from the south whose integration into national politics served to counterbalance the power of the urban nationalists and the monarchy, in a classic example of 'divide and rule' policy.[28]

A *modus vivendi* gradually developed between these fragmented elites: the *Sharifians* and the *effendis* largely occupied the institutions of the cabinet, the Royal Diwan, and the top levels of the bureaucracy, whereas the shaykhs, who through their rural clienteles controlled the majority of

[26] For a wider discussion of British tribal policy, see Dodge, *Inventing Iraq*, pp. 92–100; Batatu, *Old Social Classes*, p. 24; and Peter Sluglett, *Britain in Iraq, 1914–1932*, London: Ithaca Press for the Middle East Centre, St Antony's College, Oxford, 1976, pp. 240–243.

[27] David Pool, 'From Elite to Class: The Transformation of Iraqi Political Leadership', in *The Integration of Modern Iraq*, Abbas Kelidar (ed), London: Croom Helm, 1979, p. 76.

[28] Davis, *Memories of State*, p. 56.

the population, mostly occupied the parliament.[29] This way, the new state came to be dominated by an alliance of predominantly Shi'i landlords in the south, with a large minority of Sunni landlords in the central areas and of Kurdish *aghas* in the north, and the urban Sunni *Sharifian-effendi* politico-bureaucratic elite at the centre, coupled with the traditional merchant and religious elites who retained most of their erstwhile influence. This political system remained essentially the same after formal independence in 1932.

In this complex situation, Sunnis came to dominate the state. Though the Iraqi population was mostly Shi'i, the old Ottoman bureaucratic 'aristocracy' had been exclusively Sunni, which also was the predominant religious affiliation among the new *Sharifian* political elite. This did not mean that Shi'is were totally devoid of influence, however. Landownership, the single most important source of independent wealth and hence socio-political influence, was spread among Iraq's ethnic and religious groups as a result of the tribal division of the country. Trade had historically been controlled by the Jewish minority and by Shi'i merchants, the so-called Chalabis.[30] Following the creation of the state of Israel and the subsequent Arab-Israeli War of 1948–49, however, most of the Jewish community left for Israel, and thus further advanced the position of Shi'i Chalabis.[31] The role of Shi'i urban notables was consequently enhanced. In addition, during the monarchical period, the Ministry of Education was usually given to a Shi'i, which meant that the urban Shi'i notables were in control of important resources. Consequently, many Shi'is received scholarships to study abroad, leading to a high level of education among some sectors of the urban Shi'ah. This in turn had the effect that more and more Shi'is started to fill the upper levels of the bureaucracy and the diplomatic corps.[32]

The Kurdish situation was more complex. As Sunnis, Kurdish leaders had long been integrated into the Ottoman state; many held positions within the high bureaucracy in Istanbul. As such, they had no interest in seeking independence, and it was therefore only when the collapse of the Ottoman Empire seemed inevitable at the end of World War I that they

[29] Pool, 'Politics of Patronage', p. 124.

[30] For a description of these two merchant groups, see Batatu, *Old Social Classes*, ch. 9, pp. 224–318.

[31] Pool, 'Politics of Patronage', p. 180.

[32] Ibid., p. 142.

actively developed the first notions of Kurdish nationalism.[33] At the close of the war, two broad strands within the emerging Kurdish national movement had come to the fore—those favouring autonomy and those favouring separation.[34] During Ottoman times, the notion of Kurdish national identity had generally been weak. Until the beginning of the twentieth century, being a 'Kurd', or indeed a 'Turk', usually had the negative connotation of being uneducated and rural to progressive-minded cosmopolitan Kurds living in Istanbul. In addition, among some of the more backward elements in Kurdistan there were people who found comfort in the certainties of the Ottoman caliphate against the pervasiveness of a rapidly changing world. 'The "Kurdishness" of their existence,' commented McDowall, 'was defined essentially by the pursuit of traditional, usually tribal, identity which the *ancien régime* seemed willing to foster.' Even those Kurds who had taken up political activity did so mostly as a response to the despotic rule of Sultan 'Abd al-Hamid, and as Ottoman citizens.[35] This activity, however, was not nationalistic, but rather reflected political ambitions among some Kurdish notables aiming for the widening of their regional influence.[36] During the war, three currents regarding the future of Kurdistan developed among the Kurds. Some remained pro-Ottoman; others became pro-Allies, while some favoured complete independence. But due to the uncertainties of the time, no group wanted to commit themselves firmly to either cause.[37]

Early Kurdish responses to British rule were divided. While some *aghas* accepted British administration, others favoured complete local autonomy with separation from Baghdad and direct administration from London. This early pro-Britishness among the old Kurdish elites was hardly surprising in view of the seemingly unambiguous promises for Kurdish self-determination that had emanated from the British occupational power since the early days of British control.[38] At this point, nationalistic sentiments among leading Kurdish notables became more pronounced,

33 Hakan Özoğlu, '"Nationalism" and Kurdish Notables in the Late Ottoman-Early Republican Era', *International Journal of Middle East Studies* 33, no. 3, Aug. 2001, p. 383.

34 McDowall, *History of the Kurds*, p. 89; Özoğlu, 'Kurdish Notables', p. 384.

35 McDowall, *History of the Kurds*, p. 88.

36 Özoğlu, 'Kurdish Notables', p. 383.

37 McDowall, *History of the Kurds*, p. 125.

38 Ibid., p. 152.

although the essence of this 'nationalism' for the most part was a desire to establish and expand Kurdish emirates on the historical pattern. This uneasy mix of tribalism and nationalism was in Iraq epitomised by the rebellions of Shaykh Mahmud. In December 1918, he was appointed *hikimdar* of the Sulaymaniyyah district by the British, but in May 1919, he proclaimed himself 'ruler of all Kurdistan'. Though eventually defeated and exiled by the British, his attempt at rebellion later became a potent symbol of Kurdish nationalism, despite the fact that he had acted more from a religious platform—calling for a *jihad* against the British—than from a nationalist perspective.[39] Following the defeat of the rebellion, most Kurdish *aghas* accepted British rule and entrusted the British with ensuring that Baghdad would grant the Kurdish areas local autonomy and equal rights with the Arab population. Thus, as they learnt that Britain had been complicit in Baghdad's negligence of those rights in the proposed treaty of independence negotiated between Iraq and Britain in 1929, this led to social unrest in parts of the Kurdish areas, especially in al-Sulaymaniyyah.[40] Nevertheless, following that incident, Kurdish notables seemed quietly to accept the fact that the Kurdish areas had been irrevocably integrated into the Iraqi state and that their own positions would be secure under King Faysal.[41]

At the bottom of the political spectrum were impoverished peasants, workers, and *lumpenproletarians* living in rural areas and in the ever-growing shantytowns that developed around the larger urban centres. Iraq's integration into the world capitalist market had since the mid-nineteenth century started to change patterns of social organisation in the countryside. As tribesmen increasingly were transformed into landless peasants, huge sections of the rural population (especially in the south) headed for the cities to escape the oppression of the landlord-shaykhs or in the hope of finding alternative livelihoods. This led to a virtual explosion of poor squatter shantytowns inhabited by *shurugis*[42] ('easterners') around Iraq's larger cities, especially Baghdad.[43] During the hardships that followed World War II, the large-scale rural to urban migration

[39] Ibid., pp. 156–158.

[40] Ibid., pp. 173–176.

[41] Ibid., p. 287.

[42] For a discussion of the *shurugis* and the hardships they faced when migrating to the cities, see Batatu, *Old Social Classes*, pp. 134–138.

[43] Davis, *Memories of State*, p .52.

intensified. Although it is difficult to say exactly how this mass migration affected the social status of the urban workers, it is beyond doubt that a large section among them suffered a considerable loss in real income, owing to the abundance of cheap peasant labour.[44] The number of these workers, i.e. people earning their income from selling their physical labour in Iraq's growing industry, increased during this period. Though constituting only a small fraction of the population, in some areas manual labourers abounded, especially in the growing oil industry. Most modern Iraqi manufacturing plants, with the noteworthy exception of the oil industry, were located in Baghdad and other large cities.[45] At the inception of the mandate in 1920, oil had played only a minor, if any, role in the Iraqi economy. Soon, however, it became the paramount concern for anyone involved in the running of the Iraqi state. In fact, the British reluctance to give into Turkish claims on Mosul was largely informed by the realisation that without the oil-rich province, the new state would not be viable. Since at least 1934, the Iraqi economy was tied to oil and by 1953, the state was wholly dependent on the oil factor, as it constituted almost half the country's national income.[46]

In urban areas, these 'lower' social strata increasingly became exposed to the ideas of nationalism, anti-imperialism, socialism, communism, and general anti-British sentiments. In the period from the end of World War II until the overthrow of the monarchy in 1958, these groups started to take part in social protests against the ruling elite. From then on, protest, as Batatu has maintained, began to shift from a political to a social content. Protests were no longer directed against any one government, but rather against the system itself.[47] Maintaining the view that the main challenge was that posed by anti-British nationalists belonging to the Iraqi elite, the British failed to appreciate the danger of this rise of popular

[44] Batatu, *Old Social Classes*, pp. 137–138.

[45] Batatu has calculated that the number of workers in companies with more than 100 employees rose from 13,140 in 1926 to 62,519 in 1954, and that out of all industrial workers in 1954, ca. 33 per cent worked in the Greater Baghdad area and approximately 17 per cent in the Basra region. In comparison, the *shurugis* of Greater Baghdad numbered some 92,000 in 1956, ibid., p. 482.

[46] Marion Farouk-Sluglett and Peter Sluglett, *Iraq since 1958: From Revolution to Dictatorship*, London: I.B. Tauris, 2001, p. 35. The growing importance of oil is shown by Iraqi oil revenues, which 1941–1958 rose from £1.5 million to £79.8 million, Batatu, *Old Social Classes*, p. 34.

[47] Ibid., p. 470.

politics. Instead, they thought that only those invested with power could actually challenge the system. True to their condescending views of the political potential of the 'mob', which is well documented in the archives, the British thought this would remain the case for the foreseeable future, thereby failing to recognise the signs of what was to come.[48] The failure to institutionally incorporate the 'lower' social strata into the state and thereby create a sense of national community was one of the main reasons for these groups' increasing radicalisation. During the 1940s and 1950s, political mobilisation carried out by new political parties further exacerbated the growing feeling that the state was but the tool of the elite and the British.[49]

Sharifian Pan-Arabist Ideology and Its Gradual Demise

The intellectual roots of *Sharifian* pan-Arabist ideas lay in the thought of the Islamic modernists of the nineteenth century, such as Muhammad 'Abduh, 'Abd al-Rahman al-Kawakibi, and Muhammad Rashid Rida.[50] However, within early Arab nationalism there was also a strand of mostly non-Muslim Arabs propagating Arab cultural revival through a literary *nahdah*.[51] The Islamic modernists for their part had argued for the necessity of modernising and revitalising Islam mirroring an imagined older form of 'pure' Islam. This modernised Islam would incorporate all the ancient peoples of the Middle East into the 'Arab Nation', whose nucleus was Egypt, Iraq, Syria and Arabia. These thinkers, particularly al-Kawakibi, developed an Arab self-view based on a 'Semito-Arab history' seen

[48] See Johan Franzén, 'Development vs. Reform: Attempts at Modernisation During the Twilight of British Influence in Iraq, 1946–58', *The Journal of Imperial and Commonwealth History* 37, no. 1, 2009.

[49] Davis, *Memories of State*, p. 72.

[50] C. Ernest Dawn, 'The Formation of Pan-Arab Ideology in the Interwar Years', *International Journal of Middle East Studies* 20, no. 1, Feb. 1988: p. 69.

[51] Mahmoud Haddad, 'The Rise of Arab Nationalism Reconsidered', *International Journal of Middle East Studies* 26, no. 2, May 1994, pp. 202–203; For a more in-depth treatment of the ideas of the individual thinkers mentioned above, cf. Albert Hourani, *Arabic Thought in the Liberal Age 1798–1939, n.p.*: Cambridge University Press, 1962; see also C. Ernest Dawn, 'From Ottomanism to Arabism: The Origin of an Ideology', in *From Ottomanism to Arabism: Essays on the Origins of Arab Nationalism*, Chicago: University of Illinois Press, 1973.

as divided into two periods of greatness (the ancient Semitic and the Islamic periods), each followed by a period of *Jahiliyyah* ('ignorance'). The present era was thus likened to the pre-Islamic *Jahiliyyah*.[52] In this view, Islam was not only a religion but also a unifying national, political and social bond. However, although Islam had brought greatness to the Arab nation, it had failed to eradicate the main weaknesses of Arab society, namely individualism, egotism and tribal *'asabiyyah*. The second *Jahiliyyah* (the present stage) had been caused by the ruling classes' proselytisation of 'false religion' to pacify the masses with ignorance and superstition so that they more easily could be economically exploited.[53] From this notion arose the idea that the revival of the 'Arab nation' would require also the addressing of socio-economic issues and possibly the overthrow of the existing social order.

A further radicalisation of this intellectual current took shape as a response to the 1908 coup by the Turkish nationalist Committee of Union and Progress (CUP) in Istanbul. Reacting to its policy of 'Turkification' of the provinces, some Arab thinkers started to stress their separate political and cultural identity. Yet, it is important to note that at the time most Arab nationalists did not envisage a breakaway from the Ottoman Empire. In fact, the programme of the *al-'Ahd* society that was formed in 1912 by Iraqi and Syrian middle-ranking officers serving in the Ottoman army and in which many of the Iraqi *ex-Sharifian* officers started their political careers, demanded internal independence and federalism, while calling for Arab-Turkish cooperation to preserve the Caliphate in Ottoman hands. Nevertheless, Ottoman territorial losses before and during World War I, gradually changed the face of Arab political consciousness as dismemberment of the Empire became a real possibility.[54] This crystallised the idea of an independent 'Arab nation' on the lines propagated by the Islamic modernists.[55]

Following the formation of the Iraqi monarchy in 1921, most *Sharifians* followed Faysal and settled in Iraq. Among them and other nationalists inspired by the ideals of pan-Arabism, various political constellations

[52] Dawn, 'Formation of Pan-Arab Ideology', pp. 69–71.

[53] Ibid., pp. 72–75.

[54] Haddad, 'Arab Nationalism', pp. 214–215.

[55] For developments during this period, see also Reeva S. Simon, *Iraq Between the Two World Wars: The Militarist Origins of Tyranny*, upd. ed., New York: Columbia University Press, 2004, pp. 24–31.

took shape over the coming years. Central to these parties was 'Arab Unity', i.e. the idea of uniting the various newly established Arab states into a single polity. The *Sharifians'* original political organisation, *al-'Ahd*, split in 1919 into Syrian and Iraqi organisations. In Iraq, *Jam'iyyat al-'Ahd al-'Iraqi* was formed with branches in Baghdad and Mosul. This organisation called in its programme for a constitutional monarchy with the throne given to one of Sharif Husayn's sons, preferably 'Abdallah. It also desired a form of union of the Arab regions (*aqtar*) under Sharif Husayn, who at the time was still ruler of the Hijaz. To achieve its objectives, the organisation advocated the use of peaceful methods and dialogue.[56] The same year saw the formation in Baghdad of *Jam'iyyat Haras al-Istiqlal*. Like *al-'Ahd al-'Iraqi*, it advocated the formation of a democratic constitutional Iraqi monarchy whose throne was to be handed to one of the scions of Sharif Husayn. It envisaged Iraq forming part of an Arab unity project as a separate *liwa'*.[57]

Yet, despite the formation of these organisations, politics in the new Iraqi state was mostly conducted through a patronage system in which central patrons distributed bureaucratic resources at their disposal in order to build clienteles. In this set-up, government posts were very important. 'Becoming a minister', Pool explained, 'was the institutional recognition of the influence of the Iraqi politician'.[58] Through the logic of political institutionalisation, *Sharifian* and *effendi* politicians gradually started to adapt their ideological outlooks to the new political situation. Their pan-Arabist ideology, which before undoubtedly had been heartfelt, now more and more developed into a medium of parliamentary politics. In this way, their nationalism was mostly employed as a coating to a real intention of building clienteles and followings. For those in power, nationalism became an empty rhetoric, while for those temporarily out of power opposition was largely a tactical choice,[59] using nationalism as a means to put pressure on the central politicians and the Monarch, eventually forcing them to concede political or bureaucratic positions that could be used for patronage purposes. The formation and dissolution of political 'parties'

[56] Hadi Hasan 'Alaywi, *al-Ittijahat al-Wahdawiyyah fi al-Fikr al-Qawmi al-'Arabi al-Mashriqi 1918–1952*, Silsilat Atruhat al-Dukturah 38, Beirut: Markaz Dirasat al-Wahdah al-'Arabiyyah, 2000, pp. 66–67.

[57] Ibid., p. 67.

[58] Pool, 'Politics of Patronage', p. 136.

[59] Ibid., p. 152.

among these groups followed a well-known pattern: parties were mostly paper creations formed prior to parliamentary elections and lasted for the most part little longer than the election campaign itself. A case in point is Nuri al-Sa'id's *Hizb al-'Ahd*, formed in 1930, which, although following his political vision of establishing a federal unionist state, nevertheless clearly was at its master's behest and ceased political activity whenever the other parliamentary parties did or when told to do so by Nuri.[60] This pattern was repeated later with his *Hizb al-Ittihad al-Dusturi* (Constitutional Union Party) formed in 1949.[61]

Thus within a few years, the brand of pan-Arabist nationalism which had sought to create a pan-Arab state across the Middle East after the end of World War I had become institutionalised into an Iraqi Arab nationalism that was much more conservative and bent on preserving the status quo.

Modern Education and the Constitution of a New Intelligentsia

During the late Ottoman period, educational reforms were introduced in Iraq. These formed part of the wider centralisation and reformation campaign that had been launched by the Ottoman state in 1839 and which lasted until 1876 (the *Tanzimat*), but in Iraq the reforms were also intended to counter British influence.[62] For the formation of Arab nationalism, this development was of tremendous importance as it wrested educational monopoly from the *'ulama'*, created the embryo of independent intellectuals, and thus paved the way for modern secular ideas and ideologies.

After the establishment of the monarchy in 1921, a disagreement developed between British officers and the *Sharifians* over the nature of state education. Keen to forge national unity based on notions of pan-Arab ideology, the nationalists wanted to promote their ideas on a mass scale throughout the country's educational system. The British for their

[60] 'Alaywi, *Ittijahat al-Wahdawiyyah*, p. 109.

[61] Charles Tripp, *A History of Iraq*, Cambridge: Cambridge University Press, 2000, p. 127.

[62] A military school was founded in 1869, a civilian school in 1870, and the first vocational school in 1871. Later three preparatory schools in Mosul and one in Basra opened, and four elementary schools were established in Baghdad in 1889, Davis, *Memories of State*, pp. 34; 40.

part thought education should be limited. However, 'with a frequently inactive minister and an Advisor whose powers were less extensive than those of his colleagues in other Ministries, Education became the Department of State in which the permanent Iraqi civil servants had greatest control.'[63] Consequently, pan-Arab ideologues, such as Sati' al-Husri, Fadil al-Jamali and Sami Shawkat, who all served as Directors-General of the Ministry of Education in the 1920s and 1930s, could utilise this venue to imbue pan-Arabist ideas to a new generation of Iraqis. Despite British opposition, these nationalists managed to expand the educational system and increase its budget allocations throughout the mandate.[64] Nevertheless, the British tried to check educational expansion and thus at the end of the mandate there were less than 2,000 secondary school places in the whole of Iraq.[65] 'It was the dangers rather than the benefits inherent in education', wrote Peter Sluglett, 'which were most readily apparent to the experts in the various Imperial services.' The British feared that education would create a class of young educated people for whom there would be no employment, and who, as a result, would form a nucleus of political agitators working against British rule.[66]

British apprehensions proved correct as the expansion of education, which accelerated rapidly following the termination of the mandate, exposed young men from social groups traditionally excluded from modern education to new ideas based on notions of national community. Eventually this produced new strata of young educated people, who started to take political action in a fundamentally different fashion than

[63] Sluglett, *Britain in Iraq*, p. 277.

[64] Ibid., p. 285.

[65] Ibid., p. 275. However, some noteworthy developments in higher education did take place in the 1920s and 1930s. The College of Law reopened in 1920–21 and the College of Education was founded in 1923. A College of Medicine was established in 1927 and a College of Pharmacy in 1936, Davis, *Memories of State*, p. 72.

[66] Sluglett, *Britain in Iraq*, p. 274. Similar concerns made the British work against *Sharifian* efforts to establish a national army. Due to more favourable salaries, the British-run Iraq Levies, an army of mostly Assyrian soldiery and a British officer corps, prevented recruitment to the national army during the mandate. The imbalance was only remedied with the introduction of conscription in 1934, Mohammad A. Tarbush, *The Role of the Military in Politics: A Case Study of Iraq to 1941*, London: KPI, 1982, pp. 73–94.

the previous generation of political actors had done. Sometimes termed the 'new effendiyyah', the 'young effendiyyah' or plainly 'the effendiyyah',[67] in reality this group was markedly different from the old elite *effendiyyah*. The social function of the old *effendiyyah* had been a direct result of its economic status and social origins, but for the new educated groups, their political socialisation was mainly the result of having access to modern education.[68] From these mostly urban, predominantly Baghdadi, strata most political activists originated during the monarchy. These intellectuals were of pivotal historical significance as producers of political ideology.

For the *Sharifians*, nationalist education eventually turned into a double-edged sword, as the lofty ideals of pan-Arabism could be turned against its promoters when they failed to deliver.[69] Among the young educated generation that grew up after the establishment of the Iraqi state, who all had been recipients of pan-Arabist education, two separate strands of nationalism started to take form—one firmly pan-Arabist and the other distinctively Iraqi nationalist—both of which were essentially more radical than the institutionalised nationalism of the *Sharifian-Effendi* politico-bureaucratic elite.

This radicalisation was further assisted by the emergence of a national press during the 1920s, which began calling for complete independence for Iraq, evacuation of British troops and democratic reforms.[70] In addition, clubs and professional organisations became platforms for the proselytisation of radical nationalism.[71] The early 1930s witnessed the establishment of several such clubs, each of which were linked to a different political current. For instance, *Jam'iyyat al-Ahali* ('the Peoples' Society'), founded in 1931, was the focal point of the 'social democratic' *Ahali* movement, a conglomeration incorporating several Iraqist trends.

67 See Davis, *Memories of State*, p. 41; Eppel, 'Effendiyya'; and Peter Wien, 'The Youth and the Nation: Generational Conflict as a Trigger of National Consciousness in Iraq during the 1930s', Paper presented at the 6th Mediterranean Social & Political Research Meeting of the Mediterranean Programme of the Robert Schuman Centre for Advanced Studies at the European Univ. Institute, Mar. 2005, pp. 3–6.

68 Eppel, 'Effendiyya', pp. 229–231.

69 Wien, 'Youth and the Nation', p. 20.

70 Between 1920 and 1929, no less than 105 newspapers were established, many with explicitly radical agendas, Davis, *Memories of State*, p. 49.

71 Ibid., p. 50.

In 1934, the Iraqist *Nadi Baghdad* ('the Baghdad Club') opened. *Nadi al-Tadammun* ('the Solidarity Club'), in which some of the future members of the Iraqi Communist Party experienced their first encounter with radical ideas, was established in 1926, and *Nadi al-Muthanna* ('the Muthanna Club'), a radical pan-Arabist club that fostered many of the later participants in the 1941 anti-British movement, was founded in 1935.[72] The members of these organisations, who stemmed from the new educated strata, in various disparate and asymmetrical ways, began to constitute a new radicalised intelligentsia.

Alongside the expansion of an intellectual white-collar class brought about by the increase of education and the expansion of state bureaucracy, coffeehouses, which traditionally had functioned as venues for political socialisation, now more than ever filled that function and radicalised new socio-political groups.[73] There members of the intelligentsia would read aloud newspapers and popular poetry, transmitting radical ideas to the wider illiterate masses of urban workers and peasant toilers who had migrated from the countryside. Many coffeehouses were associated with particular political currents, and thus became 'quasi-public institutions in which the clientele was inculcated with political views and information.'[74] The role of the underground press was also crucial. For instance, in 1954–55, the outlawed communist paper *al-Qa'idah* was published in seventeen issues, totalling 92,000 sold copies, i.e. an average of 5,400 copies/issue. In comparison, *al-Bilad*, which was one of the most widespread legal newspapers, sold only ca. 4,500 copies/issue.[75] Gradually, the radical intellectuals, through the press and public meeting grounds built a popular counterculture undermining the legitimacy of the state.

[72] Note that Davis claims *Nadi al-Tadammun* was established in 1935, ibid., p. 73.

[73] The coffeehouse as a public institution for entertainment had been established in the cities of the Ottoman Empire since the sixteenth century. Initially part of the 'high culture', by the eighteenth and nineteenth centuries it had become a place of business and commerce and its social status had consequently dropped. Thus, by the twentieth century, it was a meeting place frequented by most urban groups, see Brian W. Beeley, 'The Turkish Village Coffeehouse as a Social Institution', *Geographical Review* 60, no. 4, Oct. 1970.

[74] Davis, *Memories of State*, p. 95.

[75] 'Aziz Sbahi, *'Uqud min Ta'rikh al-Hizb al-Shuyu'i al-'Iraqi*, vol. 2, Damascus: Manshurat al-Thaqafah al-Jadidah, 2003, p. 154.

Qawmiyyah vs. Wataniyyah: Ideology and Political Radicalisation, 1932–46

The common denominator among the various and diverse political constellations that arose as a result of the political coming-of-age of the new intelligentsia was their radical approach to politics. For the most part excluded from official politics, these intellectuals gradually sharpened their views. Thus, to varying degrees all of these constellations were opposed to the British presence and sought 'complete independence' for Iraq. But whereas they resembled each other in sentimental disposition, attitude and general outlook, there was one important difference—ideology. A dividing line could be drawn between two strands of these new radicalised political groupings, namely between those of a predominantly *qawmi* disposition and those of a more *watani* approach, or, in other words, between those whose lofty ideal was pan-Arabism and those whose political aim was firmly set within the existing borders of the Iraqi state.

As metaphysical entities, *Qawmiyyah* and *Wataniyyah* are not entirely easy to grasp, and indeed, to each of the political groupings they had varying significance and meaning. The concept of 'nationalism' is usually translated as 'qawmiyyah' in Arabic, but it is important to recognise that the Arabic language essentially makes use of two separate notions of 'nationalism'—'qawmiyyah' and 'wataniyyah'. For those unaccustomed with the Arabic language, it is essential to grasp both concepts when trying to understand the development of nationalism in the Arab world. 'Qawmiyyah' relates to the 'qawm', which originally meant the kinspeople and denoted blood relation, but which today sometimes is taken as meaning 'nation' in the European sense. 'Wataniyyah', on the other hand, derives from the verb 'watana', which means to settle or dwell. Thus, 'watan' is commonly translated as 'homeland', or, erroneously, as 'fatherland'. Accordingly, when discussing 'pan-Arabism', this study refers to the ideas that are encapsulated in the Arabic notion of *al-qawmiyyah al-'arabiyyah* (which may also merely be translated as Arab nationalism). Iraqi nationalism, on the other hand, or, more accurately, Iraqist nationalism(s) are (sometimes) termed *al-wataniyyah al-'iraqiyyah*, but are also frequently not formally named in Arabic at all. To add to this definitional problematic, nationalist writers and political actors rarely adhere to this strict division, but frequently overlap in their usage of 'qawmiyyah' and 'wataniyyah' and also use the equally problematic term 'ummah' with its awkward religious connotation to describe the 'Arab nation' (*al-ummah al-'arabiyyah*).[76]

Members of the new intelligentsia would have been recipients in the 1920s and 1930s of the writings of Sati' al-Husri, one of the most prominent and prolific *qawmi* writers of the time, and who, crucially, during this period was Director-General of the Ministry of Education in Iraq and thus was in control of the Iraqi school curriculum. To al-Husri, *Wataniyyah* meant 'love of the homeland' (*hubb al-watan*) and *Qawmiyyah* 'love of the nation' (*hubb al-ummah*). In his view, they were two sides of the same coin, because 'the homeland' was nothing but 'a patch of land' (*qut'ah min al-ardh*), whereas 'the nation' was 'a community of people' (*jama'ah min al-bashar*). Accordingly, *Wataniyyah* differed little from *Qawmiyyah*, as 'love of the homeland' would entail love of its inhabitants as well, just as 'love of the nation' comprised love of the land on which the nation lives.[77] He was adamant, however, that the fundamental bond of *qawmiyyah* was not of a racial nature, rejecting the myth of a common origin of the Arabs. 'All the nations that we know today', he wrote, 'are formed by the meshing of tens of descents (*'uruq*) and races (*ajnas*), during different turns of history, until the races that lived during the advanced centuries of history were also very mixed and meshed.'[78] Instead, to al-Husri, the important factors leading to the creation of a 'spiritual kinship' (*al-qarabah al-ma'nawiyyah*) were language and history.[79] Language, in his view, was the strongest bond, binding individuals to collectives because it was a means for understanding, a tool of contemplation, and, importantly, a vehicle for transmitting ideas from generation to generation. 'Nations differ one from the other', he wrote, 'on the first level by their languages, and the life of nations rests before anything else on their languages'. Thus, if a nation lost its language, it lost its life.[80] Accordingly, history was tantamount to the nation's consciousness and memory. But

[76] For more on these terms, see Richard F. Pfaff, 'The Function of Arab Nationalism', *Comparative Politics* 2, no. 2, Jan. 1970.

[77] Sati' al-Husri, 'al-Wataniyyah wa l-Qawmiyyah', from lectures given at the Dar al-Mu'allimin al-'Aliyyah in Baghdad, in *Abhath Mukhtarah fi al-Qawmiyyah al-'Arabiyyah 1923–1963*, vol. 1, Beirut: Dar al-Quds, [1974], p. 28.

[78] Sati' al-Husri, 'Awamil al-Qawmiyyah', from a lecture given in 1928 at Nadi al-Mu'allimin in Baghdad, in *Abhath Mukhtarah* 1, p. 39.

[79] Ibid., p. 42.

[80] Ibid., pp. 42–43.

al-Husri made clear that it was not history recorded in books and manuscripts that were of value to him, but rather 'history living in the souls, spread to the ears and received from traditions'. As with language, historical memory created a 'spiritual kinship' between individuals, which in al-Husri's view was stronger than any material kinship. Thus, he concluded that language and history were 'the two essential factors that most strongly influences the creation of nationalisms.'[81]

The main difference between the pan-Arabism being taught in Iraqi schools in the 1920s and 1930s and the earlier *Sharifian* pan-Arabism was the former's staunch proselytisation of secularism as a basis of nationalism. Since in al-Husri's view religion created a rival feeling of unity among its followers and stirred them into action, religion was one of the most important social bonds binding individuals together and influencing the course of politics and history. This was particularly true with internationalist religions, such as Islam and Christianity, whereas national religions, such as Judaism, developed into one of the fundamental national traits.[82] Qustantin Zurayq, another prominent *qawmi* thinker of Greek Orthodox Syrian origin, resembled al-Husri's thoughts on religion and race. To him, religion offered particular views on life and existence and as such united peoples, but it was not the decisive factor or enough to define their *Qawmiyyah*. In his view, the relationship between the Arabs and Islam was of an essential character, and the Prophet Muhammad was the founder of the Arab civilisation and the unifier of the Arab people. Importantly, however, Zurayq argued that the Arabs needed to be a 'modern people' and adopt western democracy.[83] To Zaki al-Arsuzi, a prominent *qawmi* nationalist of Syrian 'Alawi origin and later one of the founders of the Ba'th Party, religion had a more central place. While, like al-Husri and Zurayq, awarding first prominence to language in the creation of *Qawmiyyah*, al-Arsuzi is less dismissive of religion. In his more mystical approach, the 'Arab nation' enjoys a 'halo of holiness', and thus, rather than al-Husri's 'history', the 'spiritual dimension' (*al-bu'd al-ruhi*) is the second genuine factor determining the existence of a nation.[84] Sami Shawkat, an Iraqi *effendi* of Turkish origins, who, similar to al-Husri, acted

[81] Ibid., p. 44.
[82] Ibid., pp. 45–46.
[83] 'Alaywi, *Ittijahat al-Wahdawiyyah*, pp. 84–85.
[84] Ibid., pp. 89–90.

as Iraqi Director-General of Education and was equally influential over the young generation, was more forceful in his approach than his colleague. While dismissing religion and calling for a 'secular state' (*al-dawlah al-'almaniyyah*), arguing there was no place for religion in politics, he nevertheless thought the meaning of *Qawmiyyah* was 'spiritual homogeneity' (*al-tajanus al-ruhi*), which was a natural result of the milieu and surroundings in which the nation lived. As for the traits of *Qawmiyyah*, they were language, blood, nature, culture and the unity of desire and history.[85]

At the inception of the mandate, however, pan-Arab ideas had not been widespread in Iraq.[86] However, as recipients of continuous pan-Arabist history teaching, a new generation of Arab nationalists emerged in the 1930s and 1940s contending that only the 'Arab nation' could prevail over Iraq's profound internal divisions. Taking a lead in this development was Sami Shawkat, who with his message of power as the only solution to combat imperialism was particularly influential in bringing sections of the young generation in line with fascist ideas propagated at the time from Berlin and Rome. In his infamous 1933 speech entitled 'Sina'at al-Mawt', he argues that only military strength can save the Arab nation from foreign domination, quoting as historical models to emulate the successful nationalist unifications of Atatürk, Mussolini and Prussia.[87] In line with these ideas, Shawkat instructed the Iraqi youth to refrain from a life of luxury and adopt the lifestyle of the early Arabs. To put his ideology into action he helped set up and became the leader of a fascist, paramilitary organisation called *al-Futuwah*, which directly targeted secondary school students and their teachers.[88]

Another similar militarist organisation was *Jam'iyyat al-Jawwal*, which in 1934 received a government licence to pursue openly political work

[85] Ibid., pp. 96–97.

[86] Peter Sluglett, 'From the Politics of Notables to the Politics of Parliamentary Government: Iraq 1918–1932', Paper presented at the 6th Social & Political Research Meeting of the Mediterranean Programme of the Robert Schuman Centre for Advanced Studies at the European Univ. Institute, Mar. 2005, p. 12.

[87] Sami Shawkat, 'The Profession of Death', in *Arab Nationalism: An Anthology*, ed. Sylvia Haim, Berkeley: University of California Press, 1962.

[88] 'Alaywi, *Ittijahat al-Wahdawiyyah*, pp. 97–98. For a more extensive description of al-Futuwah, see Peter Wien, *Iraqi Arab Nationalism: Authoritarian, Totalitarian, and Pro-Fascist Inclinations, 1932–1941*, London and New York: Routledge, 2006, pp. 89–105.

after having worked clandestinely since 1929. It particularly targeted the army, seeking to instil a sense of courage and chivalry in the young generation. Like Shawkat, it desired the militarisation of Iraq and it foresaw a future in which Iraq would take the lead in Arab unification, just as Prussia had done in the German and Piedmont in the Italian unification. Crucially, *al-Jawwal* advocated the use of military force to achieve its objectives. In 1935, *al-Jawwal* eventually joined *Nadi al-Muthannah* and was later a participant in the Rashid 'Ali movement of 1941.[89] The Muthannah Club brought together various currents of militarist pan-Arabism into a single structure. Famous *qawmi* nationalists, such as Muhammad Mahdi Kubbah and the above-discussed Sami Shawkat were among its members. The club's objectives were to spread an Arab nationalist spirit, conserve traditions in which the 'Arab nature' were contained, educating the youth and strengthening the spirit of masculinity among them and giving birth to a new Arab culture bringing together what was sound in the Arab heritage with western culture. The club put its trust in the government, especially King Ghazi, to carry out Arab Unity. However, following Ghazi's death in 1939 and the outbreak of World War II the same year, despite public denunciation of Nazism, the club was eventually closed down by the British and the Regent 'Abd al-Ilah following the 1941 Anglo-Iraqi War.[90]

To these organisations and the new generation of *qawmi* nationalists who sympathised with them, the national army was an important tool of state building. Consequently, when during the early 1930s a series of tribal rebellions occurred that were put down by the army, and when in 1933 the so-called 'Assyrian question' was 'solved' by a massacre of civilian Assyrians, this was seen as striking blows to Britain's policy of 'divide and rule', as the British had promoted minorities to keep the country fragmented.[91] The 1936 Bakr Sidqi coup[92] opened up an era of military involvement in politics in which the pan-Arabists sought to impose their vision of Iraqi society. During the period 1937–1941, they gradually managed to displace the *Sharifians* at the top of the state but in 1941 their

[89] 'Alaywi, *Ittijahat al-Wahdawiyyah*, pp. 77–79.

[90] Ibid., pp. 79–82.

[91] Davis, *Memories of State*, pp. 59–60.

[92] For more details about the Sidqi coup, and the ICP's involvement in it, see the next chapter.

spell in government was ended by the British who after a coup by Rashid 'Ali al-Gaylani that had ousted the Regent, re-occupied the country militarily. The influence of the pan-Arabists declined as a result.[93]

Despite the efforts of educationalists like al-Husri and Shawkat and organisations like *al-Jawwal* and *al-Muthannah*, this particular brand of militarist pan-Arabism never fully managed to penetrate wider layers of the population. After the debacle of the Rashid 'Ali movement in 1941 and the general turn of fortunes for the Axis powers in the war, it lost most of what little popular appeal it had. The general idea of pan-Arabism did of course not die with these organisations, and after the Egyptian Revolution in 1952 and increasingly after the Anglo-French-Israeli tripartite attack on Egypt in 1956 (the Suez War), pan-Arabism had a revival, but this was more the result of the influence of Jamal 'Abd al-Nasir rather than that of domestic pan-Arabists. Instead, from the end of World War II in 1945, the scene of oppositional politics in Iraq belonged almost exclusively to various *watani* Iraqist groups, which, stressing democracy and social reform, gained immense popular support.

This Iraqist nationalism, although not constituting a coherent ideology or commanding a unified following, and although to varying degrees professing loyalty to the idea of pan-Arabism, was clearly distinct from its *qawmi* counterparts. To all Iraqist groups, the political objective of liberating the territorial entity of 'Iraq' was an end in itself, rather than a stepping-stone to the achievement of a pan-Arabist union as it had been to the various pan-Arabist groupings. During a brief liberalisation spell following the end of World War II under the premiership of Tawfiq al-Suwaydi, a range of new distinctively Iraqist political parties were formed. Thus, the National Democratic Party (*al-Hizb al-Watani al-Dimuqrati*, NDP) developed out of *Jam'iyyat al-Ahali*. Much of its activity was centred around the persona of Kamel al-Chadirchi, a well-known and respected political figure with roots in the old *effendiyyah*. Its programme spoke of working toward general reform in accordance with 'a well-ordered scientific plan'. Its main political goals were complete Iraqi independence, Arab unity, liberation of colonised Arab countries, resisting the establishment of a Jewish national home in Palestine, representative parliamentary democracy, defence of general liberties, reformation of the governmental system and the army and independence of the judiciary.

[93] Davis, *Memories of State*, pp. 68–71.

The programme further called for Iraqi unity on the ground that none of its citizens should be discriminated and that 'the Iraqi homeland is a field for free cooperation on the basis of common interest between Arabs and Kurds and others....'[94] A similar development took place in Iraqi Kurdistan, where the Kurdistan Democratic Party (*Parti Dimukrati Kurdistan*) was formed as a merger of several Kurdish parties during the failed 1946 Kurdish Mahabad Republic in Iran. Its founding congress was held in August 1946 and elected Mulla Mustafa Barzani (who was then Commander-in-Chief of the Republic's armed forces) as its president.[95] While sentimentally adherent of pan-Kurdism as an ideal, in its practical politics and indeed, to some extent, in ideology (owing to the fact that many of its founding members were ex-members of the ICP and other leftist organisations) it was unmistakably Iraqist.

The same period also saw the formation of a new pan-Arabist party, *Hizb al-Istiqlal* (the Independence Party), with origins in the Muthannah Club. In socio-economic terms, the members of this pan-Arabist grouping had similar backgrounds to those of the Iraqists. However, in contradistinction to the Iraqists they continued the ideals of a unified 'Arab nation', which had been the watchword of the earlier pan-Arabists. In pragmatic terms, however, the Istiqlalists differed little from the activists in the NDP. Although their long-term objectives were pan-Arabist in orientation their 'immediate demands' focused on very much the same issues as the NDP, such as amendment of the 1930 Treaty and strengthening of Arab unity through a federal system, something that included solving the Palestine question. One of the main differences, however, was that their programme called for education of the youth with national (*qawmi*) consciousness and unionist orientation.[96] In general, the main difference between the Iraqist parties and the modern pan-Arabists was

[94] Kamel al-Chadirchi, *Mudhakkirat Kamel al-Chadirchi wa Ta'rikh al-Hizb al-Watani al-Dimuqrati*, Cologne: Manshurat al-Jamal, 2002, pp. 128–129. For a history of the Ahali group, see Fu'ad Husayn al-Wakil, *Jama'at al-Ahali fi l-'Iraq 1932–1937*, Baghdad: Dar al-Hurriyyah li l-Taba'ah, 1980.

[95] François-Xavier Lovat, *Kurdistan Democratic Party, n.p.*: G.I.D. Editions, 1999, p. 13.

[96] Fadil Muhammad Husayn al-Badrani, *al-Fikr al-Qawmi lada l-Ahzab wa l-Harakat al-Siyasiyyah fi l-'Iraq 1945–1958*, Beirut: *n.p.*, 2005, pp. 56–57; see also Muhammad Mahdi Kubbah, *Mudhakkirati fi Samim al-Ahdath, 1918–1958*, Beirut: Dar al-Tali'ah, 1969, pp. 112–113.

the social content of their respective ideologies. The Iraqists were more inclined towards socialist-inspired ideas, whereas the pan-Arabists were more socially conservative.

2

THE IRAQI COMMUNIST PARTY AND THE ADVENT OF IDEOLOGICAL POLITICS

Origins of Iraqi Communism

The founding of the Iraqi Communist Party (*al-Hizb al-Shuyu'i al-'Iraqi*, ICP) in 1934 marked the beginning of a new era in which politics ever more was represented by political parties functioning from an ideological basis. As discussed in Chapter 1, the introduction of modern secular education was pivotal for this development. The new educated social groups, and in particular students, were exceptionally receptive to the new form of ideological politics offered by the ICP. Their radicalism and inclination to question the established 'truths' of Iraqi society made them a fertile recruitment ground for the party. In fact, numerous communists joined the party as students. Many within its higher echelons also worked as civil servants, lawyers, teachers, or held other forms of educated occupations.[1] Baqer Ibrahim al-Musawi, a prominent ICP leader, relates how he as a youngster in the 1940s attended the elect King Faysal II College. Despite its privileged status, the school became in his words, 'a fortress for *watani* activity', especially for the ICP and its front organisation *Hizb al-Taharrur al-Watani*, along with its secret student organisations.[2]

1 The trial of ICP leader Baha' al-Din Nuri in 1953 is a good illustration of its support among the intelligentsia, especially lawyers. Facing a military court, Nuri was defended by a legal team of no less than twenty-six lawyers, all of whom were members or sympathisers of the party, Sbahi, *'Uqud min Ta'rikh*, p. 120.

2 Baqer Ibrahim, *Mudhakkirat Baqer Ibrahim*, Beirut: Dar al-Tali'ah, 2002, p. 22.

Most early ICP members were thus intellectuals whose political ideas had been shaped by the traditional 'coffeehouse culture' that had developed since the 1920s. Few were workers and hardly any accustomed to clandestine work. Many had been educated at the Law College or the Higher Teachers' Training College in Baghdad but forced into unemployment or taking jobs below their training. Their reason for joining the communists was often more to do with the ICP's anti-imperialist position rather than an advanced understanding of Marxist-Leninist ideology.

The origins of communist ideas in Iraq lay in the growing intellectual milieu of political radicalism that started to emerge in the 1920s. In this environment, various ideas with roots in western socialism had first begun to flourish. Communist ideas first made their way into Iraq by way of Husayn al-Rahhal.[3] In the early 1920s, he formed the first 'Marxist' study circle, called *Mutadarisi al-Afkar al-Hurrah* ('The Students of Independent Ideas'). In 1924, the group began publishing a paper called *al-Sahifah* ('The Journal').[4] Though not Marxist in the traditional sense, the journal was unmistakably socially oriented. In its quest for radicalism, it even attacked religion, which in the 1920s was more than traditional opinion could accept and the journal was eventually closed down by the authorities.[5] Nevertheless, in mid-1926 the organisation's youngsters came together again to form the aforementioned *Nadi al-Tadammun*.[6] Though only lasting two years, the club was instrumental in bringing together some of the most important persons of early Iraqi communism.[7] In southern Iraq, communist ideas were first promoted by Pyotr Vasili, a

[3] As the son of a Shi'i officer in the Ottoman army, al-Rahhal had accompanied his father on a military mission to Germany where he went through the German educational system and witnessed firsthand the tumultuous events of the communist uprising in 1919 led by the *Spartakusbund*, Batatu, *Old Social Classes*, p. 390. See also Tareq Ismael, *The Rise and Fall of the Communist Party of Iraq*, Cambridge: Cambridge University Press, 2008, pp. 17–20.

[4] Salah al-Kharsan, *Safahat min Ta'rikh al-'Iraq al-Siyasi al-Hadith: al-Harakat al-Marksiyyah 1920–1990*, Beirut: Mu'assasat al-'Arif li l-Matbu'at, 2001, pp. 16–17.

[5] Batatu, *Old Social Classes*, pp. 393–5.

[6] al-Kharsan, *Safahat min Ta'rikh*, p. 17.

[7] Zaki Khayri, 'Asim Flayyeh (ICP founding member), 'Abd al-Qader Isma'il (*Ahali* founder and ICP member 1959–63), and Husayn Jamil (*Ahali* co-founder in 1932 and of NDP in 1946), were all in some way associated with al-Rahhal and *Nadi al-Tadammun*, Batatu, *Old Social Classes*, p. 403.

Georgian Assyrian who entered the country in 1922 as a professional revolutionary. Before being expelled in 1934 he worked to spread communist doctrines in Iraq. Vasili introduced communism to Yusuf Salman Yusuf (Fahad), Daud Salman (Fahad's brother), and Ghali Zuwwayed, who were all from al-Nasiriyyah.[8] In 1927, they formed Iraq's first communist study circle in Basra and a year later another one in al-Nasiriyyah.[9]

The new study circles had a slender following—no more than a dozen people at the outset. Like al-Rahhal's *al-Safihah*, attacks on religion was the main focus. For this purpose, they set up *al-Hizb al-Hurr al-Ladini* ('The Independent Atheist Party'). But like their counterparts in *Mutadarisi al-Afkar al-Hurrah*, the southern communists soon realised that rather than undermining the *'ulama'*, radical anti-religious agitation actually strengthened it, and so in late 1929 anti-religious propaganda was dropped altogether.[10] By 1933, Lenin's initial 'infantile disorders'[11] had been overcome, and the ranks of the various circles had swelled accordingly. Later that year, Ja'far Abu al-Timman, a Shi'i and a staunch Iraqist nationalist announced that his *al-Hizb al-Watani* ('The National Party') would withdraw from politics. Through his party, the communists had been able to venture their ideas legally. Now, however, the need for a separate organisation became clear. The various currents of Iraqi communism thus came together mainly through the leadership of 'Asim Flayyeh.

In the annals of Iraqi communism, the date 31 March 1934 is marked as the day of ICP's founding. However, agreement on this date as the founding date was reached much later. No documents, manifestoes or contemporary accounts have survived that would enable the establishment of a definite account of the party's founding.[12] Whenever the actual found-

[8] The Salman brothers (Yusuf and Daud) were from a Chaldean Christian family, while Ghali Zuwayyed was a slave of the mighty Sa'dun family, ibid., 411; 487.

[9] Ibid., pp. 404–6.

[10] Ibid., pp. 406–9.

[11] Lenin in his 1920 pamphlet 'Left-Wing Communism: an Infantile Disorder' had pointed out that radical leftism was a common trait of newly established communist organisations, see V. I. Lenin, 'Left-Wing Communism: an Infantile Disorder', in *Collected Works* 31, Moscow: Progress Publishers, 1964.

[12] 'Aziz Sbahi, 'Fusul min Ta'rikh al-Hizb al-Shuyu'i al-'Iraqi: al-Ta'sis', *al-Thaqafah al-Jadidah*, p. 297. For various, mutually contradicting, versions of the introduction of communism into Iraq, see Ismael, *Rise and Fall*, pp. 20–21.

ing took place, it is nevertheless clear that the newly unified party immediately increased communist activities. During 1935 it published a new organ, *Kifah al-Sha'b* ('The Struggle of the People'), took part in the country's incipient trade union movement, participated in a Congress of Arab Communist Parties, and dispatched Qasim Hasan, member of the new Central Committee, as an observer to the Seventh World Congress of the Communist International (Comintern) in Moscow. But the activities of the new party soon drew the attention of the authorities, and in November it was subjected to a wide clampdown that saw the arrest of the leading members.[13]

Following King Faysal's death two years earlier, in 1933, the throne had been taken over by his more nationalist-minded son, Ghazi, who until his violent death in a car crash in 1939 was a constant thorn in the side of the British. Ghazi's ascendency to the throne coincided with a militarisation of Iraqi society whereby military officers, through the medium of the army, would directly intervene in politics. The period 1936–41 witnessed a series of military interventions, all but two of which merely involved the exchange of one government for another. The other two, the 1936 Bakr Sidqi and 1941 Rashid 'Ali coups, were however of a different nature as they challenged the nature of government in a more profound way. As a nascent organisation, the ICP certainly was in no position to influence events at these junctures, but the two incidents serve as informative case studies of the way the party was prepared to collaborate with and support regimes that appeared to have popular support.

On 29 October 1936, General Bakr Sidqi together with other military officers and the support of the civilian *Ahali* group launched a coup d'état. This was the first in a long series of military coups that would shake the Arab World in the years to come. The ICP supported the new government, in which the *Ahali* nationalists received half the seats. Combined ICP and *Ahali* efforts helped to popularise the new regime.[14] During the

[13] al-Kharsan, *Safahat min Ta'rikh*, p. 21.

[14] Batatu, *Old Social Classes*, pp. 439–40. Note that Gabbay claims the ICP initially hesitated to support the new regime, Rony Gabbay, *Communism and Agrarian Reform in Iraq*, London: Croom Helm, 1978, pp. 51–2. This too is maintained by Laqueur who claims the ICP had to await instructions from the Comintern and as a result did not offer its support until Jan.-Feb. 1937, Walter Laqueur, *Communism and Nationalism in the Middle East*, London: Routledge, 1956, p. 178.

winter of 1936–37 the new regime held general elections in which two people close to the ICP, 'Abd al-Qader Isma'il and 'Aziz Sharif, managed to win seats in the parliament. Soon, however, the rising communist influence alarmed the officers who were running things behind the scenes. In March 1937, Bakr Sidqi attacked the communists and declared his loyalty to the monarchy, saying he was prepared to crush any movement threatening the throne.[15] From then on, the government grew increasingly anti-communist, eventually forcing the ICP to withdraw from open work completely. When Sidqi was murdered on 11 August 1937, the situation further worsened. The incoming civilian government launched a repression campaign against the ICP.[16]

During this period and increasingly after the Bakr Sidqi coup had shown the growing importance of military power in the young Iraqi state, ICP had undertaken a campaign of secret propaganda work in the army. The task was also partly a way of fulfilling the requirements of Comintern membership for which the ICP was accepted in 1936. One of the membership clauses stipulated that member parties had to have a military organisation.[17] The work had initially been centred on military instalments in Baghdad, but as successful military cells were formed, they multiplied and spread also to Kirkuk and Gawurpaghi in the north. Eventually, following Sidqi's assassination, ICP's secret army network was discovered and broken up. According to Batatu, at its height the movement comprised no less than 400 soldiers and non-commissioned officers. Yet, only sixty-five of them were brought to justice and in the end, only twenty-two were sentenced. Three of the officers were given death sentences, but after the intervention of Ja'far Abu al-Timman[18] these were eventually commuted to imprisonment. This incident fundamentally rocked the ruling elite and forever changed ICP's operational context. On 1 May 1938, an amendment to the Baghdad Penal Law added an Annexe—Article 89a—essentially criminalising communism as an ideology and made its proselytisation among the army punishable by death.[19]

[15] Batatu, *Old Social Classes*, p. 442.

[16] Gabbay, *Agrarian Reform*, p. 52.

[17] al-Kharsan, *Safahat min Ta'rikh*, p. 25.

[18] In a later ICP article written in 1960, Ja'far Abu al-Timman was described as a 'patriotic fighter', *Iraqi Review* 1, no. 23, 25 Jan. 1960, p. 2.

[19] Batatu, *Old Social Classes*, 444–6. Article I (i) of the 1938 Bagdad Penal Code An-

With the arrest of the ICP leadership and the remainder of the party forced to work clandestinely, the field laid open for other anti-British movements to seize the leadership of those sectors of society that were opposed to foreign domination. The period 1937–41, thus witnessed the rise of radical *qawmi* nationalists. In April 1941, in the midst of World War II, a constellation of right-wing military officers came to power through another military coup. These officers established a 'Government of National Defence'[20] (*Hukumat al-Difa' al-Watani*) placing Rashid 'Ali al-Gaylani, a respected Arab nationalist *effendi* and a member of the prominent Gaylani family, as a figurehead of their regime. Furthermore, they replaced the Regent with his cousin. After a gradual escalation of the situation, Britain decided to take military action against Iraq. In a short war lasting only a month, Britain re-conquered Iraq and returned the Regent 'Abd al-Ilah and his entourage of *Sharifian* politicians to Baghdad.[21]

Though the ICP had its misgivings about the new regime, the party realised it had evoked a genuinely 'popular enthusiasm' of the street, and therefore cautiously supported it. ICP-veteran Baqer Ibrahim, for instance, remembers how as a youngster in al-Kufah he witnessed the mass demonstrations in support of the Rashid 'Ali movement. He relates how the peasants from the surrounding countryside poured into the city, answering the call for a *jihad* against the British, and how they fired into the air. While acknowledging that they mostly were organised along 'traditional tribal' lines, i.e. following orders from their tribal chiefs, in his opinion the movement was not without its nationalist spur.[22]

---

nexe stated that Communist Party membership was an offence punishable with life imprisonment; Article I (iii), that the 'dissemination' of 'Communism' in the army and the police was punishable by death, see TNA: PRO FO 371/104668 1012/75/1953: Jul. 20 1953 'Bromley to British Embassy, Bagdad'. Later, Ordinance No. 16 of 1954 equated 'Fellow Travelling' with 'Communism' and put it within the scope of the 1938 Law, see TNA: PRO FO 371/115748 1012/1/55: Jan. 11 1955 'Chancery to British Embassy, Bagdad'.

[20] For a description of the 'Government of National Defence' and a wider discussion of events during this period, see Muhammad Hamdi al-Ja'fari, *Britaniya wa l-'Iraq: Hiqbah min al-Sira' 1914–1958*, Baghdad: Dar al-Shu'un al-Thaqafiyyah al-'Ammah, 2000, pp. 103–106.

[21] Tripp, *History of Iraq*, pp. 103–105.

[22] Ibrahim, *Mudhakkirat*, p. 19.

On 3 May, a day after the outbreak of the war, the Communist Party called upon the people to rally around the regime. Some days later, on 7 May, ICP First Secretary, Fahad, personally sent a letter to Rashid 'Ali urging him to rely on the people in the encounter with the British, and to grant them their constitutional rights. He also expressed his repugnance with the treatment of Jews at the hands of the regime, stressing that the reliance on the Axis powers was as much a menace to Iraq as dependence on British imperialism. According to Fahad, the only friend the regime could rely on was the Soviet Union.[23]

In an article issued less than a month after the collapse of the Rashid 'Ali regime, ICP maintained it had been correct to support it,[24] but when Germany attacked the Soviet Union on 22 June, this prompted a worldwide communist re-evaluation of fascism and British imperialism, something that reverberated also in Iraq. In a leaflet issued in July, ICP thus claimed Rashid 'Ali had been a 'fascist hireling'.[25] Two years later, it toned down the language, merely asserting its support had been a 'political mistake', but a year later Fahad stated the movement had been a 'foolhardy adventure', and in 1953 the Rashid 'Ali al-Gaylani movement was finally categorised as 'fascist' and 'criminal'.[26]

A New Type of Party—ICP under Fahad's Leadership, 1941–49

In 1941, Yusuf Salman Yusuf (Fahad), who had received training in Moscow during the previous years, took over the reins of the ICP. He led the party with an iron fist until his death at the gallows in 1949. Under Fahad's leadership, ICP became a political party of a new type. Its secretive and clandestine party apparatus introduced a new pattern of political organisation in Iraq, which in the decades to come was the model of success. It was fruitfully copied not only by the Free Officer Movement that overthrew the monarchy in 1958, but also by the Ba'th Party in the 1960s. ICP's new organisation was an organisational response to the increasingly

[23] Rashid 'Ali established diplomatic relations with the Soviet Union and following pressure from Fahad he also released the communist prisoners from 1937, Batatu, *Old Social Classes*, pp. 453–55.

[24] Ibid., p. 461.

[25] Gabbay, *Agrarian Reform*, p. 53.

[26] Batatu, *Old Social Classes*, p. 461.

repressive Iraqi state, but also a result of the party's turning into a Soviet-style communist party.

During Fahad's period in charge, ICP was transformed into a highly organised and centralised party, with local committees gradually covering the country. The party thus markedly distinguished itself from the other radical parties formed in the aftermath of World War II (the NDP, the Istiqlal and the KDP). Whereas those parties mostly had a strong presence in Baghdad and a few other big cities and were centred around charismatic leaders such as Kamel al-Chadirchi (NDP), Muhammad Mahdi Kubbah (Istiqlal), or Mulla Mustafa Barzani (KDP), ICP had a more inconspicuous approach. While it before had functioned trough the political activity of a handful intellectuals, ICP now developed into a mass organisation.

Fahad managed to transform the ICP from a 'traditional' urban political association of intellectuals to a wide-ranging party that attracted followers from all walks of life and with branches throughout the country.[27] Structurally, ICP was now organised in branch, district, and local committees. The secretariat of branches and districts would be in charge of city committees, consisting of party 'organisers' (*munazzimun*), each responsible for a cell. Furthermore, there were workers, peasants, 'national' (*watani*), students, factory, rural and school committees, all organised on the local level.[28] The smallest unit in the structure was the cell (*al-khaliyyah*). It constituted the basis of party work, as it was the main point of contact between party members and the 'masses'. It would consist of between two and five members who worked in a common place (e.g. a school, a factory, a farm, and so on).[29] The ICP was divided into Kurdish and Armenian sections, the Baghdad Local Committee, regional committees, and various local and city committees. Its hierarchical structure was made up of the National Congress—its highest authority, followed by the Central Committee, and finally, the Politburo and the Secretary-General, which were the main bodies that carried out the daily work in between regular meetings.[30]

[27] Ibid., p. 510.

[28] 'al-Nizam al-Dakhili li l-Hizb al-Shuyu'i al-'Iraqi', in *Kitabat al-Rafiq Fahad: Min Watha'iq al-Hizb al-Shuyu'i al-'Iraqi*, Beirut: Dar al-Farabi, 1976, pp. 169–183.

[29] Ibid., pp. 177–178.

[30] Ibid., pp. 156–9.

Communist mobilisation was usually carried out on a personal eye-to-eye basis; friends and acquaintances were approached in an indirect manner, observed, and if deemed sufficiently committed to the political cause, would be offered candidate membership in the local party organisation. The ICP never advertised its presence and membership was secret. Baqer Ibrahim al-Musawi's first encounter with the party is a case in point. In his memoirs, he remembers how he was introduced to political life by a fellow student while at secondary school. His friend introduced him to a study circle (*halqah*) that supported the party. During their meetings, they would study secret political literature and listen to the political commentaries of the *mas'ul* of the study circle, but, importantly, during their studies, the Communist Party or indeed the word 'communism' was not mentioned once.[31]

Under Fahad's iron fist leadership, ICP convened its First Conference in 1944. The more relaxed attitude of the authorities during the latter parts of World War II provided the necessary circumstances for its realisation. The conference took place in Baghdad in March,[32] approving the party's National Charter—a collection of principles aimed at public consumption. It avoided radicalism so as not to alarm the authorities and to appeal to as broad popular support as possible. Hence, among other things, communist support for petty traders and small producers was established, while also calling for complete Iraqi independence, revival of the constitution, and equality of women, Kurds, and other minorities.[33] The conference also adopted the Syrian Communist Party's motto: *Watan Hurr wa Sha'b Sa'id* ('A Free Homeland and A Happy People'),[34] which until this day has remained the ICP watchword.

A year later, in February 1945, the ICP also successfully convened its First Congress.[35] By now, Fahad's grip on the leadership was unchallenged and the congress was accordingly an attestation of his dominance. While nothing in the party's general policy was changed, internal rules were adopted in traditional Marxist-Leninist fashion. All proposed articles

[31] Ibrahim, *Mudhakkirat*, p. 22.

[32] Note that al-Kharsan maintains it took place in February, al-Kharsan, *Safahat min Ta'rikh*, p. 39.

[33] For the complete charter, see *Kitabat al-Rafiq Fahad*, Beirut: Dar al-Farabi, 1976, pp. 133–137.

[34] Batatu, *Old Social Classes*, p. 515.

[35] al-Kharsan, *Safahat min Ta'rikh*, p. 43.

were approved, and the congress added some new interesting ones to the effect that the ICP was struggling for 'political cooperation' with the 'Arab peoples' to achieve independence for Palestine and the colonised Arab countries, and an 'honest alliance' to enable these goals. Other articles called for social and economic cooperation among Arab peoples.[36]

ICP and the Problem of the 'National Bourgeoisie'

The main dilemma for any communist party operating in a Third World colonial or 'semi-colonial' context, was that the material forces of the working class—the 'proletariat'—had not reached the same level of maturity as its western counterpart, and was thus a minority in society. Since the beginning of the communist movement in the colonial world in the early twentieth century, this problem had grappled Third World communist parties, and indeed their European counterparts. It was generally acknowledged that the so-called 'national bourgeoisie' might be able to play some part in the revolution, at least in its first 'national-democratic' stage, which, in communist theory, sought to unite as wide as possible social forces in opposition to imperialism (widely conceived) to rid the country of foreign influence, and to thereby proceed to the next phase—the social revolution. Support for the national bourgeoisie was thus in the self-interest of the communists, as Lenin had pointed out in his seminal article 'The Right of Nations to Self-Determination'. 'The working class', he wrote, 'supports the bourgeoisie only in order to secure national peace…, in order to secure equal rights and to create the best conditions for the class struggle.'[37] After achieving this, the struggle would shift from national to class struggle and attain a distinctly social character. At this stage, tensions would show between the various national classes who before fought side by side.

For the Iraqi context in the 1940s, the term 'national bourgeoisie' is rather problematic. Not only was Iraq relatively unindustrialised at the time, but also the little industry that did exist (e.g. oil) was mostly foreign owned. In economic terms, a 'national bourgeoisie' in the Marxist-Leninist sense can thus not be said to have existed. Instead what the Iraqi com-

[36] See 'al-Nizam al-Dakhili', pp. 151–183.

[37] V.I. Lenin, 'The Right of Nations to Self-Determination', in *Selected Works*, vol. 1, Moscow: Progress Publishers, 1963, p. 609.

munists arguably meant by the term was individual members of the *Sharifian-effendi* elite, who had started incipient industries in Iraq's main cities, or traders who were involved in traditional Iraqi export, such as date and barley production. In political terms, the 'bourgeois-nationalists' were not necessarily members of the 'national bourgeoisie' economically, but rather intellectuals who were perceived to uphold the interests of this imagined group, that is, members of political parties such as the newly-formed NDP or the Istiqlal.

The problem of this potentially treacherous national bourgeoisie was at the heart of the anti-imperialist revolution; without its support, the revolution could not succeed, yet with its support there was always the possibility of betrayal at the most sensitive moment or, in the case of a successful revolution, its desire to assume the leadership of the nation. Due to the fluctuating nature of class relations, and because each country had its own specific historical and socio-economic circumstances, Lenin had early on advised communists in the colonial world not to assume dogmatic positions vis-à-vis the national bourgeoisie but to use any possibility of achieving mass support, even though their allies would be unreliable. In fact, at the Second Comintern Congress (held in Moscow 19 July—7 August 1920), two opposing views on the national bourgeoisie had crystallised. Lenin's generally positive position on the possibility of cooperation was challenged by Manabendra Nath Roy, an Indian communist. Roy, who had negative experience from working with the reformist Indian National Congress, argued that in countries with a prevailing 'reformist' nationalist movement, Comintern should avoid alliances with nationalist leaders as they were destined to abandon the struggle and join the 'imperialist camp' in a revolutionary situation. Instead, Roy argued, focus should be on building the communist movement and organise the 'masses' for the interest of that movement.[38] In an unusual move, the congress adopted both theses, but the final draft incorporated Roy's ideas into Lenin's thesis, which thus read:

> the Communist International should support bourgeois-democratic national movements in colonial and backward countries only on condition that, in these countries, the elements of future proletarian parties, which will be communist not only in name, are brought together and trained to understand their special

[38] John Patrick Haithcox, *Communism and Nationalism in India: M.N. Roy and Comintern Policy 1920–1939*, Bombay: Oxford University Press, 1971, p. 11.

tasks, i.e. those of the struggle against the bourgeois-democratic movements within their own nations.[39]

In the Iraqi context, there was very little of this struggle against the 'bourgeois-democratic movement'. The ICP instead adopted a conciliatory attitude towards what it perceived to be the 'national bourgeoisie'. In Iraq, Fahad explained, there were two types of 'national bourgeois' politicians: on the one hand, there was what he described as 'imperialism's cadre among us'—the 'pro-British' who served 'imperialism as civil servants and ministers',[40] i.e. *Sharifians* and members of the upper echelons of the *effendiyyah*. On the other side of the spectrum, there were two groups, according to Fahad. Firstly, patriots [*wataniyyun*] feeling the need for reform, and secondly, people with interests in the national industry, such as owners of barley, dates, and other national products, who had 'clashed' with foreign companies. These people, Fahad explained, would 'offer resistance defending their personal and class interests' and their opposition would thus 'on defined points' be 'in congruence' with 'the national interest [*al-maslahah al-wataniyyah*]'.[41]

In the above-cited 'Draft Theses on the National and the Colonial Questions', Lenin had instructed the Comintern to 'enter into a temporary alliance with bourgeois democracy in the colonial and backward countries', but had also warned it 'should not merge with it, and should under all circumstances uphold the independence of the proletarian movement even if it is in its most embryonic form'.[42] This, however, necessitated a fine balancing act on the part of the local communist parties. If they were to propagate their long-term objectives of establishing socialist states through the 'dictatorship of the proletariat', this would inevitably alienate large sections of the intelligentsia and the 'national bourgeoisie'.

The solution to this predicament was to have one secret programme, whose objective was a socialist state and eventually a communist society,

[39] V.I. Lenin, 'Preliminary Draft Theses on the National and the Colonial Questions', 28 Jul. 1920, in *Theses, Resolutions and Manifestos of the First Four Congresses of the Third International*, Alan Adler (ed), Alix Holt and Barbara Holland (trans.), 2nd ed., London: Pluto Press, 1983, p. 80.

[40] Fahad, 'Taqrir al-Rafiq Fahad Hawla l-Wad' al-'Alami wa l-Dakhili: Alqahu fi l-Mu'tamar al-Watani al-Awwal li l-Hizb al-Shuyu'i al-'Iraqi', in *Kitabat Fahad*, p. 146.

[41] Ibid., p. 147.

[42] Lenin, 'Draft Theses', p. 80.

attained through the dictatorship of the proletariat, and a second public programme focusing on principles providing common ground for unifying the 'masses'. For the ICP, this overt programme had been spelt out by Fahad at the First Conference in 1944. In the document, called 'the National Charter', he echoes the Iraqist parties demanding 'national sovereignty', 'real' independence, 'a government working for the interest of the people and a befitting democratic government apparatus and a real democratic system', the 'return of the constitution', taxing of 'speculators and monopolists', 'exploitation of our national riches', 'raising the level of agriculture', and 'ridding our people from the foreign monopolist companies', among other things.[43]

As for the long-term goal, this was much more sparsely commented upon, but it was clear from Fahad's polemics with various ICP factions that opposed his hard-line leadership in the early 1940s that his views did not differ from those of traditional Marxist-Leninist parties. For instance, in the seminal work *Hizb Shuyu'i, La Ishtirakiyyah Dimuqratiyyah* ('A Communist Party, Not Democratic Socialism') written in 1943, Fahad clearly stated that:

> We say that the ultimate goal of the Bolshevik Party, as documented in its programmes, was the overthrow of the bourgeoisie and the establishment of the dictatorship of the proletariat. And there is no Communist Party in the world that does not stand on this basis, just as that is also one of the requirements of the Communist International.[44]

In his February 1944 preface to the above text, Fahad's close aide, Husayn Muhammad al-Shabibi (Comrade Sarem), stressed the need for the party always to have 'in front of its eyes the remote goals which all Communist Parties aim for', i.e. the establishment of the dictatorship of the proletariat. 'Communist Parties are not', he underlined, 'whatever stage they pass through, anything but revolutionary proletarian organisations', warning the oppositional factions that they would 'not see their grandest programmes realised save by the revolution of the proletariat and its dictatorship.' He continued, explaining that the proletarian revolution 'is a long-term goal [*hadaf ba'id*] that we do not disavow, and are not afraid to mention, and we do not stray from it, or violate it, and we do

[43] *al-Mithaq al-Watani li l-Hizb al-Shuyu'i al-'Iraqi*, in *Kitabat Fahad*, pp. 133–34.
[44] Fahad, 'Hizb Shuyu'i, La Ishtirakiyyah Dimuqratiyyah', in *Kitabat Fahad*, p. 36.

not allow ourselves—or others—to call for it while following a road that will not reach it.'[45] Many of the early sympathisers, and indeed some of the early party members, did not agree with Fahad's 'undemocratic methods', and accused him of implementing a 'dictatorship' also on the party itself. However, in his polemics with these groups, Fahad insisted on the need for the ICP to be a centralised, fighting party during the stage of national liberation. He explained that:

> Communist Parties are able to carry out their obligations at this stage—the stage of imperialism [*al-imbiriyalism*]—by prescribing for themselves that they are fighting parties, mass parties, which have firm general methods (when it comes to the role in the struggle of the working class), just as the Party is centralised—not disjointed—so that it is able to fight the united enemy, monopoly capitalism..., and so that it is free from foreign influence, the influence of the antagonistic classes, which utilise opportunists connected to them inside the party.[46]

The strategy envisaged by the ICP, as indeed by other Third World communist parties, to overcome the problem of the weak working class and the potentially treacherous national bourgeoisie was the establishment of a national anti-imperialist front. This strategy had been advocated by Comintern at its Seventh Congress in 1935, when it, as a response to the growing threat of European fascism, had instructed the European parties to form popular fronts with Social Democratic and socialist parties in the interest of countering fascism. For the colonial and semi-colonial world, the counterpart was the national front with nationalist parties and groups opposed to imperialism.[47] However, when Lenin first had advised colonial communist parties to form anti-imperialist alliances with the national bourgeoisie, these were seen as temporary solutions to cease upon independence whence the emphasis would return to class struggle.[48]

For the purpose of uniting the biggest possible number of people, the ICP established a front organisation during World War II called *Hizb*

[45] Husayn Muhammad al-Shabibi (Sarem), foreword to 'Hizb Shuyu'i, La Ishtirakiyyah Dimuqratiyyah', by Fahad, in *Kitabat Fahad*, p. 20.

[46] Fahad, 'Hizb Shuyu'', p. 37.

[47] M.S. Agwani, *Communism in the Arab East*. Bombay: Asia Publishing House, 1969, p. 21.

[48] Erica Schoenberger and Stephanie Reich, 'Soviet Policy in the Middle East', *MERIP Reports* 39, Jul. 1975, p. 22.

al-Taharrur al-Watani ('The National Liberation Party'), led by Fahad's trusted right-hand man, Husayn Muhammad al-Shabibi. It was initially able to conceal its real affiliation from the authorities, and was eventually granted a licence in the brief liberalisation attempt that followed World War II. Its membership in 1947 was estimated by British intelligence officers at ca. 5,000.[49]

The writings of al-Shabibi are highly informative as they reveal core tenets of ICP thought on the concept of the front. In one of his key texts, he outlined the classes of the 'people' which were to make up the front. It shows profound knowledge of Iraqi society and the fragmented nature of Iraqi social 'classes'. The text is thus in stark contrast to the party's ideological propaganda material which categorically talked about the 'working class' and the 'national bourgeoisie' as unproblematic existing entities. First of all, al-Shabibi explained, 'a big class of peasants which comprise approximately three-fifths of the country's individuals' would constitute a significant part of the front. Despite their numbers, however, al-Shabibi argued that their political usefulness was not the best, as they were 'subjugated to old and antiquated feudal relations of production', and were the most miserable class in Iraq 'who do not derive from their pursuit and their struggle anything but misery, poverty, sickness and ignorance….' Secondly, classes [*martabat*] of professionals [*mihniyyin*] and skilled workers [*hirafiyyin*] would provide support against imperialism because they were 'engrossed by oppressive taxes' and, faced by foreign competition, wanted to defend their economic and social rights.[50] Thirdly, there were earners [*kasabah*][51] and petty traders, suppressed by the same phenomena as 'their brothers the *mihniyyin* and the *hirafiyyin*', and 'subjugated to the control and influence of foreign monopolist companies and prices'. The main support, of course, would come from 'the continuously growing working class', upon whose shoulders was the task of 'constructing our economic future and our national [*qawmi*] awakening'. The front would also include a class of intellectuals that had been 'prohibited from

[49] TNA: PRO FO 624/116/300/7/47: 27 Jan. 1947 'Fraser to Brewis: MEMORANDUM. National or International Organisations in Iraq in which Communist Influence is overtly or covertly predominant'.

[50] Husayn Muhammad al-Shabibi, *al-Jabhah al-Wataniyyah al-Muwahhadah Tariquna wa Wajibuna al-Ta'rikhi*, in *Kitabat al-Rafiq Husayn Muhammad al-Shabibi: Min Watha'iq al-Hizb al-Shuyu'i al-'Iraqi*, Baghdad: Matba'at al-Sha'b, 1974, pp. 34–35.

[51] Poor workers without regular employment who survive by doing odd jobs.

a place of work and *watani* service'. They would join the front, al-Shabibi explained, because they 'do not own the means with which to increase their talents, their capabilities, [or] their numbers'.[52] The front would even include a class of capitalists, consisting of industrialists and merchants. The industrialists, according to al-Shabibi, 'sees in imperialism an obstacle without [the possibility] to develop their national industrial projects due to foreign monopolist companies' monopolisation of the country's sources of wealth'. Similarly, those merchants whose trade was linked to foreign interests had lost their position as 'free merchants' due to 'the existence of the controlling monopolist companies'. As for those merchants whose trade was primarily based on local production and the domestic market, they too had seen their trade decline as a result of 'the existence of monopolies on dates and barley'.[53] Perhaps the most noteworthy group to be included by al-Shabibi was a class of large feudalists and landowners, who were worried that the country would remain 'backward in the economic, agricultural and industrial arenas, and that this backwardness would lead to the widening of the space for foreign influence which threatens our independence and demolishes our national sovereignty.'[54] Thus, on balance, the ICP envisioned a very wide front at this point. In fact, only the 'agents', that is, those who actively worked for 'imperialism', such as the Regent and his close entourage of pro-British politicians, were seen as bona fide enemies.

Arab Unity and the National Question

In a country like Iraq, made up of two main nationalities—Arabs and Kurds—the 'national question' was of particular importance for any political party targeting a mass audience. The ICP was no exception to this rule. This was later seen with an emphasis in the aftermath of the 14 July 1958 Revolution, after which much of the ideological and power struggles in the country became centred around the 'Kurdish question' and the 'question of Arab unity'. These were, of course, not entirely novel concerns. Prior to the 1958 Revolution, the ICP had expressed principled opinions on both issues. Fahad's view on the Kurdish question was

[52] al-Shabibi, *Jabhah al-Wataniyyah*, pp. 35–36.
[53] Ibid., pp. 36–37.
[54] Ibid., pp. 37–38.

explained in an article in *al-Qa'idah* in 1945, which was subsequently taken as the starting point for any discussion of the subject by ICP leaders. 'The right of all nations and nationalities to decide their own fate', read the article,

> is a fundamental principle of the world's Communist Parties, with which the Iraqi Communist Party agrees.... [Our Party] struggles to achieve the complete interests of the masses of the people as regards freedom for all... and in so doing it guarantees the Kurdish people and its working masses the necessary democratic organisations which will enable it to demonstrate its opinion, either by choosing to stay—or choosing separation, whenever Iraq's liberation from the control of imperialism has been completed or in a situation when it suits the Kurdish people and is in the interests of the working masses.[55]

Generous as that pledge may sound, it was tacitly understood that the Kurds would join the Arab national liberation movement and jointly fight against imperialism. Consequently, Fahad criticised what he saw as US attempts to extend American influence in Iraq at the end of World War II, using the Kurdish issue to create 'a social base' in the country. These fears were augmented by the visit of an American journalist to Iraqi Kurdistan during which 'imperialist pledges' to the Kurds for unification of the Kurdish areas purportedly had been made. At the First National Congress in February 1945 Fahad thus sounded the following warning: 'We remind our Kurdish brothers that their national question is linked with the question of Iraq's liberation and that the freedom of the Kurds in Iraq will not come to them by way of imperialist pledges from this or that person, but through joint struggle with the Arabs for the sake of complete independence for Iraq.'[56]

In an article celebrating the twenty-sixth anniversary of the October Revolution, Fahad dealt at length with the national problem, treating it from a historical point of view. He explained how, despite the many theo-

[55] *al-Qa'idah*, Nov. 1945, quoted in Najm Mahmud, *al-Sira' fi l-Hizb al-Shuyu'i al-'Iraqi wa Qadaya l-Khilaf fi l-Harakah al-Shuyu'iyyah al-'Alamiyyah*, Paris: *n.p.*, 1980, p. 18. However, the National Charter of 1944 gave witness to a much more cautious line. Its tenth clause stated: 'We struggle to create equality of rights for the Kurdish national minority taking into account the rights of the small national and racial groups such as the Turkmen, the Armenians and the Yazidis.', *Mithaq al-Watani*, p. 135.

[56] Fahad, 'Taqrir', p. 144.

ries put forward to solve the problem, none had been successful. In Tsarist Russia, there had been those who advocated incorporation of small nationalities into the dominant nationality of the metropolis, which led to prohibition of minority schools and institutions and the use of their language. This policy had also been followed by the Ottomans and by France in North Africa. These policies all failed, according to Fahad. 'But we do not deny', he went on,

> that this oppressive and barbarous policy was able to bury the history of those nationalities and hinder their general and cultural progress, and fragmentise their unity, and this is the main desire of the imperialist policy. In the light of this 'brilliant' policy, Hitler's 'nationalist' servants in Iraq contrived a new practical theory to solve the national problem in Iraq by liquidating the non-Arab elements and getting rid of them.[57]

This Iraqi policy, according to Fahad, tried to solve the problem by focusing on the 'pure Arabs', thus denying nationality to Jews, Kurds, Shi'is (because they were Persians), Christians (because they were non-Arabs), and some of the Sunnis (because they were Turks), 'but with this kind of counting', Fahad ironised, 'there would not have been left more than ten inhabitants of Iraq'. He also pointed out the fact that most of those calling for this policy were non-Arabs, such as Sami Shawkat.[58]

Another theory trying to solve the national problem had been espoused by the socialists of the Second International, who were in favour of granting cultural independence and linguistic rights to European minorities. 'When it came to the colonised peoples', Fahad critically explained, 'they had to remain colonised even during "their future socialist system"'. The pretext used by these 'socialists' was that as Europe went through socialist revolution and started to industrialise it would need raw materials, and since these raw materials were to be found in the colonies, there was no other way than to maintain these colonies. Out of these Second International theories, Fahad argued, the politicians of imperialist countries found 'a well that never dried out'. Thus, the Zionist notion of a 'home-

[57] Fahad is here referring to those *qawmi* organisations such as *al-Futuwah* and *al-Jawwal* that had emulated and started to propagate fascist ideas in Iraq during the course of the 1930s, see ch. 1.

[58] Fahad, 'al-Dhikra al-Sadisah wa l-'Ishrun li Thawrat Uktubir al-Ishtirakiyyah al-Majidah: Tahiyat al-Hizb al-Shuyu'i al-'Iraqi ila Shu'ub al-Ittihad al-Sufiyati', *al-Qa'idah*, Nov. 1943, in *Kitabat Fahad*, pp. 385–86.

land' in Palestine had its roots in 'Bundism', a socialist organisation that argued for Jewish cultural independence in Tsarist Russia, and which was linked to the Mensheviks who were members of the Second International. Similarly, Fahad continued, the Mandate idea as a whole had also emerged out of the theory of cultural independence that was intended for European minorities.[59] Lambasting these ideas and the 'opportunist position' of the leaders of the Second International, Fahad wrote the following:

> Their position was non-Marxist and anti-socialist because they did not see any connection between the national question and the proletarian revolution and the dictatorship of the proletariat, they did not understand the great benefit to be drawn from linking the toiling peoples' struggle in the colonies and the dependent countries with the proletarian class' struggle in the great industrialised countries against the common enemy, and that is because [the issue of] the dictatorship of the proletariat was not written down in their lists.[60]

In the 1940s, Arab unity had become a focal point for Iraqi politicians and had gradually started to receive cautious British backing. During the earlier mandate period, however, Britain had been wholly against attempts at unification of the newly-established Arab states, as it was detrimental to its own imperial policy of strengthening its mandates, but above all because it would seriously impede relations with the French. Nevertheless, Britain eventually realised that pan-Arabism as a political idea would not disappear. Following a series of negotiations during World War II, a Preparatory Committee for Arab Unity was thus able to convene with British support in Alexandria during the autumn of 1944. The resolution of the meeting, known as the Alexandria Protocol, called for the formation of a League of Arab States (*Jam'iyyat al-Duwal al-'Arabiyyah*), which eventually came into being in March 1945.[61]

These schemes were categorically viewed negatively by the ICP, who insisted that any Arab unity should be 'a voluntary union of the Arab peoples, not a union of Arab kings and princes and of the ruling classes.' The union, in the party's view, should 'draw its strength from its real source—the Arab people—in all its classes and from the international

[59] Ibid., pp. 386–88.

[60] Ibid., p. 388.

[61] Yehoshua Porath, *In Search of Arab Unity 1930–1945*, London: Frank Cass, 1986, pp. 277–286.

democratic movements.'[62] Against the critics of this cautious position, the ICP made a response in an article in *al-Qa'idah* in September 1943 entitled 'Our position on the Union'. 'Some interpret our position', the article read,

> to the effect that we take a position of opposition against Arab union, and that is correct. We cannot support a project whose goals and results we do not know, and the moving force behind which we do not know. All that is apparent with it is that it is a union of Arab kings and emirs and that the people do not have any affair in it. But at the same time we announce our sincere desire to support every project that leads to rapprochement and cooperation between the Arab peoples on the basis of an Arab union as we have outlined it...[63]

Attempts at Revolution—the 1948 Wathbah and the 1952 Intifadah

ICP's restructuring and consolidation under Fahad's leadership coincided with a general political radicalisation of Iraqi society following World War II. The period witnessed two serious attempts by the communists to challenge the *ancien régime* in 1948 and 1952. Yet it also witnessed the shattering of the organisation built by Fahad and his own arrest in 1947 and execution in 1949. Nonetheless, during this era the ICP developed into a major political force, but, as a result, it was also from this period onwards that it suffered the full repressive force of the British-backed *Sharifian* political elites. Although eventually subdued by the authorities, the 1948 *Wathbah* and the 1952 *Intifadah* marked the crumbling of patrimonialism and the 'politics of personalities'.[64] The eruption of popular politics consciously guided by ideological political parties showed with stark clarity that the ruling elites were no longer able to control politics through their usual pattern of clientelism and patronage distribution.

Fearful that the combination of economic crisis caused by the end of the war economy and the growing number of unemployed politicised students and civil servants along with wider segments of the population

[62] Fahad, 'al-Ittihad al-'Arabi al-ladhi Tanshuduhu al-Shu'ub al-'Arabiyyah', in *Kitabat Fahad*, p. 347.

[63] Fahad, 'Mawqifuna min al-Ittihad', *al-Qa'idah*, no. 8, Sept. 1943, in *Kitabat Fahad*, p. 353.

[64] Pool, 'Politics of Patronage', p. 244.

might erupt into detrimental social disturbances, even revolution, the British advised the Regent 'Abd al-Ilah to instigate reforms at the end of the war. Crucially for the ICP, the same insight that had propelled the Regent towards liberalisation had also made him and members of the establishment realise that the communists constituted a real problem and they thus launched a police campaign against the party in 1947.[65] While the attempted reforms largely failed, the repressive campaign towards the ICP proved more successful. In January 1947, Fahad was seized by the police. More arrests followed and soon the whole Politburo was apprehended.[66] Fahad was sentenced to death, but Britain, fearing bad international publicity from execution of civilians in peacetime, asserted pressure on the Iraqi government and his death sentence was eventually commuted to life imprisonment.[67]

Yet, with the failed liberalisation attempt Britain and the ruling circles realised that arrest of communist leaders would not suffice to extinguish the fervour of communist ideas, which through their focus on anti-imperialism and social justice counted considerable mass support. Thus, in a bid to appease the intelligentsia, the British government and some senior Iraqi politicians set out to secretly renegotiate the 1930 Anglo-Iraqi Treaty in December 1947. To most nationalists, the treaty was a symbol of the country's subordination as it stipulated the terms under which Anglo-Iraqi relations operated. In early January 1948, the negotiations could no longer be concealed and when the terms[68] of the new treaty that had been signed at Portsmouth were published on 16 January, the

[65] For earlier British views of the Iraqi communists, see Johan Franzén, 'Education and the Radicalization of Iraqi Politics: Britain, the Iraqi Communist Party, and the "Russian Link", 1941–1949', *International Journal of Contemporary Iraqi Studies* 2, no. 1, Jun. 2008.

[66] al-Kharsan, *Safahat min Ta'rikh*, pp. 51–52.

[67] Batatu, *Old Social Classes*, p. 541. Both Nuri al-Sa'id and the premier Saleh Jabr (Nuri's protégé) were 'intent on seeing the sentences carried out', a course of action also approved by the Regent, but were eventually swayed by the British, TNA: PRO FO 624/116/300/19/47: 30 Jun. 1947 'COMMUNISM—IRAQ S.F. 5/5, 27.6.47'.

[68] The more important terms were: Article 1 committed Iraq to a 'firm alliance' with Britain and a foreign policy congruent with her interests; Article 1a of the Annexe established Iraq's air bases as links in Britain's 'essential' communications; and Article 1b stipulated that in case of war or 'threat of war' Iraq had to 'invite' British troops and provide them with all facilities, see Batatu, *Old Social Classes*, p. 550.

public's anger was unleashed. A vitriolic press campaign against the new treaty, which was seen as a sell-out agreement by the nationalists, stirred popular unrest on an unprecedented scale.

Public fury was boundless; street fighting became common practice. Eventually the Regent lost his nerve and on 21 January issued a statement repudiating the new treaty.[69] However, since Saleh Jabr's government was still intent on seeing it through, the protests did not subside; instead, throughout the coming months demonstrations and strikes escalated and brought the country to a standstill. The ICP, having suffered from the blow to its leadership, was initially caught unawares, handing the initiative to the pan-Arabist Istiqlal Party, which for the first couple of days was the driving force behind the protests. Soon, however, the ICP came to terms with the situation and gradually took over the leadership of the protests by virtue of its superior organisational skills and its being more attuned to the protestors' radical mood. These events, additionally fuelled by the worsening situation in Palestine, led to 'the most formidable mass insurrection in the history of the monarchy',[70] popularly referred to as *al-Wathbah* ('the Leap').[71]

During the spring of 1948, protests continued and as the situation in Palestine deteriorated, increasing pressure was put on the government to take a firm stand against Zionism and British designs for the Palestine Mandate. It has been suggested that the Iraqi decision to join the Arab invasion of the new Israeli state, upon its proclamation in May, was a result of the unrelenting impact of the *Wathbah*.[72] Despite having the largest Arab force in Palestine at the end of the conflict, the Iraqi army mostly took up defensive positions for the duration of the Palestine war. The real intention of the Iraqi elite had instead been to try to displace domestic criticism and languages of social revolution through using radi-

[69] Wm. Roger Louis, *The British Empire in the Middle East 1945–1951: Arab Nationalism, The United States, and Postwar Imperialism*, Oxford: Clarendon Press, 1984; reprint, 1998 (page citations are from the reprint edition), p. 335.

[70] Batatu, *Old Social Classes*, p. 545.

[71] For a detailed account of these events, see ibid., ch. 22. Saleh Jabr, Iraq's first Shi'i PM, had to resign due to the protests. On 29 January, he was succeeded by fellow Shi'i Muhammad al-Sadr, whose appointment was intended to appease the Shi'i community; see Khadduri, *Independent Iraq*, p. 270.

[72] See Michael Eppel, *The Palestine Conflict in the History of Modern Iraq: The Dynamics of Involvement 1928–1948*, Ilford: Frank Cass, 1994, pp. 177–189.

Fig. 1. Commemoration of martyrs (*shuhada'*) killed during the *Wathbah* of January 1948 taking place on the *Arba'in* (fourtieth day) of the original event. Baghdad, 7 March 1948.

cal rhetoric and advocating military action against the Zionists.[73] However, with the Palestine adventure ending in military defeat, many instead questioned the ruling elite's Arab nationalist credentials.

As a direct result of the *Wathbah* and by using the outbreak of war in Palestine on 15 May 1948 as a pretext, martial law was declared. Later, in January 1949, the real strongman of Iraqi politics and one of the closest allies of the British and the Regent, Nuri al-Sa'id, was called back to head the government, as was customary in times of crisis. Despite having arrested hundreds of ICP members and effectively crushed its party apparatus, student protests continued unabated. On 6 January 1949, the same day as Nuri al-Sa'id's tenth government came into office, student strikes took place in the College of Medicine, the Pharmaceutics College and

[73] Charles Tripp, 'Iraq and the 1948 War: Mirror of Iraq's disorder', in *The War for Palestine: Rewriting the History of 1948*, Eugene L. Rogan and Avi Shlaim (eds), Cambridge: Cambridge University Press, 2001, p. 128.

the College of Law, while demonstrations raged in al-Hillah, al-Najaf, Basra, Kirkuk and al-Sulaymaniyyah. This prompted Nuri to state angrily in the senate, 'the present government has no other goal… than to settle the account with the communists and to combat communism to the last breath in this country.'[74] Accordingly, he brought back severe repression and clamped down on all the opposition parties, and, with special emphasis, on the Communist Party.

Following the crackdown, the police was able to arrest hundreds of other ICP members and re-try some of its leaders. On 10 February 1949, Fahad and two other members of the ICP Politburo, Zaki Basim and Muhammad Husayn al-Shabibi, were convicted of having led the party from prison and were sentenced to death. The sentences were carried out at daybreak on 14 and 15 February. They were hanged in public in different squares around Baghdad. The ICP was shattered; its organisation lay in ruins and all its senior cadres had been arrested. From November 1948 to June 1949, the party was fragmented and in utter confusion. Not only was it run by unauthorised *mas'uls* and youngsters, but it also split into five separate groups: *al-Haqiqah* ('The Truth'), *al-Najmah* ('The Star'), *al-Sawab* ('The Rightness'), *al-Ittihad* ('The Union'), and those who remained faithful to the old centre around the party journal, *al-Qa'idah*. The fragmentation and the scarcity of members essentially meant that by mid-1949, the ICP was no more.[75]

Yet, the popularity of the party and its message of anti-imperialism and social justice meant that a handful of surviving activists soon were able to rebuild the shattered organisation. Thus, the period following Fahad's death in 1949 until the revolution in 1958 saw the ICP bounce back and regain its position as the biggest and most influential opposition party on the Iraqi political scene. Although organisationally, the party had been seriously hit by the government clampdowns of 1947–49, in terms of ideological impact the *Wathbah* proved to be the ICP's real baptism of fire. In addition, over the course of the 1950s the party slowly rebuilt its battered structures and began spreading its influence into new areas of political and social activity.

[74] Mahadir Majlis al-Nuwwab, 'al-Ijtima' al-I'tiyadi li Sanat 1948', in 'Abd al-Razzaq al-Hasani, *Ta'rikh al-Wizarat al-'Iraqiyyah fi al-'Ahd al-Maliki*, vol. 8 (*n.p.*: Dar al-Shu'un al-Thaqafiyyah, *n.d.*), p. 88.

[75] Batatu, *Old Social Classes*, pp. 568–71; al-Kharsan, *Safahat min Ta'rikh*, p. 61.

Fig. 2. Communist prisoners in al-Kut Prison in 1948. Standing first from the right is Husayn Muhammad al-Shabibi (Comrade Sarem), member of the Politburo of the Communist Party. Third from the right is Zaki Basim (Comrade Hazem), also member of the Politburo, and fifth from the left is the First Secretary, Yusuf Salman Yusuf (Comrade Fahad).

While work among 'the masses' had been preached already during Fahad's period in charge and although some success had been achieved in this regard prior to his arrest in 1947, it was in the decade following the *Wathbah* that the ICP truly emerged as a mass party on the Iraqi political scene. Key areas that the party focused its mobilisation work on were among students, youth, women and 'patriots'. The *Wathbah* had showed the key role played by students, and although the party's student organisations had been forcibly dissolved during the *Wathbah* and many students had been arrested, the party remained influential in their midst. Attempts to revitalise the General Student Union (*Ittihad al-Talabah al-'Amm*) were made immediately after the *Wathbah* and by autumn 1950 the party managed to put together a new student leadership, which was drawn from ICP members and was headed by Hamdi Ayub al-'Ani, a communist student in the College of Arts (*Kulliyat al-Adab*). The Union enjoyed considerable support among secondary and college students. Starting in 1952, it clandestinely published a special student journal called *Kifah al-Talabah*.[76]

[76] Sbahi, *'Uqud min Ta'rikh*, p. 46.

The party also gained considerable influence among the youth in general during the 1950s. Young Iraqi communists and supporters of the ICP increasingly started to travel to Europe in the early 1950s, and whilst there gained experience of various political activities and youth festivals that had been organised by European leftist and communist organisations. Following on these experiences, Iraqi communist youngsters set up an Iraqi branch of the international Organisation of Democratic Youth (*Munazzamat al-Shabibah al-Dimuqratiyyah*) in 1951. The organisation gained considerable support among Iraqi youth, especially students. Its High Committee was made up of 'Aziz al-Shaykh, 'Abd al-Jabbar Wahbi and Muhammad Saleh al-'Abli, among others. The organisation remained clandestine until the 1958 Revolution following which it received a government licence.[77]

Work among women also intensified in the early 1950s. In 1951, a separate organisation was set up specifically to mobilise women. In due course the party even felt strong enough to apply for a government licence for a front organisation called *Rabitat al-Difa' 'an Huquq al-Mar'ah* ('The League for the Defence of Women's Rights'). However, the Ministry of Interior refused to grant a licence for the organisation, which included prominent communist and non-communist women, such as Dr. Nazihah al-Dulaymi, Dr. Khalidah al-Qaysi and Dr. 'Adwiyyah Adib. Instead the League continued to pursue its activities secretly.[78] As with the youth organisations, following the 1958 Revolution the League emerged into the open and dramatically expanded its activities and influence. According to its own estimates, it comprised some 25,000 members in the aftermath of the Revolution and by 1959 it had reached a membership of 40,000.[79]

Another key area in which the ICP managed to gain influence during this period was the bourgeoning peace movement. Again, this was an international initiative that eventually spread to Iraq as well. As the Cold War intensified, international intellectuals concerned with the growing threat of nuclear war came together in a World Congress of Intellectuals for the Defence of Peace, which was held in Wroclaw, Poland in August 1948. Among those attending were Aldous Huxley, Berthold Brecht and

[77] Ibid., pp. 47–48.

[78] Ibid., p. 48.

[79] Batatu, *Old Social Classes*, p. 897.

Pablo Picasso. The only Arab at the conference was the famous Iraqi poet Muhammad Mahdi al-Jawahiri, who was very close to the ICP.[80] In Iraq, the peace movement took off in earnest the following year. In mid-1950 a preparatory committee under al-Jawahiri's leadership was set up to coordinate peace activities in Iraq. The Iraqi peace movement soon counted among its followers prominent cultural and political personalities, such as 'Abd al-Wahhab Mahmud (chairman of *Hizb al-Ahrar*), and the renowned poets Badr Shaker al-Sayyab and Muhammad Saleh Bahr al-'Ulum.[81]

Reflecting its background as a party that had emerged out of the new radicalised intelligentsia, the ICP was also extremely influential among various professional groups, especially lawyers. In fact, several future leaders of the party were themselves trained lawyers, such as 'Amer 'Abdallah. In this period, the party therefore set up a separate front organisation intended to mobilise lawyers for the communist cause. The organisation's name was *Lajnat Mu'awinat al-'Adalah* ('The Committee for the Support of Justice') and it included a large number of communist and non-communist lawyers. The primary objective of the organisation was to offer legal services to the numerous communists and 'patriots' that were arrested and brought to trial, but the organisation also saw it as its task to defend democratic rights in general against the repressive measures of the state.[82]

The successful formation of these 'mass organisations' and their gradual growth throughout the 1950s meant that the ICP developed into a true *Iraqi* political party that was ever-present on the political scene—a political force loathed by some and admired by many. These developments were crucial for the later political and ideological development of the party following the 1958 Revolution. Many of the new party members that joined the ICP during the 1950s had received their first notions of political awareness during the crucial events of the *Wathbah*. Although many of these youngsters initially joined the ICP primarily for its nationalist anti-imperialist stance, the party was now strong enough to impose its own distinctive ideology on its members. Thus, in contradistinction to the 1930s and early 1940s when most joined after having formed their political consciousness as members of other political organisations and

80 Sbahi, *'Uqud min Ta'rikh*, pp. 50–51.

81 Ibid., pp. 51–52.

82 Ibid., pp. 54–55.

were heavily influenced by the new radicalised intelligentsia, for many of the future leaders who joined the ICP during the latter parts of the 1940s and the 1950s, the communist party was their first experience of organised political activity. Crucially, therefore, although in socio-political terms they did not differ much from earlier generations of communists, they now increasingly began to constitute a *communist* intelligentsia.

Husayn Ahmad al-Radi, who became leader of the party in 1955, is a case in point. He was born in the Shi'i holy town of al-Najaf in 1922. His father was an impoverished shop owner who had been forced into taking a salaried job as a flourmill clerk. Following secondary school, he left for Baghdad to attend *Dar al-Mu'allimin al-Ibtida'iyyah* ('The Elementary Teachers' Training School') in al-'Azamiyyah. Upon graduation in 1944, he became an elementary school teacher in al-Diwaniyyah *Muhafazah*. There, he became exposed to communist ideas through *al-Qa'idah* and eventually joined the ICP.[83] Senior ICP leader Saleh Mahdi Duglah had a similar background. Born in al-'Amarah in 1930 to a merchant father, he had been sent to a *Kuttab* as a young child. After having finished secondary school, he briefly worked as a teacher in al-Hillah.[84] As he was younger than al-Radi, Duglah was still in school at the time of the *Wathbah*. Although initially a supporter of the Istiqlal Party, he gradually became attracted to the communists because Istiqlal's activities were unorganised and sporadic.[85] Another example is Rahim 'Ajinah. Like al-Radi, he was born in al-Najaf, but in 1925. His family belonged in his own description to 'the upper echelons of the middle classes'. Like the others, 'Ajinah's conversion to communism came not out of socio-economic hardship but intellectually through ideas. From then on, 'it developed into a political stand and from there into organisational affiliation'.[86]

After the dark year of 1949, the party had eventually managed a slow recovery. In November 1949, an internal journal called *al-Injaz* ('The Accomplishment') started to circulate, and in February 1950, the party

[83] Thaminah Naji Yusuf and Nazzar Khaled, *Salam 'Adel: Sirat Munadil*, vol 1., Damascus: Dar al-Mada, 2001, pp. 17–26.

[84] Saleh Mahdi Duglah, *Min al-Dhakirah: 'Sirat Hayah'*, Damascus: Dar al-Mada, 2000, pp. 20–24.

[85] Ibid., pp. 28–29.

[86] Rahim 'Ajinah, *al-Ikhtiyar al-Mutajaddad: Dhikriyat Shakhsiyyah wa Safahat min Masirat al-Hizb al-Shuyu'i al-'Iraqi*, Beirut: Dar al-Kunuz al-Adabiyyah, 1998, p. 13.

journal *al-Qa'idah* re-emerged.[87] At that point, a policy of 'orderly retreat' was announced. The party started afresh and everyone had to reapply for membership and go through a probationary period.[88] The party's quiet and innocuous—but successful—approach during this period was mainly dictated by a young Kurdish communist called Baha' al-Din Nuri. He led the party from mid-1949 until 1953, a period marking the beginning of increased Kurdish party membership. When Nuri became party leader, he was merely twenty-two years old. He was born in 1927 in the village of Takih, situated outside al-Sulaymaniyyah, into a well-known religious family. Both his father and grandfather were prominent *'alims* in al-Sulaymaniyyah and wealthy landowners. He was related to Shaykh Mahmud Barzinji, who in 1920 as *hikimdar* of 'southern Kurdistan' had proclaimed Kurdish independence and thereafter been arrested by the British. The family later moved to al-Sulaymaniyyah, where Baha' in 1946 started his political activity in *Hizb al-Taharrur al-Watani*, the ICP front organisation. During the 1948 *Wathbah*, he had been elevated to cell organiser, and following the draining of the communists' ranks he rose to *mas'ul* of the Sulaymaniyyah Local Committee in April 1949. Less than two months later, he became First Mas'ul of the ICP by default.[89] Despite his tender age and revolutionary inexperience, Baha' al-Din Nuri proved to be a capable leader who managed to bring the party back to its feet. During his leadership, the party, having drawn valuable lessons from the disastrous period preceding Nuri's ascendance to power, the so-called *Naksah* ('The Degeneration'), was slowly able to rebuild some of its organisations.

The first real test of the rebuilt ICP came in late 1952 when parts of the country erupted into protests, very much on the same lines as the 1948 *Wathbah*. Throughout the year, the regime was rocked by a series of well-organised strikes. In June and again in September, the British military bases at al-Habbaniyyah and al-Shu'aybah were targeted. These strikes, which were of a political rather than an economic character, had a great impact on the mood of the public.[90] In the autumn, protests, which

[87] *al-Injaz* was later replaced by *Munadil al-Hizb*, which until the present has remained ICP's internal journal, Sbahi, *'Uqud min Ta'rikh*, p. 37.

[88] Batatu, *Old Social Classes*, p. 659.

[89] Sbahi, *'Uqud min Ta'rikh*, pp. 32–34.

[90] Ibid., pp. 62–63.

led to *al-Intifadah* ('The Shaking Off'), started because of oppositional reform demands on the Regent. The opposition consisted at this point of the Istiqlal Party, the NDP, the newly founded 'United Popular Front' led by the *effendi* Taha al-Hashemi, and the ICP front organisation *Ansar al-Salam* ('The Peace Partisans'). At a meeting on 17 November, they agreed to set up a 'Liaison Committee' (*lajnat al-irtibat*) to coordinate the protests.[91] The demands that had been presented to the Regent in late October were essentially a call for direct elections instead of the traditional two-tier system. However, on the advice of the British the Regent, 'Abd al-Ilah, rejected the demands. Former Prime Minister Saleh Jabr, who had fallen out with his erstwhile patron Nuri al-Sa'id, also opportunistically took up the popular calls for direct elections putting additional pressure on the ruling circles.[92]

On 22 November, Baghdadis took to the streets to protest against the government and the Regent. Clashes with the police followed leaving one dead and fifty-two wounded, forcing Prime Minister Mustafa al-'Umari's government to resign. Yet, the next day protests intensified and new clashes followed, this time with twenty-five wounded. Now the ICP managed to get a more firm hold over events on the street by actually having its leaders on the scene and handing out direct orders, something that gave it a distinct advantage vis-à-vis the other oppositional parties. The mood of the demonstrators grew more radical, attacking police stations, looting and burning the US Information Service Library to the ground. The American Ambassador, Burton Y. Berry, in a meeting with his British counterpart, John Troutbeck, explained that he and his staff were 'much upset' by the attacks, which they regarded as 'proof' that American influence was waning in Iraq.[93] The police shot dead twelve of the demonstrators, further incensing the crowds. At the end of 23 November, the situation was out of control and the army was called in to restore order. The Kurdish Chief of Staff, General Nur al-Din Mahmud formed a new government and proclaimed martial law, deployed armoured cars and tanks on Baghdad's streets, arrested the opposition leaders, dissolved their

[91] Batatu, *Old Social Classes*, pp. 666–7; Sbahi, *'Uqud min Ta'rikh*, p. 65.

[92] TNA: PRO FO 624/209/1012/77/52: 20 Oct 1952 'J.M.T. Minutes', and FO 624/209/1012/71/52: 25 Oct. 1952 'Maitland Minutes' have reference.

[93] See TNA: PRO FO/209/1012/122/52: 26 Nov. 1952 'Confidential Minutes J.M. Troutbeck'.

parties, suspended a total of seventeen newspapers and journals, and arrested people on a massive scale.[94] But through its clandestine nature, the ICP avoided the arrests, and on the next day, the demonstrations continued. In the evening of 24 November, troops again opened fire on the demonstrators, this time killing eighteen and wounding eighty-four. In the end, however, protests were quashed by the repression of the new government.[95]

Ideological Struggle, Splits and Re-Unification, 1952–56

Whereas in the 1930s and early 1940s, there had been much overlapping between the political activities of the ICP and other organisations formed by members of the new intelligentsia, by the 1950s such intersections almost stopped by virtue of the Communist Party's ideological and organisational maturity. The communist intellectuals emerging from the ranks of the ICP now distinguished themselves significantly from other intellectuals in that they had become professional revolutionaries who were committed ideologically to their cause to the degree that they were prepared to face incarceration and possible death. In such an organisation, it was only natural that ideological differences erupted when it lost its leadership.

Following the *Intifadah* and as result of international developments, the ICP began to radicalise its views on the nature of the regime it wanted to set up in Iraq and its views on the 'stage of national liberation'. This development was spurred on by the advance of 'Peoples' Democracies' across Eastern Europe and Asia. Whereas Fahad's old National Charter had been a careful attempt to incorporate as broad as possible social elements into the party's sphere of influence, a tougher stance was now crystallising as a result of the experiences of Eastern European communist and leftist parties who had managed to obtain the leadership of the social movements in their countries. Since February 1949, calls had been made in the party organ, *al-Qa'idah*, for replacing Fahad's 1944

[94] Sbahi, *'Uqud min Ta'rikh*, p. 69.

[95] Batatu, *Old Social Classes*, pp. 668–70. According to the statistics of the Ministry of Defence, 2,999 people were arrested during the *Intifadah*. Two were sentenced to death, 958 to imprisonment, while hundreds were fined and had to pay bail, Sbahi, *'Uqud min Ta'rikh*, p. 70.

notion of a 'genuinely democratic regime' with the more radical 'People's Democratic Republic' on the eastern European pattern.[96]

As the draft for a new National Charter was published in December 1952, a heated debate ensued, bringing to light all the differences of opinion that existed within the party, which Fahad's charismatic persona and iron-fist leadership alone had managed to suppress. Eventually, after the new charter had been formally adopted in March 1953, its opponents, in total seventy-three people, were expelled. The expellees, who were predominantly from the Sulaymaniyyah and Arbil branches, called themselves the 'disciples of Fahad'. Some later very influential communists were in their ranks, among others future First Secretary 'Aziz Muhammad, 'Abd al-Salam al-Nasiri, 'Abd al-Razzaq al-Safi and Jamal al-Haydari. They set up a paper, *Rayat al-Shaghilah* ('The Banner of the Workers'), with which they attacked the party leadership, criticising it for having exaggerated the strength of the 'revolutionary forces'. Fahad's old charter still held true, they maintained, and instead of an 'empty' slogan like a 'People's Democratic Republic', they suggested their own: 'a national, democratic, and peace-loving government'.[97]

In April 1953, Baha' al-Din Nuri was arrested and the helm of the party was taken over by 'Abd al-Karim Ahmad al-Daud, a Kurdish ex-teacher.[98] He began to formulate a more radical party policy. In June, *al-Injaz* claimed 'the immediate task of the workers, peasants, and toiling masses' was 'the seizure of power by the proletariat',[99] thereby giving evidence to the somewhat unrealistic direction the party was taking. It has to be remembered that this happened after the party had suffered heavy blows during the repression that followed the *Intifadah*, and just having had its leader arrested and sentenced to life imprisonment. The new policy therefore seems to have been out of touch with the party's actual capabilities.

[96] Batatu, *Old Social Classes*, p. 671.

[97] Jamal al-Haydari, from a prominent Kurdish landowning family of Arbil, was the leading force behind the new faction. Having joined the Party in 1945, he had spent most of his time in opposition, either in the anti-Fahad faction *Wahdat al-Nidal* or in the Kurdish leftist organisation *Shurish* ('Revolution'). The party centre was also challenged by another faction called *Wahdat al-Shuyu'iyyin al-'Iraqiyyin* ('The Unity of the Iraqi Communists'), a group formed in 1952, ibid., pp. 672–73; al-Kharsan, *Safahat min Ta'rikh*, p. 72.

[98] Sbahi, *'Uqud min Ta'rikh*, p. 119.

[99] Batatu, *Old Social Classes*, p. 673.

Meanwhile a more moderate stance was developing among some ICP leaders. The moderates gathered around Husayn Ahmad al-Radi, a Shi'i from a family of *sayyids* and the son of a flourmill clerk. They managed to impose a decision to consolidate Fahad's old National Charter at a meeting in January 1954. The final report of the meeting, issued under the title *Jabhat al-Kifah al-Watani Didd al-Isti'mar wa l-Harb* ('The Front of National Struggle Against Imperialism and War'), included a call to form a 'National Front Government' in which the ICP would take part. This stand was also echoed by al-Radi in his speech to the 'Conference of Communist and Workers' Parties in countries within the sphere of British Imperialism', held in London 21–24 April 1954.[100] Radi later acknowledged that he had been instrumental in the formulation of the document and that it had essentially outlined 'his vision'.[101] Thus, two diametrically opposed sets of thoughts were developing within the ICP leadership at that point.

From about the same time, al-Radi had started to rise within the ranks of the party; in 1949, he had been arrested during a demonstration in Baghdad and incarcerated for four years. While under police supervision in the summer of 1953, however, he managed to escape and make his way back to Baghdad. There he was made *mas'ul* of the southern region[102] by his friend, Karim Ahmad al-Daud, who, following Baha' al-Din Nuri's arrest in April 1953, had taken over as First Mas'ul of the party. After having successfully led a strike in Basra in December 1953, al-Radi was co-opted into the Central Committee. From that position, he was instrumental in formulating the major policy change outlined in the above-mentioned document.[103]

The document, which was the ideological forerunner of later policy changes, focused on the problem of the national front, a question re-actualised by the 1948 *Wathbah* and the 1952 *Intifadah*. During both

[100] al-Kharsan, *Safahat min Ta'rikh*, p. 74. During his stay in London, al-Radi allegedly received £3,000 from ICP's London Branch, headed by Anis 'Ajinah. According to 'Ajinah, this gave al-Radi 'more clout' within the CC back in Iraq, which was in financial dire straits. Interview by Ismael with Anis 'Ajinah, 17 Mar. 1974, Ismael, *Rise and Fall*, p. 50.

[101] Interview by Ismael with Husayn Ahmad al-Radi, 8 Dec. 1959, Ismael, *Rise and Fall*, p. 47.

[102] Comprising Basra, al-'Amarah, and al-Nasiriyyah.

[103] Yusuf and Khaled, *Salam 'Adel*, 1, pp. 36–56.

these events, the lack of a unified national front had allowed the authorities to quell the uprisings. The document, which was the report of a Central Committee-meeting, was therefore very pragmatic in nature and focused on unifying the 'national forces' at any cost. 'We have to understand', the document read, 'that the question of the front is not a question of agreement or signing of the front's charter, nay it is a question of agreeing on joint action.'[104] While theoretically discussing the government to be set up after a defeat of imperialism, the document listed some key actions to be taken by the future government, which included annulment of the 1930 Treaty and evacuation of 'the occupying English armies', oil nationalisation, cancellation of 'all the reactionary laws' and release of political prisoners, and finally, what appeared as a much less radical policy toward the Kurdish question, as the document merely stated that the coming government would have to allow 'the Kurdish people's exercising of its political, administrative, and cultural rights', but without mentioning Fahad's pledge to allow the Kurds to decide their own fate.[105]

Remarkably, the party was even prepared to give up its own stake in a future government if that meant it would come into fruition. Thus, although contending that the 'best of national governments' would include the ICP, its participation was not an absolute demand. The document thus went on:

> But this is not the only sort of government that we can support, irrespective of whether we participate in it or not, nay, some governments generally take positions against imperialism, and [even] if they are in phases where they are the least resolute and courageous in striking the positions of imperialism, our position toward them will be that we will support their patriotic [*watani*] positions by propping them up from below, although that does not mean that we will not criticise their reactionary or wavering positions that are harmful to the interest of the people.[106]

The new conciliatory policy towards so-called 'national governments' now became the backbone of the party's ideology, and later constituted the theoretical blueprint from which it acted following the 1958 revolution.

[104] *Jabhat al-Kifah al-Watani didd al-Isti'mar wa l-Harb*, in Yusuf and Khaled, *Salam 'Adel*, 1, p. 58.
[105] Ibid., pp. 60–61.
[106] Ibid., p. 61.

The more mollified approach of al-Radi's faction, which was close in outlook and disposition to the other Iraqist parties, led to the formation of a National Front with the NDP and the Istiqlal in May 1954. This was intended as an election front for the general election that took place during the liberal premiership of Fadil al-Jamali. The front's charter demanded democratic liberties, free elections, annulment of the 1930 Treaty, evacuation of foreign troops, repudiation of all 'imperialist and military alliances', refusal of American military aid, while calling for Arab solidarity in getting rid of 'imperialism', independence for Arab countries and liberation of Palestine, and toward realising 'social justice'.[107] Although the ICP leadership of course knew that the electoral approach would not win them any real power during the reign of the *ancien régime*, it argued that the legalist approach was of benefit due to the many propaganda opportunities that came with an election campaign.[108]

Nevertheless, the failure of al-Jamali's brief liberalisation attempt resulted in a new wave of repression against the oppositional forces that lasted until the 1958 Revolution. As the struggle increasingly became ideological, the government issued a decree that forced political prisoners (mostly communists) to renounce their principles or face being stripped of their Iraqi nationality, something that befell many prominent communists while incarcerated (e.g. Baha' al-Din Nuri and Zaki Khayri). The ideological struggle targeted students as well; they had to reveal their political sympathies through the presentation of a so-called *bara'ah* ('disavowal') in order to enter college.[109]

The radical faction within the party leadership, for its part, was backed by veteran ICP-member Hamid 'Uthman, a Kurd from Arbil with a big following in the party, especially among communist inmates in al-Kut Prison where he had been incarcerated. In June 1954, 'Uthman managed to escape from prison and take over the party leadership. From the position of new leader, he accused al-Radi of 'right deviationism' and threw him out of the Central Committee. He then gradually steered the party

[107] See the complete text of *Mithaq al-Jabhah al-Wataniyyah* ('the Charter of the National Front') in al-Chadirchi, *Mudhakkirat*, p. 560.

[108] During the elections, the front had thirty-seven candidates: NDP fourteen, Istiqlal eight and fifteen independents (mostly tied to the ICP), Sbahi, *'Uqud min Ta'rikh*, p. 139.

[109] Ibid., pp. 149–150.

back to the radical track.[110] During 'Uthman's reign, the ICP gradually started to radicalise its stance. In December 1954, party activity was resumed in the armed forces through its newly created military organisation, *al-Lajnah al-Wataniyyah li Ittihad al-Junud wa l-Dubbat* ('The National Committee for Unity of Soldiers and Officers'). This committee issued a secret publication called *Hurriyat al-Watan* ('The Freedom of the Homeland'),[111] whose first number came out the same month.[112]

But the ICP was still a comparatively weak party, ill-prepared for 'Uthman's radical course. For instance, when he in September 1954 had called for a 'general political strike' and when in January 1955 he called for 'armed struggle' these were policies that were out of accord with the party's resources and capabilities. Though some, like Batatu, ascribe the root of his radicalism to Maoist influence,[113] others have rejected such assertions. Long-time party renegade Hesqil Kojaman, for example, maintains that while 'Uthman was 'very loyal to the Party and loyal to the Revolution' he was 'not a Marxist'.[114] Be that as it may, 'Uthman's leadership coincided with attempts made by the Iraqi ruling elite, headed by Nuri al-Sa'id, to tie Iraq firmer to the West through the launching of the so-called 'Baghdad Pact'. This was seen by many as an attempt to sneak the failed Portsmouth Treaty of 1948 in through the backdoor. Hamid 'Uthman thought as much and ordered the party onto the streets in an all-out battle to defeat the government and the new Pact. But unprepared for such an immense task, it was defeated and suffered heavily.[115]

Incensed by 'Uthman's disastrous policies and critical of his 'individualistic' leadership style, the Central Committee-majority eventually staged an internal coup against him in June 1955. The change of leadership steered the ICP back in the moderate direction it had been heading before 'Uthman's brief interlude in power. 'Uthman was criticised for having pursued a 'leftist, isolationist policy' towards the 'masses', as a result

110 Batatu, *Old Social Classes*, 676–77; Sbahi, *'Uqud min Ta'rikh*, pp. 145–146.

111 Not, as Ismael translates it, 'the liberation of the motherland', see Ismael, *Rise and Fall*, p. 57.

112 *Hurriyat al-Watan*, no. 1, Dec. 1954.

113 Batatu, *Old Social Classes*, p. 677. At least superficially 'Uthman was influenced by Maoism as he advocated building 'revolutionary strongholds' and a revolutionary army on the Chinese pattern, *Supplement to al-Qa'idah*, no. 7, Jan. 1955.

114 Interview by author with Hesqil Kojaman, London, 12 Oct. 2005.

115 Batatu, *Old Social Classes*, p. 709; al-Kharsan, *Safahat min Ta'rikh*, p. 76.

of underestimating the possibility of legal work. To underline its departure from 'Uthman's radicalism the new Central Committee decided that more focus should be put on legalistic 'mass' propaganda.[116] The new moderate leadership under al-Radi also paved the way for a reunification of the ICP with the erstwhile antagonistic factions, *Rayat al-Shaghilah* and *Wahdat al-Shuyu'iyyin*. Following negotiations, *Rayat al-Shaghilah* was dissolved on 13 June 1956.[117] Briefly thereafter, the *Wahdat al-Shuyu'iyyin*-group was also welcomed back in the party, as were other individuals who had drifted from the party.[118] All the old journals, *Rayat al-Shaghilah*, *al-Nidal*, and *al-Qa'idah*, ceased publication in favour of a new joint organ called *Ittihad al-Sha'b* ('The Unity of the People'),[119] thereby signalling a departure from 'Uthman's radicalism to the new line of 'unifying the people'.[120]

The resulting unified party was a far cry from Fahad's well-oiled organisational machine obeying his every demand. The new Politburo was effectively divided between three strongmen. At its helm stood Husayn Ahmad al-Radi, who in the period after the 1958 Revolution became known under his then party name—Salam 'Adel. The 'second man' was 'Amer 'Abdallah, a Sunni Arab Lawyer from al-'Anah who stemmed from a family of *sayyids* and who was the son of a *mu'adhdhin*.[121] He had only joined the ICP as recently as 1951, but nonetheless stood out as the party 'ideologue'. Along with party old-timer Zaki Khayri, he was the most theoretically minded of the ICP leaders. The 'third man' was Jamal al-Haydari, who had led the *Rayat al-Shaghilah* faction.[122]

[116] In July it issued a manifesto to this effect entitled *Fi Sabil al-Hurriyah al-Dimuqratiyyah, Fi Sabil al-Masalih al-Hayawiyyah li Jamahir al-Sha'b*, Sbahi, *'Uqud min Ta'rikh*, p. 164. In Nov., a similar manifesto was issued under the title *Fi Sabil Siyasah Wataniyyah 'Arabiyyah, Fi Sabil al-Hurriyat al-Dusturiyyah, Fi Sabil Inqadh Iqtisadina al-Watani wa Takhfif Mashakil al-Jamahir*. It also contained a call to the other oppositional parties to join the ICP in a front. The rapprochement, it argued, was 'the only way to win the victory', *al-Qa'idah* 14, no. 1, Feb. 1956, quoted in Sbahi, *'Uqud min Ta'rikh*, p. 167.

[117] Interview with Salam 'Adel, *Ittihad al-Sha'b*, 26 Jan. 1960, in Sbahi, *'Uqud min Ta'rikh*, p. 173.

[118] Sbahi, *'Uqud min Ta'rikh*, p. 174.

[119] Batatu, *Old Social Classes*, pp. 710–11.

[120] Sbahi, *'Uqud min Ta'rikh*, p. 174.

[121] Batatu, *Old Social Classes*, pp. 674–75.

[122] Ibid., pp. 719–20.

Once the successful reunification of the party had been carried out in July 1956, the new leadership went on to convene a party conference. This was only the second conference in the party's history. In addition to sealing the unification of the party, it was also intended to debate the historical resolutions of the Twentieth Congress of the Communist Party of the Soviet Union (CPSU), held earlier that year. The Second ICP Conference took place in Baghdad in September 1956.[123] Apart from the attendance of two Spanish communists, representatives from Iraqi nationalist parties had also been invited, such as Dr. Kamal Fu'ad, a member of the politburo of the Democratic Union of Kurdistan and Saleh al-Haydari, the former leader of *Shurish*.[124] At the meeting, a new politburo consisting of the aforementioned trio was formally elected.[125] The conference came to be noted for the significant change of the general political course it prompted within the party. Its resolutions were heavily influenced by the Twentieth CPSU congress, which only half a year earlier had transformed communist politics worldwide. The new political line adopted at that congress, the so-called 'peaceful co-existence' theory in international relations and the possibility of a 'peaceful road' to socialism, dominated the agenda of the Second ICP Conference.[126] But what appeared as a radical transformation of communist policy in fact merely consolidated the pacifist direction that the ICP had taken under Husayn Ahmad al-Radi's leadership, following the ousting of Hamid 'Uthman in 1955. The Conference thus continued the route outlined in the document 'Jabhat al-Kifah al-Watani' which the ICP Central Committee had approved in 1954.

The main issue discussed at the Second Conference was a political report presented to the meeting by al-Radi, Jamal al-Haydari and 'Amer 'Abdallah outlining the political developments on the world level and within the national liberation movement in the Arab world. The report, entitled *Khittatuna al-Siyasiyyah fi Sabil Taharrurina al-Watani wa l-Qawmi* ('Our Political Plans for Our Patriotic and National Liberation'), strictly followed the new Soviet line and argued for a 'peaceful road' also for the local Iraqi situation. Although the recent Iraqi history suggested

123 Sbahi, *'Uqud min Ta'rikh*, p. 177.

124 Duglah, *Min al-Dhakirah*, p. 51.

125 al-Kharsan, *Safahat min Ta'rikh*, p. 79.

126 See Adam B. Ulam, *Expansion and Coexistence: Soviet Foreign Policy, 1917–73*, 2nd. ed., New York: Praeger Publishers, 1974, p. 573.

that the coming battles would be anything but 'peaceful' (e.g. the *Wathbah* of 1948 and the *Intifadah* of 1952), the party leadership still adopted the new Soviet 'pacifist' approach. The change in political line within the CPSU, the principal communist party in the world and the symbolic and practical leader of the world communist movement, undoubtedly added another dimension to the *problématique* of ideological change within the ICP's ranks. Not only was the party now exposed to the internal pressures and strains brought on it by years of relentless struggle against the *ancien régime*, but it was also challenged by external pressures coming from the most senior ideologues within the global communist movement.

The decision to adopt the 'peaceful road' was taken despite the fact that many of the senior leaders and much of the rank-and-file were behind the bars of the regime, and that this regime, in collaboration with the British, had set as its goal the annihilation of the Iraqi communist movement. Yet, the report argued: 'We, the Iraqi Communists, have no desire for violence or to follow the road of force, we, on the contrary, endeavour to accomplish the liberating goals of our movement in the easiest way and with the least sacrifices.'[127] Heavily influenced by the idea of the 'power of the masses', as witnessed in the popular outbursts of 1948 and 1952, the report argued that 'leaning on the national movement's past experiences, it is possible to draw the conclusion that the balance of power is on the side of the popular masses in a definite manner…', and this was so '[b]ecause the enemies of the people are not in a position in which they can put a stop to the will of the rising united people.' Therefore, the report argued, the coming battle would be of a 'predominantly peaceful character'. It would:

> count essentially on the mobilisation of the national forces in a wide front, and the application of pressure on it in a concentrated manner and in various, influencing, forms with the aim of exchanging the existing policy for an independent Arab national policy, one that lets the country follow the course along the road of development.[128]

The document also adopted the new Soviet notion of a 'gradual' (*tadriji*) transition to socialism. Discussing the nature of the government to be set up after the ridding of imperialism, the report argued that:

[127] *Khittatuna al-Siyasiyyah*, quoted in Mahmud, *al-Sira'*, p. 20.

[128] *Khittatuna al-Siyasiyyah*, quoted in Sbahi, *'Uqud min Ta'rikh*, pp. 178–179.

The first big victory will be protected by the people; it will ignite the energy of popular enthusiasm to a great extent. This government… will be given splendid conditions to make the people take its destiny into its own hands, in addition to the resources of Iraq and its vast revenues, and the nature of revolutionary outbursts prevalent among the Iraqi people, and the captivating force of progressive, democratic and socialist ideas in Iraq, and the favourable disposition of the balance of power to the benefit of the workers, the peasants, and the nationalist intellectuals, which put forth the evidence that Iraq never will require more than a short time to proceed with great steps along the road of economic, cultural and social prosperity within the framework of the allied Arab family, proceeding united under the leadership of the working class, along the road of peaceful and gradual transition to Socialism.[129]

But, even a 'peaceful and gradual transition' to Socialism was not on the immediate agenda; such a transition was seen more as an inevitable outcome in the long run, resulting from the favourable 'balance of power'. Instead, for the moment, the Iraqi 'masses' would have to continue to endure their hardships, because the report concluded that 'the task of transition to Socialism and the transfer of political power to the hands of the workers and the peasants and their allies is not a task that our movement envisage in the present circumstances.'[130]

At the time, the Second Conference was heralded by the party leadership as a great victory for unity, but some members have later asserted that the alleged unity was fictional. They have criticised the conference for its new policies and strategies; the way in which the 'peaceful road' was adopted and dogmatically carried out is generally believed to have been erroneous. The relationship between the ICP and the CPSU has also been singled out as a root of the party's coming problems. Critics have held that the conference adopted the new general theory without conducting any analysis of the local situation in Iraq. 'Aziz Sbahi, for instance, argues that 'the Party leadership did not reach its conclusion regarding peaceful development relying on any serious study of the social reality in Iraq at the time.' He adds that it is 'unavoidable to recall how the reactionary regime did not hesitate to use bullets to suppress the uprisings of the people.'[131] Saleh Mahdi Duglah, who attended the con-

129 al-Taqrir al-Siyasi li l-Lajnah al-Markaziyyah li l-Hizb al-Shuyu'i al-'Iraqi, p. 34, quoted in Sbahi, *'Uqud min Ta'rikh*, pp. 180–181.

130 *Khittatuna al-Siyasiyyah*, quoted in al-Kharsan, *Safahat min Ta'rikh*, p. 79.

131 Sbahi, *'Uqud min Ta'rikh*, p. 180.

ference as a candidate member of the Central Committee, is also critical in his memoirs. Although generally positive to official ICP policies, of which he was an integral part, he nevertheless concludes that the 'Conference's assessments on the "peaceful road to Socialism" did not themselves prove valid, and soon the Party abandoned this policy and embarked upon a policy more in touch with the reality of Iraqi conditions, because the government would resort to suppressing it for any opposition with the utmost savage violence.'[132] A more severe critique of the conference is offered by Hesqil Kojaman, ICP member from 1945 until 1959. He regards the document as a 'real anti-Marxist' document,[133] and is especially critical of the notion of the 'peaceful road', which he argues 'in fact was the hardest road with the dearest sacrifices'.[134] To him, the new Soviet ideas were nothing but a development of the old notion of peaceful transition to socialism, which had originally been propagated by the Second International. Thus, in his view, the programme of the conference was 'petty bourgeois reformist and opportunist..., with no relation to Marxism-Leninism.'[135]

Another sticking point for the critics was the apparent willingness on the part of the ICP leadership to give up the claim for the sharing of power in the coming 'national government', a position, as we have seen, already formulated in the 1954 document 'Jabhat al-Kifah al-Watani'. In that document, the party had cautiously stated that it was its 'duty' to support such a government 'without imposing as a condition the participation in it as long as it endeavours with sincerity and enthusiasm to carry out the tasks presented before it and respects the will of the people.'[136] In Kojaman's opinion, this was a policy of self-denial. By assuming this position, he argues, the party surrendered not only its own immediate interests of obtaining some ministerial posts in the coming national government, but also the interest of the working class. An equally critical position is echoed by Najm Mahmud,[137] who relates ICP's predicament

132 Duglah, *Min al-Dhakirah*, p. 51.

133 Interview by author with Hesqil Kojaman, London, 12 Oct. 2005.

134 Hesqil Kojaman, *Thawrat 14 Tammuz 1958 fi l-'Iraq wa Siyasat al-Hizb alShuyu'i*, Guildford, UK: Biddles, 1985, p. 54.

135 Ibid., pp. 52–53.

136 'Taqrir al-Siyasi', quoted in Sbahi, *'Uqud min Ta'rikh*, p. 182.

137 His real name was Ibrahim al-'Alawi. After the split in 1967, he was prominent in

to its ideological and political subservience to the CPSU. 'It is possible to say without being overly cautious', he asserted,

> that one of the main reasons for the Party's relapses and the great losses that afflicted the revolutionary movement in Iraq was because of the Party leadership falling under the ideological and political influence of international revisionism starting in 1956 specifically. And, since the Twentieth Congress of the Soviet Communist Party, the revisionism appeared as a complete line for the international and internal policy, capitalist in its direction...[138]

Mahmud, too, criticises the main conference decisions for not having taken into account the political situation in Iraq or other Arab countries. He is adamant that the proximity to the convening of the Twentieth CPSU Congress made the party leadership stretch its own report to suit the new conditions.[139] This is corroborated by Sbahi, who acknowledges that 'the Party paid special attention to the Twentieth Congress of the Communist Party of the Soviet Union, to its proceeding and to the documents that were presented in it.'[140]

There is little doubt the ICP leadership felt a close affinity with the CPSU. In an official congratulatory message written by the ICP Central Committee on 30 January 1956 and published in *al-Qa'idah*, it clearly showed its adoption of the Soviet notions of 'peaceful coexistence' and 'peaceful competition' between world systems, as had been outlined by the Twentieth Congress. 'As for the imperialists', the message read, '[who] exploit the peoples, and the enemies of peaceful competition [*al-tanafus al-silmi*] between various systems, they are the ones that are frightened by the colossus of the Soviet Union's creative methods ... The leadership of the great Communist Party is superior, and the Soviet peoples comprise indefatigable developments...'[141]

In Iraq, the new line soon met with failure. Only weeks after the conference had ended, in late October, the pivotal Suez Crisis erupted. The

---

the 'Central Command' faction, and after the detention and killing of its two main leaders, he became its unofficial leader.

[138] Mahmud, *al-Sira'*, p. 21.

[139] Ibid., p. 19.

[140] Sbahi, *'Uqud min Ta'rikh*, p. 176.

[141] 'Tahiyat al-Lajnah al-Markaziyyah li l-Hizb al-Shuyu'i al-'Iraqi ila al-Lajnah al-Markaziyyah li l-Hizb al-Shuyu'i fi al-Ittihad al-Sufiyati bi-Munasabah In'iqad al-Mu'tamar al-'Ishrin al-'Adi li l-Hizb al-Shuyu'i fi al-Ittihad al-Sufiyati', 30 Jan. 1956, published in *al-Qa'idah* 14, no. 1, Feb. 1956.

British-French-Israeli attack on Egypt and Jamal 'Abd al-Nasir's defiant decision to offer resistance in the name of Arab nationalism showed with unmistakable clarity that the communist proclamation of a new era of 'peaceful competition' had been dreadfully premature. Instead of peaceful co-existence, British and French imperialist ambitions in the region had led to violent confrontation. The outcome of the Suez Crisis, the fact that Britain and France had to back down following crucial American and Soviet intervention and in the Arab world the elevation of Nasir to the position of Arab hero, marked a watershed in the modern history of the Middle East. The crisis effectively meant the end of Britain as the dominant power in the Middle East and the rise of the United States to that position.[142] The Americans, whose esteem among the Arabs temporarily increased after they forced Britain and France to withdraw from Egypt in late 1956, just as quickly lost this new moral high ground when they issued the 'Eisenhower Doctrine' in January 1957. This was an attempt to formalise the new American position in the Middle East and contain the threat of growing Soviet influence in the area by offering economic and military aid to countries that needed 'assistance against armed aggression from any country controlled by international communism',[143] and came to include Iraq, Jordan, Lebanon and Saudi Arabia.[144]

Coming as it did just a few weeks prior to this crucial event, it is thus beyond doubt that the new policy adopted at the Second ICP Conference was exceptionally ill-timed. In Iraq's major cities, the situation was almost as explosive as in Egypt. People poured onto the streets in their masses demonstrating against 'imperialism' and for Nasir and Egypt's independence. In a manner that proved beyond any doubt that Nuri al-Sa'id and the ruling clique in Iraq were unimpressed with the ICP leadership's newfound peace-loving inclinations, these demonstrations were brutally suppressed, just as demonstrations always had been in the past. When

[142] Wm. Roger Louis, 'Britain and the crisis of 1958', in *A Revolutionary Year: The Middle East in 1958*, Wm. Roger Louis and Roger Owen (eds), London and New York: I. B. Tauris, 2002, p. 17.

[143] Ibid., pp. 18–19.

[144] For a comprehensive study of the Eisenhower Doctrine and the compelling argument that it was as much about containing the radical pan-Arabism espoused by Nasir as it was an attempt at keeping the Soviets at bay in the region, see Salim Yaqub, *Containing Arab Nationalism: The Eisenhower Doctrine and the Middle East*, Chapel Hill, N.C.: University of North Carolina Press, 2004.

the attack on Egypt went under way in earnest in early November, a popular uprising prompted by anti-imperialist fervour erupted in al-Najaf. The uprising was dominated by communists and nationalists who made common cause in issuing calls for the downfall of Nuri al-Sa'id and in support of Nasir; it lasted throughout November and into December, prompting support demonstrations and strikes all over Iraq—in Baghdad, Mosul, Kirkuk, al-Sulaymaniyyah and Arbil.[145]

With these new developments, the ICP leadership realised it had made a serious error of judgment when adopting the new Moscow line. The idea that the coming battles for national liberation in Iraq and the rest of the Arab world would be of a 'predominantly peaceful nature', as argued by the conference, thus within weeks of its inception died a quiet death, and so on 11 November the party issued a Manifesto in which the reversal was made public. However, rather than acknowledging that the whole concept of a 'peaceful road' was flawed, the ICP leadership merely argued that violence might be needed for the specific Iraqi circumstances. 'The question of violence', the Manifesto read,

> is for us a question that is determined by the antagonist's behaviour, when he is unwilling to yield to the will of the people. For that reason, the "violent way" is the preponderant way for our people's struggle and for its national movement decisively to overcome the aggression and violence of imperialism and its agent rule in Iraq.[146]

Following the British-French-Israeli withdrawal from Egypt, Nasir became the undisputed nationalist hero throughout the Arab World. He was seen to have single-handedly defeated the three mighty enemies; in reality, of course, US and Soviet pressure had been decisive. Nevertheless, the fact that Nasir put up a violent resistance made an inextinguishable impression on the general public, which more or less forced the ICP leadership to adapt its position to the new reality.

Having thus abandoned the concept of the 'predominantly peaceful road', the party went on to organise a popular uprising in al-Hayy, a small town of no more than 25,000 inhabitants and with a significant sympathy for communism. Throughout December 1956, the party and its sym-

145 For a detailed account of these events, see Sbahi, *'Uqud min Ta'rikh*, pp. 194–214; Batatu, *Old Social Classes*, pp. 752–754.

146 'Manifesto of the Iraqi Communist Party', 11 Nov. 1956, quoted in Sbahi, *'Uqud min Ta'rikh*, p. 180.

pathisers held much of the city despite desperate police attempts to penetrate the barricades. The city was defended by armed contingents but eventually fell to the overwhelming onslaught of the reinforced police units. On 21 December, the uprising's two main leaders, 'Ali al-Shaykh Hamud, secretary of the local party committee, and 'Ata Mahdi al-Dabbas were arrested, and subsequently executed on the gallows.[147] On the same day, the ICP issued a manifesto in support of the uprising entitled *Anhadu Da'aman li Jamahir al-Hayy al-Shaja'ah fi Intifadatiha al-Musallahah* ('Render Support to the Courageous Masses of al-Hayy in their Armed Uprising').[148]

Later, in May the following year, the party published a pamphlet with the heading *Intifadat 1956 wa Mahammuna fi l-Waqt al-Rahin* ('The 1956 Uprising and Our Tasks at the Present Moment'). In it, the party leadership made a frank self-criticism of its position at the Second Conference and its having been caught off guard when spontaneous demonstrations in support of Egypt erupted in November 1956. The self-criticism read:

> ...when the aggression against Egypt occurred and our people started to move towards the struggle, it followed completely clearly from the facts of the local, the Arab, and the international situation, what we in the past had been unable to diagnose.... since we were not capable.... of appraising, with precision, that the ruling reactionary forces in the interior would protect their positions and commit to the defence of the interests of imperialism with such mad tenacity....[149]

Yet, overall the categorically positive view of the Twentieth CPSU Congress prevalent among the ICP leadership was unshaken. This could be seen even five years later when, at the Twenty-second CPSU Congress in 1961, ICP First Secretary Husayn Ahmad al-Radi delivered a speech on behalf of the party in which he praised the Twentieth Congress. 'The Twentieth Congress of the Communist Party of the Soviet Union', he stated in the speech,

> was a historical bend that changed the course of events and opened up vast horizons.... For our Party, the decisions and conclusions of that Congress had a huge

[147] For a more in-depth account of these events, see Sbahi, *'Uqud min Ta'rikh*, pp. 206–210; Batatu, *Old Social Classes*, pp. 754–756.

[148] Sbahi, *'Uqud min Ta'rikh*, p. 209.

[149] 'Intifadat 1956 wa Mahammuna fi l-Waqt al-Rahin', quoted in Mahmud, *al-Sira'*, p. 22.

impact on its life and its activities.... The Twentieth Congress helped us liquidate the splitting and opportunist organisations in the Communist movement in our country, and it helped us attend with greater determination to ideological inflexibility and isolationism and [fight] against bureaucracy. The Central Committee summoned our Party for the Second General Conference to be held in 1956, despite the difficult circumstances and the grave terror against the Party and the National movement at that time, in order to revise the complete policy of the Party in the light of the historical achievements of the Twentieth Congress.[150]

He thus conceded that not only did the ICP leadership accept the new Soviet general line; it also used it in order to unite the oppositional groups prior to the conference.

It is therefore clear that the Second Conference of the Iraqi Communist Party, like its Soviet counterpart, played a crucial role in the future ideological and political development of the communist movement in Iraq, as indeed the Twentieth Congress did for the development of Soviet communism.

The 14 July 1958 Revolution

Given that the ICP voluntarily had chosen to pursue its new pacifist line, which was based on a fundamentally positive reading of the capabilities of the so-called 'national bourgeoisie' to take a lead in the national struggle against imperialism, it is perhaps not a surprise that when the British-installed Iraqi monarchy finally was overthrown on 14 July 1958, it was not the communists but a group of secretive military officers that were the masterminds behind the move. The military initiative that led to the overthrow of the *ancien régime* was carried out by a group of nationalist military men calling themselves *al-Dubbat al-Ahrar* ('The Free Officers').

In socio-economic terms, these Free Officers came from the poorer and middle strata of society. In their majority, they were Sunni Arabs, either from provincial towns or born in Baghdad to recent migrant parents. They were all colonels or lieutenant colonels, and all in their late 30s or early 40s. Ideologically, most of them belonged to the new generation of pan-Arabists who had clashed with the British in 1941, but some were more Iraqist in orientation.[151] The structure of the new organisation was

[150] From a speech on behalf of the ICP at the Twenty-second CPSU Congress in 1961, in Mahmud, *al-Sira'*, pp. 20–21.

[151] Batatu, *Old Social Classes*, pp. 764–765; 787–788.

very secretive and highly centralised, working through small cells of no more than three or four people. This was almost identical with the ICP cell. Throughout its existence, membership in the organisation counted very small numbers. In 1957, it had only 172 members, while on the eve of the Revolution, they were little more than 200—less than 5 per cent of the officer corps as a whole.[152]

The radicalisation of the army had been ongoing for a long time. The army's unsuccessful venture for power in 1941 under the aegis of Rashid 'Ali al-Gaylani and the ensuing defeat at the hands of the British army had led to an irreparable break between pan-Arabist officers and the Monarchy. This further worsened later on with the debacle in Palestine in 1948–49. To this disillusionment, a gradual deterioration of the economic situation, although abated from the mid-1950s when money started to be poured into the army for fear of waning loyalties, further accounted for the spread of anti-British and anti-Monarchy sentiments in the army. A series of events starting in the mid-1950s convinced the officers that immediate action needed to be taken. The ruling elite signed up Iraq to the Baghdad Pact,[153] thereby unequivocally putting Iraq within the western sphere in the Cold War. This was in clear break with the will of most nationalists who favoured neutralism in foreign affairs. When emotions were already running high, the 1956 tripartite attack on Egypt led to an unprecedented upsurge in nationalist feelings in the Arab world. Finally, as a response to Egypt forming an alliance with Syria, the so-called United Arab Republic (UAR), the old regime in Iraq announced in early 1958 that it too was to form an alliance with its Hashemite brothers in Jordan.[154]

152 Ibid., pp. 776–783.

153 The Baghdad Pact was formed as a strategic response to Nasir's rise in Egypt. As he gradually developed into Britain's main antagonist in the region, British strategists sought to boost Iraq's role in regional defence arrangements, enthusiastically encouraged by their local Iraqi allies, see Elie Podeh, *The Quest for Hegemony in the Arab World: the Struggle over the Baghdad Pact*, Leiden: Brill, 1995, pp. 53–9. The pact was formally established in 1955. Initially, only Iraq and Turkey were members, following the signing of a military co-operation agreement between them on 14 February 1955. However, in April Britain joined the pact as well and later in 1955 Pakistan and Iran were also added to the list of members, Sbahi, *'Uqud min Ta'rikh*, 156.

154 Batatu, *Old Social Classes*, pp. 765–67.

The ICP leadership, for its part, had observed the gradual politicisation of the army and had increasingly stressed the need for work in its midst. Since the army's deployment against popular demonstrations during the 1952 *Intifadah*, the necessity to win over soldiers and officers to the side of the revolution had been firmly imprinted on the minds of ICP's leaders. However, due to the factional struggles that lasted until the mid-1950s, no work in the army had been carried out, with the exception of uncommissioned propaganda work pursued by Husayn Ahmad al-Radi in 1954 while he headed the Baghdad Local Committee.[155] But from 1955 onwards, the ICP rapidly built up a strong support base, not only among the soldiery but also among senior officers.[156]

In accordance with the party's new political line of seeking cooperation with other nationalist groups, the ICP now also opened up more to the civilian oppositional movement. Thus, the major political parties (the KDP, the Istiqlal, the Ba'th Party and the ICP) formed a Front of National Union with the intention of coordinating oppositional activities. The front, formed in February 1957, called in its first manifesto in March for the removal of Nuri al-Sa'id's government, Iraq's withdrawal from the Baghdad Pact, unification of Iraq's policies with those of the 'liberated Arab countries', constitutional democratic liberties, annulment of martial law, and release of political prisoners and reinstatement of relegated students, sacked civil servants and teachers who had lost their jobs for political reasons.[157] Moreover, the front set up a Higher Committee and a Central Organisational Committee to liaise between the parties. Below them, there were local and professional committees throughout the country, and in addition, principal committees in most *liwa's*.[158] The Free Officers were worried that independent political activity in the army might spoil the plot before it could be executed, and hence passed a warning to members of the front. As a result, Ba'thi activities in the army ceased and officers supporting the Ba'th joined the Free Officers.

[155] Sbahi, *'Uqud min Ta'rikh*, pp. 246–248.

[156] To mention but a few, the ICP had direct relations with retired Air Force General Jalal Ja'far al-Awqati, Staff Brigadier Muhyi al-Din 'Abd al-Hamid, Staff Brigadier Nazem al-Tabaqchali, Staff Brigadier Daud al-Janabi, Staff Brigadier Hashem 'Abd al-Jabbar, Brigadier General Ibrahim al-Jaburi, and Colonel Fadel al-Mahdawi. For a more exhaustive list, see ibid., p. 250.

[157] al-Chadirchi, *Mudhakkirat*, p. 592; Sbahi, *'Uqud min Ta'rikh*, p. 229.

[158] Sbahi, *'Uqud min Ta'rikh*, p. 230.

Contacts between the Free Officers and the front were formalised in 1958.[159] The ICP also agreed to cease publication of its military journal *Hurriyat al-Watan*, following a demand from the Free Officers.[160]

Then, on 14 July 1958, troops loyal to the Free Officers entered the capital and seized the Ministry of Defence and other vital areas of the capital. The action was swift; everything went as planned except that Nuri al-Sa'id managed to escape.[161] At about the same time, the ICP, which had been informed in advance of the planned military attack,[162] had the whole party on its feet and out on the streets of Baghdad. According to 'Amer 'Abdallah, the party had been aware of the coup plans already in 1956. First Secretary Husayn Ahmad al-Radi had seemingly given his approval to such an endeavour. In this account, 'Abd al-Karim Qasim, the leader of the Free Officers, desired Soviet backing for the coup and wanted the ICP to act as a liaison with the USSR.[163]

Although the initial move had been military in nature, which through its meticulous planning had been able to swiftly eliminate key persons of the old regime, the event could not have been such an all-encompassing success had it not been for its popular support. People poured onto the streets in their masses. Low estimates calculate that at least 100,000 people took part in the early events in Baghdad alone.[164] This figure indisputably grew over the coming days. The clogging up of the main streets of Baghdad and other cities thus effectively eliminated any hope the old regime might have nurtured for a counter-revolution. The crowds transformed what started as a purely military operation into a popular revolution.[165]

A plethora of academic literature focusing on the events that ended the Monarchy on 14 July 1958 has been produced. Much of the debate has centered on whether the events constituted a 'revolution' or merely a

[159] Batatu, *Old Social Classes*, p. 794.

[160] Sbahi, *'Uqud min Ta'rikh*, 249.

[161] During the coup, the whole Royal family was killed. The following day, Nuri al-Sa'id was caught and killed on the spot by a sergeant, Batatu, *Old Social Classes*, pp. 800–801.

[162] As alleged by the *mas'ul* of the party's Military Organisation, Thabet Habib al-'Ani in *al-Thaqafah al-Jadidah*, no. 266, quoted in Sbahi, *'Uqud min Ta'rikh*, pp. 250–251.

[163] Ismael, *Rise and Fall*, pp. 75–76

[164] Batatu, *Old Social Classes*, p. 805.

[165] The crowds were so agitated that the new revolutionary authority actually had to declare a curfew and briefly martial law soon after installing itself, ibid., p. 805

military 'coup'. In general, writers linked to the *ancien régime*, or who adhere to the 'patrimonialist school' denying ideological agency to Iraqi political actors, have maintained that the changes merely constituted a coup d'état.[166] Batatu, on the other hand, offers perhaps the best explanation when he stresses the role played by the general public, especially in Baghdad, in transforming the coup into a revolution. He maintains the reason for the coup's swift and conclusive success was 'because it expressed a basic bent in society.'[167] Norman Daniel goes even further and claims the 'Iraqi Revolution was a decisive moment in the history of imperialism.' He also maintains that there is no real contradiction between regarding the events either as a coup or as a revolution, arguing that coups can be revolutionary and that it would be wrong to 'disqualify coups from being revolutionary only because some coups have been reactionary'. Taking a relativist position, in his view 'it is not popular endorsement that makes a revolution' or even 'the extent of changes that result' from it, but rather 'such indisputable changes as are seen to occur and are recognized as revolutionary at the moment they occur.' Fittingly, he concludes philosophically 'that a revolution is when everyone thinks it is.'[168] Joe Stork, for his part, thinks, 'Iraq's experience in 1958 was unquestionably revolutionary'.[169] Agreeing with Batatu, Peter Sluglett and Marion Farouk-Sluglett underline how the regional and international political conjuncture in the 1950s combined with the inflexibility of the political system precipitated the military coup that then became a revolution.[170]

[166] See for instance the arguments of the former American Ambassador to Iraq Waldemar J. Gallman, *Iraq under General Nuri: My Recollections of Nuri al-Said, 1954–1958*, Baltimore: Johns Hopkins University Press, 1964, p. 205; see also former British Ambassador to Iraq, Humphrey Trevelyan, who despite including the word 'revolution' in the title of his book, staunchly maintains the events of 14 July were 'essentially an Army coup', Humprey Trevelyan, *The Middle East in Revolution*, London: Macmillan, 1970, p. 136. Among historians, Charles Tripp is the most prominent of the coup advocates; see Tripp, *History of Iraq*, pp. 143–147.

[167] Batatu, *Old Social Classes*, p. 805.

[168] Norman Daniel, 'Contemporary Perceptions of the Revolution in Iraq on 14 July 1958', in *The Iraqi Revolution of 1958: The Old Social Classes Revisited*, Robert A. Fernea and Wm. Roger Louis (eds), London: I.B. Tauris, 1991, pp. 20–21.

[169] Joe Stork, 'The Soviet Union, the Great Powers and Iraq', in Fernea and Louis, *Iraqi Revolution*, p. 95.

[170] Marion Farouk-Sluglett and Peter Sluglett, 'The Social Classes and the Origins of the Revolution', in Fernea and Louis, *Iraqi Revolution*, p. 139.

Roger Owen, while agreeing that it was a process of political and social revolution, points to how the events created a new type of Iraqi state, based on unity, coherence and monopoly of power.[171] Abdul-Salaam Yousif stresses that the changes brought about by the events of 14 July, in addition to constituting a social and political revolution, also crucially was a cultural revolution, and that as such it was 'a truly genuine revolution'.[172] Sami Zubaida, finally, makes the crucial point of the role of ideology in the period leading up to the revolution, underlining how the participants of the revolutionary movement were fighting over the national entity and its destiny. Overall, it is fair to say that most academics agree that, in Zubaida's words, 'the 1958 Revolution was a great deal more than a military coup d'état.'[173]

Arguably, the events of 14 July 1958 was a joint endeavour involving not only a military operation, but crucially also a civilian part. This civilian part was the result of oppositional activity carried out during decades by political parties in the country, overtly, but above all, clandestinely. The role played by the ICP in this oppositional activity undoubtedly stands out. The party had suffered the most under the old regime, and worked the hardest for its downfall. In the end, though, it was the army rather than the communists that took military action against the monarchy. The inaction of the communists, to be sure, was a direct result of the ICP leadership's decision to sit back and let the other 'national forces' play the role of vanguard. But while the outcome of the 1958 Revolution fitted in neatly with the party's new pacifist line and the new Iraqi president, Brigadier General 'Abd al-Karim Qasim, seemed to offer the prospect of beneficial cooperation with the 'national bourgeoisie', the voluntary decision to play second fiddle to the army would come back to haunt the communists in the decades to come.

171 Roger Owen, 'Class and Class Politics in Iraq before 1958: The "Colonial and Post-Colonial State"', in Ferna and Louis, *Iraqi Revolution*, pp. 169–170.

172 Abdul-Salaam Yousif, 'The Struggle for Cultural Hegemony during the Iraqi Revolution', in Ferna and Louis, *Iraqi Revolution*, p. 172.

173 Sami Zubaida, 'Community, Class and Minorities in Iraqi Politics', in *The Iraqi Revolution of 1958: The Old Social Classes Revisited*, Robert A Fernea and Wm. Roger Luis (eds), London: I.B. Tauris, 1991, pp. 197; 209.

3

COMMUNISTS, KURDS, AND ARAB NATIONALISTS IN REVOLUTIONARY IRAQ, 1958–1963

Political Developments, 1958–63

The 14 July Revolution opened up a new era in Iraqi history. Gone was the overt interference of Britain through local Iraqi elites, and new, hitherto marginal, socio-political forces stemming from 'lower' social backgrounds and represented by new ideological political parties emerged to the apex of the political scene to demand a stake in—or all of—the political power.

The period 1958–1963 was primarily characterised by the intense power struggle and battle of ideas precipitated by the revolution's doing away with the political power of the old elite constellation of *mallaks* and *Sharifians*. In their place, a new political elite constituted mostly of military officers supporting the Revolution and intellectuals of political parties that had emerged after World War II, such as Muhammad Hadid of the NDP and Siddiq Shanshal of the Istiqlal Party, came to fill the void. Thus, the political ideas and ideologies of this new intelligentsia were suddenly swung onto the political centre stage. Though not all members of the intelligentsia received seats in government or were close to the corridors of power, the Revolution nevertheless marked a break in the political history of Iraq as these groups now became directly involved in the ideological and political struggle over the future direction of the new Iraqi Republic. Thus, in clear distinction to political affairs under the monarchy, official politics in Iraq following the Revolution developed a marked ideological character.

'Abd al-Karim Qasim, who as leader of the Free Officers proclaimed himself president of the new Republic, did everything in his might to retain the power equilibrium through skilful manipulation. Arab nationalist Free Officers and other, unaffiliated officers, along with nationalist intellectuals from the pan-Arabist Istiqlal Party and other groupings, now spurred on by Nasir, increased their demands for influence in the new government. The KDP, which initially supported Qasim out of fear of a pan-Arabist future for Iraq, grew disillusioned with his intentions for northern Iraq. The Revolution also brought out social tensions as the new regime launched an agrarian reform that upstaged power relations in the countryside, thereby setting once powerful but now dispossessed rural landlords, shaykhs and *aghas* in motion against the new Republic.

No sooner had the euphoria of the monarchy's successful overthrow settled before various groups started to manoeuvre for power and influence. Earlier in the year, Syria and Egypt had formed the UAR, which had hastily prompted the Regent, 'Abd al-Ilah, to set up a makeshift union with his fellow Hashemite brethren in Jordan.[1] That union vanished with the revolution, but the idea of Arab unity remained. As soon as it stood clear the monarchy actually had been defeated and that the British were not going to launch a counter-revolution, Arab nationalist groupings such as the Ba'th Party and officers close to Qasim began clamouring for Iraq's immediate joining with the UAR. On the practical side, however, no-one seemed to possess a thought-out plan to achieve unity. Three days after the revolution, on 17 July, Qasim's new cabinet sent a delegation led by fellow Free Officer 'Abd al-Salam 'Aref to meet with Nasir in Damascus.[2] 'Aref, who seems to have been genuinely persuaded by the idea of 'Arab Union', put the issue on the table during his meeting with Nasir without authorisation from the Iraqi government. While Nasir at the time thought the Iraqi Revolution needed to consolidate before such a venture could

[1] For a discussion of various Hashemite unity schemes during the monarchy, see Reeva S. Simon, 'The Hashemite "Conspiracy": Hashemite Unity Attempts, 1921–1958', *International Journal of Middle East Studies* 5, no. 3, Jun. 1974, pp. 314–327.

[2] In addition to 'Aref, the delegation consisted of Muhammad Hadid (Finance Minister), Siddiq Shanshal (Guidance Minister) and 'Abd al-Jabbar Jumard (Foreign Minister), Sbahi, *'Uqud min Ta'rikh*, p. 340.

be undertaken, 'Aref became determined that the future of the new Iraqi Republic lay with Nasir's UAR. Thus, upon his return to Iraq, he joined forces with the Iraqi Ba'th Party and began propagating for 'immediate unity' with the UAR, touring the country and giving speeches drumming up support for Nasir.[3]

It was only at this point that the Iraqi branch of the Ba'th Party began to emerge as a major political force on the Iraqi political scene. Prior to the revolution, its influence had been miniscule. The Arab Socialist Resurrection Party (*Hizb al-Ba'th al-'Arabi al-Ishtiraki*), as its formal name was, had been founded in Syria in 1943 with the aim of bringing about the political and ideological unification of the Arab world. Its two main front figures, Michel 'Aflaq and Salah al-Din al-Baytar (Bitar) were both Arab intellectuals educated in France.[4] In 1954, the Ba'th Party in Syria merged with Akram al-Hawrani's (Hourani) Arab Socialist Party, which made it move somewhat to the left on the political scale. It entered into cooperation with the Syrian communists, as did the small Iraqi branch that had been formed in 1952 when it joined the National Front in 1957. Fearing the strength of the communists, however, the Syrian Ba'th advocated union with Nasir's Egypt as a way of countering communist influence.[5] Thus, although a significant force in Syria, in Iraq the party's message of a particular *Arab* socialist vision[6] had prior to the 1958 Revolution not achieved much popularity, partly on account of lacking support for pan-Arabism in Iraq but also because of the Ba'thists' staunch anti-communism, which by 1958 was becoming ever clearer. As such, the Iraqi Ba'thists decided to ally with 'Aref and live off his political prestige. Nasir's overwhelming support on the Arab street was also something they argued would work to their advantage.[7]

[3] Batatu, *Old Social Classes*, p. 817.

[4] Supporters of Zaki al-Arsuzi claim he was the real 'spiritual father' of the Ba'th, Nabil M. Kaylani, 'The Rise of the Syrian Ba'th, 1940–1958: Political Success, Party Failure', *International Journal of Middle East Studies* 3, no. 1, Jan. 1972, p. 3. Note also that Kaylani (p. 5) claims the party was founded in 1946.

[5] Kamel S. Abu Jaber, *The Arab Ba'th Socialist Party: History, Ideology, and Organization*, Syracuse, NY: Syracuse University Press, 1966, p. 44; Batatu, *Old Social Classes*, p. 743. Note that Batatu claims Hourani merged with the Syrian Ba'th already in 1952.

[6] For a discussion of Ba'thi ideology, see ch. 4.

[7] Batatu, *Old Social Classes*, p. 816.

The ICP, on the other side of the political spectrum, realised the threat posed by signing up Iraq to an 'immediate union' with Nasir's UAR. Instead, it propagated the idea of a federal Arab union comprising Iraq, the UAR and Yemen. Representing the hesitating mood of the Iraqist forces (NDP, KDP and Qasim himself), with implicit support from Qasim, the communists organised a demonstration counting hundreds of thousands in Baghdad on 5 August in support of a federal union and, crucially, against 'immediate union'.[8] The communist show of strength imprinted on the minds of the pan-Arabists the strong resistance that existed among the Iraqist forces against the idea of 'immediate union' and forced them to resort to other, clandestine, methods of achieving their objective. These contradictions between the Ba'thists, the Nasirists and the other pan-Arabists on the one side and the communists and Qasim, on the other, inevitably led to serious clashes that would come to dominate much of the period.

During the autumn of 1958, the clash came to a head between Qasim and 'Aref, who had more and more taken on the role of unofficial leader of the pan-Arabist opposition. To alleviate the situation, Qasim relieved 'Aref of his political powers and sent him to West Germany as the Iraqi ambassador. But 'Aref managed to sneak back to Iraq in secret and renewed his conspiratorial activities which were set to undermine Qasim. This eventually forced Qasim to have him arrested and put on trial for treason. 'Aref was found guilty and was sentenced to death, although in the end Qasim agreed to have his sentence commuted.[9] 'Aref's fall from grace and Qasim's handling of the dismissal caused many of Qasim's coming problems. By letting 'Aref live, Qasim had created a rallying focus for the disparate pan-Arabists, which would ultimately prove disastrous. Equally, by targeting other prominent nationalists in the reshuffles that accompanied 'Aref's removal from power, such as Fu'ad al-Rikabi, the Iraqi Ba'th's Secretary-General, who was demoted from Minister of Development to the insignificant post of Minister of State, Qasim alienated many of the pan-Arabists.[10]

8 Sbahi, *'Uqud min Ta'rikh*, pp. 340–343. Note that Batatu claims it took place on 7 Aug. Some sources also claim it had up to half a million participants, Batatu, *Old Social Classes*, p. 828.

9 See Farouk-Sluglett and Sluglett, *Iraq Since 1958*, pp. 59–60. For 'Aref's own take on the fallout with Qasim, see *Mudhakkirat al-Ra'is al-Rahil 'Abd al-Salam 'Aref*, Baghdad: Sharikat al-Tab' wa l-Nashr al-Ahliyyah, 1967.

10 Farouk-Sluglett and Sluglett, *Iraq Since 1958*, p. 60.

In December 1958, Rashid 'Ali al-Gaylani, the figurehead of the 1941 military coup and subsequent war against the British, attempted a putsch against Qasim with the support of senior Nasirist Free Officers such as Taher Yahya, Rif'at al-Hajj Sirri, Nazem al-Tabaqchali and 'Abd al-Wahhab al-Shawwaf.[11] Gaylani, who drew most of his support from tribal shaykhs and big landowners disgruntled with the new Agrarian Reform Law, failed in his attempt. As Uriel Dann has commented, the failed coup attempt showed that the old form of politics whereby politicians would enlist the support of rural and tribal armed forces to put pressure on the centre at Baghdad was no longer working.[12] The Nasirist officers were undeterred, however, and continued to undermine the Qasim regime and plan for a military takeover. In March 1959, they launched a revolt led by al-Shawwaf in the northern city of Mosul. Qasim's popularity and the communists' ever-increasing support meant the nationalists had to seek aid from all possible corners, and it is a case in point that many of the principal military officers joining the revolt belonged to the old Iraqi elites, such as the Rawis, the 'Umaris, the Tabaqchalis, and the Shawwafs.[13] It is also proof of the nationalists' difficult situation that despite the manifest backing of the old landed classes, al-Shawwaf's statement at the time of the revolt nevertheless called for 'a just social life, a socialist economic policy and a cooperative democracy', promising that the Agrarian Reform Law, despite its plotters' obvious disapproval of it, would be 'properly implemented and applied'.[14] However, it was the Ba'thists that skilfully manipulated the genuine popular sympathy for Nasir that existed in the city into precarious support for the revolt. In all these efforts, the conspirators had the full backing of the UAR and Nasir himself.[15]

The revolt erupted on 8 March 1959, after having had to be postponed since the communists, sniffing out its planned date of 4 or 5 March, had staged an impressive show of force in the city with the gathering of some

[11] Ibid., p. 61.

[12] Uriel Dann, *Iraq under Qassem: A Political History, 1958–1963*, Praeger: Pall Mall, 1969, p. 133.

[13] Ibid., p. 167. In the plotters' 'Communiqué no. 1', which was broadcast by a clandestine radio in Mosul, Brigadier Nazem al-Tabaqchali was also named as the leader of the revolt, see 'Iraq Report of Army Revolt', *The Times*, 9 Mar. 1959.

[14] Manifesto of Colonel 'Abd al-Wahhab al-Shawwaf, quoted in Dann, *Iraq Under Qassem*, p. 171.

[15] Batatu, *Old Social Classes*, p. 872.

250,000 of their supporters and Qasim loyalists to hold a conference of *Ansar al-Salam* ('The Peace Partisans'), an ICP auxiliary organisation. But by the eighth, they had all left and the nationalists went ahead with their plans. As the revolt failed to spread outside Mosul, the plotters behind it, Colonel Sirri and Brigadier al-Tabaqchali, lost their nerve and withdrew support, as did Nasir who had pledged air cover for the conspirators. Qasim, entirely reliant on ICP support, gave the communist-dominated 'People's Resistance' (*al-Muqawamah al-Sha'biyyah*) free reign, although he continued to withhold ammunition from it.[16] After days of street fighting, the communists defeated the revolt and its local supporters and thus emerged stronger and seemingly more powerful than at any moment previous in their history.[17]

In addition to the ideological and political challenges facing the communists with the triumph of the revolution, the make-up of the ICP leadership was also significantly altered as a direct result of the overthrow of the old order. Within two months of the revolution, all party members had been released from prison.[18] Before the revolution, the party had been run by the troika consisting of Salam 'Adel, Jamal al-Haydari and 'Amer 'Abdallah. The release of prisoners and the ending of repression and persecution created a unique moment in ICP history, never replicated again, in which all its senior leaders were free and the leadership could congregate with relative ease. True, the party remained clandestine, but its operational conditions were immensely improved compared to the prerevolutionary era. Prior to the revolution, the Politburo, i.e. the body with real executive power, had consisted only of the before mentioned triumvirate, but 'Amer 'Abdallah had been abroad and had not returned until after the revolution, which had left much in the hands of Husayn Ahmad al-Radi (who now became known under his *nom de guerre*, Salam 'Adel). After the revolution, however, Baha' al-Din Nuri, the former First Secretary, was co-opted back into the Politburo, thus restraining the reigns of Salam 'Adel.[19] In addition, the Central Committee, which previously

16 Ibid., pp. 880–883.

17 For a more in-depth study of the Mosul events, see Batatu, *Old Social Classes*, ch. 44, pp. 866–889.

18 Dann, *Iraq Under Qassem*, p. 100.

19 Nuri was clearly incensed when the troika was formed in 1956, saying that it was 'a strange makeup' and that 'Abdallah had been 'no more than a supporter' when

merely had consisted of Saleh Mahdi Duglah, Thabet Habib al-'Ani, George Hanna Tellu, Muhammad Saleh al-'Abli (who was studying in Moscow), Rahim Sharif 'Ajinah and 'Aziz al-Shaykh (both of whom were detained at the time of the revolution), was now expanded to also include 'Aziz Muhammad, Karim Ahmad al-Daud, Zaki Khayri,[20] Muhammad Husayn Abu al-'Iss, and 'Abd al-Salam al-Nasiri.[21] Since the Second Conference in 1956, and increasingly after the expansion of the Central Committee following the revolution, the ideological contradictions within the leadership had crystallised into two separate tendencies: one cautious current embodied by 'Amer 'Abdallah who was a personal friend of Qasim and one current headed by First Secretary Salam 'Adel and Jamal al-Haydari, which vacillated in its support and distrust of Qasim.[22]

By now, these communist leaders had all become professional revolutionaries supported by the party. Thus, the emergence of the ICP as a mass party following the revolution, coupled with the professionalisation of the communist intelligentsia, fundamentally altered the nature of ideology production in Iraq. The post-revolutionary developments undoubtedly made an imprint on the ICP leaders, who started to view themselves and the party as the real force in the country. Thus, already at the first Central Committee-meeting after the revolution, held in late July 1958, voices had been raised for caution vis-à-vis the 'bourgeoisie' and for arming 'the masses'. Nevertheless, the meeting majority voted against it. In addition, at the pivotal Extended Meeting of the Central Committee in September 1958, convened after the immense show of strength witnessed by the August demonstration in which hundreds of thousands took to the streets demonstrating their support for the ICP and the revolution, the issue of seizing power in order to safeguard the development of the revolution

---

Nuri was arrested in 1953, and that al-Haydari had 'spearheaded' the splinter group *Rayat al-Shaghilah*, quoted in Ismael, *Rise and Fall*, p. 81.

[20] Note that Batatu claims Khayri was co-opted into the Politburo, Batatu, *Old Social Classes*, p. 850.

[21] Sbahi, *'Uqud min Ta'rikh*, p. 297. Batatu claims 'Aziz Sharif and 'Abd al-Qadir Isma'il were also admitted into the Central Committee, Batatu, *Old Social Classes*, p. 850.

[22] Mahmud, *al-Sira'*, p. 24. According to Ismael, 'a *de facto* dual leadership' had been created due to this tensional relationship between Salam 'Adel and 'Amer 'Abdallah. The antagonism had its roots in 'Abdallah's close relations with Qasim and the new military leadership, Ismael, *Rise and Fall*, p. 82.

toward socialism was raised. However, proposals to this effect were also defeated. The meeting instead called for a 'joint leadership' promising the party's unconditional 'safeguarding' of the Republic. According to Najm Mahmud, this 'joint leadership' meant the party in the internal training of its cadres maintained there were in fact two leaderships of the revolution: state power, in which the 'bourgeoisie' took part, and 'leadership of the battleground' (*qiyadat al-maydan*), i.e. the leadership of the mass movement, in which the party took part.[23]

The Communists and the Revolution

Following the revolution, the ICP adhered to its newly adopted policy of cautiously supporting a 'national government' without demanding participation in it, as had been established at the Second Conference in 1956. It was quickly decided that Qasim's regime fitted the theoretical mould. According to adopted policy, the communists' duty was mainly to pressure the new government into a desirable direction. With the danger of the new government succumbing to 'imperialism' and 'feudalism', the party therefore sought to mobilise 'the widest masses' in order to force it to set up 'a popular resistance', suppress 'the enemies of the Revolution', purge the government apparatus of 'reactionary elements', establish relations with the Soviet Union and the socialist camp, implement agrarian reform, and end links with 'imperialism'.[24] Thus, on the day of the revolution, the party demanded that the new regime set up People's Committees and a People's Resistance Force to defend the Republic,[25] which it acceded to, although the arming of this force was cautiously checked by Qasim out of fear it might be used against him. The purging and suppressing of 'the enemies of the Revolution' was carried out through the so-called 'People's Court' (*Mahkamat al-Sha'b*), established to pass sentences on senior figures of the *ancien régime*.[26] Qasim implemented the Agrarian Reform

[23] Mahmud, *al-Sira'*, p. 27–30.

[24] Salam 'Adel, *al-Burjuwaziyyah al-Wataniyyah fi l-'Iraq*, in Yusuf and Khaled, *Salam 'Adel*, 1, p. 313.

[25] 'For the Sake of Preserving the Gains of the Revolution and Buttressing Our Iraqi Republic', quoted in Batatu, *Old Social Classes*, p. 847.

[26] According to an editorial in *Ittihad al-Sha'b*, 'the People's Court was from the start a popular school of patriotism, democracy and liberation as well as a weapon in the

Law limiting individual land holdings to 2,000 *dunums*[27] on 30 September 1958,[28] formally signed an agreement of technical and economic cooperation with the Soviet Union on 16 March 1959,[29] and withdrew from the Baghdad Pact on 24 March 1959 and the Eisenhower Doctrine on 14 May 1959.[30]

With these unparalleled historical developments as a backdrop, ICP's Central Committee called an extended meeting in early September 1958—the first such meeting since September 1956. At the meeting, the nature of the revolution was discussed at length, and it was decided that the 14 July Revolution, 'the greatest victory that our national movement had realised since its inception', was indeed a 'national-democratic revolution directed against imperialism and feudalism'. It was also maintained that the revolution was 'part of the Arab national-democratic revolution, which aim at establishing an all-encompassing democratic, unionist, Arab republic'.[31]

ICP's wholehearted support for the new regime was well in keeping with the new ideological direction precipitated by the Second Conference in 1956. Despite the disproval of the notion that the coming revolution would have a 'predominantly peaceful character', the other main thesis propagated at that conference, namely that the new set-up of society after the victory would necessitate a mobilisation of the 'national forces' in a 'wide front', was vigorously defended. In fact, at the time of the revolution the national front theory was so central to the ICP leaders that in their new National Charter, published in January 1960, they argued that the 'cooperation of the political forces which represent the various classes of the people is an historical necessity because no political force can alone accomplish the aims of the revolution.'[32] Given that such a national front

---

hands of the people against the traitors and plotters', 'How Did They Prepare For The Conspiracy?', editorial from *Ittihad al-Sha'b*, 11 Oct. 1959, printed in English in *Iraqi Review* 1, no. 17, 18 Oct. 1959, p. 2.

[27] 1 *dunum* ≈ 0.618 acre.

[28] Batatu, *Old Social Classes*, p. 837.

[29] Ibid., p. 863.

[30] Agwani, *Communism in Arab East*, pp. 122–23.

[31] Political Report of the September meeting presented by First Secretary Salam 'Adel, quoted in Sbahi, *'Uqud min Ta'rikh*, p. 297.

[32] 'The National Charter of the Iraqi Communist Party', *Iraqi Review* 1, no. 22, 18 Jan. 1960, p. 4.

had been successfully formed prior to the revolution, now was the time to implement the other important part of the theory it had adopted in 1956, namely that through the assertion of pressure on the new regime the party would be able to steer it in a desirable direction. 'Irrespective of the course that the leadership of the coup intended it to take', Salam 'Adel commented in a treatise written in 1960 on the 'National Bourgeoisie in Iraq', in which he explained the ICP's position on the 14 July Revolution,

> the objective characteristics of the national-democratic revolution were ripe to [such] a degree that they pushed this coup forward to a real revolution [where] its first strike led to the fall of the monarchical system, which was representing the dictatorship of the biggest landowners (the feudalists) and the bourgeois agents, and to the establishment of a *watani* Republic led by the national bourgeoisie.[33]

In other words, in the communist view, the 14 July Revolution occurred *in spite of* the desire of its executors. According to the ICP, the national front had forced the military officers to steer the new regime in a popular direction. The party's analysis of the revolution was summarised by senior party leader Zaki Khayri later the same year; the revolution, he maintained, was not 'socialist', but, corresponding to the Soviet two-stage theory, a 'national democratic' revolution directed 'against the imperialist-feudalist monarchy', and, as such, it was a 'bourgeois revolution from the point of view of social content'. It was not socialist because it did not 'aim at the abolition of private ownership', but to free it from 'imperialism' and 'the remnants of feudalism'.[34] As was made clear in its new National Charter the ICP viewed the revolution as having ended 'the semi-colonial, semi-feudal reactionary system' and put in its place 'an independent, liberational (anti-imperialist) democratic (anti-feudal, anti-reactionary) republic.'[35] Initial policies adopted by the Qasim regime, such as the implementation of agrarian reform and limited political freedoms thus provided the practical requirements to allow the communists to appropriate the revolution ideologically as their own. Accordingly, as the revolution was argued to be national-democratic, it did not represent the 'interest of

33 'Adel, *Burjuwaziyyah al-Wataniyyah*, p. 312.

34 Zaki Khayri, 'Report on Agrarian Reform', *Iraqi Review* 1, no. 29, 30 Apr. 1960. p. 7.

35 'National Charter', p. 3.

one class apart from the others', but was 'in the interest of all national classes of the people.'[36] This characterisation of 14 July as the 'revolution of all national classes' was crucial for the party's understanding of and policies towards the ensuing Republic and its political manifestation—the Qasim regime.

In a bid to make core communist tenets fit reality, Salam 'Adel explained that the military officers who, as we have seen, stemmed from comparably modest backgrounds of a predominantly Sunni Muslim disposition, in fact represented 'the military wing of the national bourgeoisie'.[37] This categorisation of Qasim and his entourage was necessary to coat the military coup with a veneer that corresponded to the communists' rigid socio-political analysis of Iraqi society, which taught that only the 'national bourgeoisie' could lead the 'national-democratic revolution'. Thus, regardless of the social background of the Free Officers, to the ICP they represented and served, 'objectively', the interests of the 'national bourgeoisie'.

Salam 'Adel further argued that the ICP's leading role in the national movement had been key to the coup's success, that it had ideologically and politically mobilised 'the masses' for revolution and made them 'support the coup, merge with it, and push it to the level of a real national revolution.' From that point onwards, he maintained, the coup developed into a national revolution with 'a clearer and more profound popular characteristic than what happened in regards to the armed coup in Egypt in 1952.'[38]

Having thus ideologically constructed the 14 July Revolution in accordance with their theory of national-democratic revolution, communist policy became characterised by a frantic desire to 'safeguard' the new Republic. From the inception of the revolutionary regime until its violent overthrow at the hands of Arab nationalists in early February 1963, the preserving of the Republic was an *idée fixe* in ICP thinking. 'It is not the question of Right and Left', the party accordingly argued, 'the basic question is that of defending the independence of the country from the danger of threats and conspiracies.'[39] At the core of this categorical and

[36] Ibid.

[37] 'Adel, *Burjuwaziyyah al-Wataniyyah*, p. 312.

[38] Ibid., p. 313.

[39] *Ittihad al-Sha'b*, in English in *Iraqi Review* 1, no. 28, 13 Apr. 1960, p. 11.

obstinate insistence on the fundamental necessity of defending the Republic, which in essence meant defending the Qasim regime, was the belief that the power of the Soviet Union and the rest of the socialist world would assert enough pressure on the regime to swing it to the party's side. The existing balance of forces in the world would thus guarantee an inevitable historic push of national liberation movements and 'liberated' countries towards socialism. 'In the current historical conditions', the party consequently wrote in its National Charter, 'the "popular" nature of the Revolution gains a more prominent and important feature, because of the rise and consolidation of the Socialist camp and the great growth of the progressive ideas and the vanguard role played by the working class in the development of society.'[40] To the communists, growing Soviet strength would inevitably be 'a reinforcement to our struggle for safeguarding our republic and completing the tenets of our complete national liberation'.[41] In the view of this historically determinist outlook, there was no need for the party to make 'insensible' demands for representation on the regime.

The Problem of Arab Unity

In practical terms, the ICP was the first organisation to raise the issue of union with the UAR. Two days before the revolution, it called for establishment of a government that would embark on a 'national Arab policy' (*siyasah wataniyyah 'Arabiyyah*) and establish a federal union with the UAR, and this was repeated on the day of the revolution in a memorandum sent to Qasim. This was also confirmed in the Central Committee's Extended Meeting of September 1958.[42] But with the gradual deterioration of relations with the pan-Arabists and the clash at Mosul in March 1959, the party dropped such policies in favour of its pro-Qasim line of safeguarding the Republic.

Due to pan-Arabism's increasing popularity at this point, the ICP became locked in an ideological battle with the various nationalist group-

[40] 'National Charter', p. 3.

[41] 'The Decisions of the Supreme Soviet Council Are An Important New Contribution in the Reduction of World Tension', editorial from *Ittihad al-Sha'b*, 17 Jan. 1960, printed in English in *Iraqi Review* 1, no. 23, 25 Jan. 1960, p. 11.

[42] Sbahi, *'Uqud min Ta'rikh*, p. 337.

ings. To confront the popularity of pan-Arabist thought, the party abandoned parts of its Marxist-Leninist ideology for an opportunist populism designed to appeal to nationalist sentiments. For this purpose, the ICP leadership tried to infuse Arab nationalism with a progressive, anti-imperialist character, purportedly tracing its roots to an imagined revolutionary past. The communists thus declared themselves to be working for the revival of 'the revolutionary national and patriotic traditions and to renew the progressive ideas in the history of the Iraqi people and the history of the Arab nation.'[43] This fusion of nationalist and communist ideas, which made a basic distinction between 'progressive' *watani* nationalism and 'reactionary' *qawmi* nationalism, became a characteristic of the party's ideology from this point onwards—a tendency that later, during the heyday of Arab Socialism in the 1960s and 1970s, would become even more pronounced.[44]

In a speech at the 'People's Hall' (*Qa'at al-Sha'b*) on 13 February 1959, entitled 'The Historical Path to Unity of the Arab Nation', ICP Politburo member 'Amer 'Abdallah outlined the party's general views on Arab unity. In the speech, he explained that due to historical and socio-economic factors the Arab countries did not follow one single style in their progress toward unity. All the evidence, he maintained, pointed to the fact that they would follow many different roads toward complete union. Anyone who tried to simplify or abstract that fact, he continued, clearly hinting at Nasir and his local backers in Iraq who at the time had seen one attempt to overthrow Qasim by Rashid 'Ali al-Gaylani in December 1958 quashed and were busy planning another in Mosul for the following month and who also had seen their informal leader, 'Abd al-Salam 'Aref, arrested, would make the issue worse and, willingly or not, would take part in the creation of obstacles in the path of its historical development.[45]

From the time of the failed Mosul revolt, Jamal 'Abd al-Nasir turned staunchly anti-communist in his rhetoric. Not only was Qasim, who in a play with words was described as the 'divider of Iraq' (*qasim al-'Iraq*), painted as an enemy of Arab unity, but the Iraqi communists by virtue of

[43] 'The Inner Rules of the Iraq C.P.', *Iraqi Review* 1, no. 23, 25 Jan. 1960, p. 3.

[44] See chs. 4 and 5.

[45] 'Amer 'Abdallah, 'al-Tariq al-Ta'rikhi li Wahdat al-Ummah al-'Arabiyyah', published in *Ittihad al-Sha'b*, nos. 19, 21, 23, and 26 of 16, 18, 22, and 25 Feb. 1959 and then collected into a pamphlet with the same title, quoted in Sbahi, *'Uqud min Ta'rikh*, pp. 357–358.

their involvement in the revolt's suppression now emerged as the main adversary in Nasirist propaganda. Thus, in a speech delivered in Damascus on 11 March 1959, i.e. in the midst of the civil strife in Mosul, Nasir spelt out his repudiation of the communists. In the speech, incidentally entitled 'Qasim al-'Iraq', Nasir unceremoniously denounced the Iraqi communists, who, he said, would:

> never in the Arab world find anyone who will answer them save agents, because the communists are [themselves] agents and they do not believe in freedom in their country nor in the freedom of the homeland [*watan*], but work for the foreigner. This, o Brothers, is communism and for that reason we have fought it while [on the other hand] we have never here [i.e. in Egypt] fought the Left under any circumstances, because the Left has voiced *watani* principles [*al-mabadi' al-wataniyyah*]. However, we have fought communism because it does not take its inspiration from its land [*ard*] but from outside its country [*bilad*]...[46]

Trying to tarnish the Iraqi communists with the brush of anti-Arabism, Nasir also picked up on the fact that the ICP enjoyed much support from Iraq's Shi'ah community,[47] and utilised this to imply that the Iraqi communists were *shu'ubis*—the worst insult that can be uttered by an Arab

[46] Jamal 'Abd al-Nasir, 'Qasim al-'Iraq', speech given in Damascus, 11 Mar. 1959, in *Nahnu wa l-'Iraq wa l-Shuyu'iyyah*, Beirut: Dar al-Nashr al-'Arabiyyah, [1959], p. 60. For excerpts of the speech in English, see 'Nasser Accuses Communists', *The Times*, 12 Mar. 1959. In the speech, Nasir is referring to his fallout with the Egyptian communists, who following the Iraqi Revolution had increasingly voiced their support of Qasim and the ICP. Within the Egyptian Communist Party, which was a tenuous conglomerate of various leftist groups, the issue of its relations with Nasir eventually caused those who had originally belonged to the Democratic Movement for National Liberation to split due to their unreserved and uncritical support of Nasir. The fragile Nasirist-communist alliance that before had existed was finally shattered on 31 Dec. 1958 when hundreds of Egyptian communists were arrested in wide clampdowns, Joel Beinin, *Was the Red Flag Flying There?: Marxist Politics and the Arab-Israeli Conflict in Egypt and Palestine, 1948–1965*, London: I.B. Tauris, 1990, pp. 205–206.

[47] The charge of 'communism' to discredit Shi'i political demands was common at the time in the Arab World. Sunni Arab nationalists would use the pun *Shi'i-Shuyu'i* to highlight the linguistic closeness of both terms to imply also a political affinity, Silvia Naef, 'Shi'i-Shuyu'i or: How to Become a Communist in a Holy City', in *The Twelver Shia in Modern Times: Religious Culture & Political History*, Rainer Brunner and Werner Ende (eds), Leiden: Brill, 2001, p. 255. In Iraq, Shi'is were indeed drawn to the ICP in large numbers, and key persons in its leadership, including

nationalist.[48] Thus in another speech the next day, entitled 'The Terror of the Communists', Nasir maintained that the Iraqi communists would never be able to 'extinguish the fire of Arab nationalism' although they for a while might be able to rely on the '*shu'ubi* elements who for hundreds of years have hated Arab *qawmiyyah*'.[49] Nasir also denied being behind the Mosul revolt, which he referred to as the Mosul Revolution.[50] He equally denied plotting with 'Aref to overthrow Qasim and maintained that the real reason 'Aref had been sentenced in the People's Court[51] was because he had called for Arab *qawmiyyah* and for the 'unity of the Arab nation'.[52]

Realising the immense appeal of Qasim and the Iraqi communists, however, Nasir was careful not to attack the 14 July Revolution or its legacy, which accordingly was referred to as the 'glorious revolution'. Instead, focus was put on Qasim's detrimental effect on the revolution and his dictatorial methods, which were said to resemble those of Nuri al-Sa'id. Qasim was thus painted as the evil mastermind who in Iraq had wanted to produce 'a *watani* separatist desire distancing itself from Arab *qawmiyyah* so that he could master it along with the communists, the

First Secretary Salam 'Adel, were Shi'i. For the period 1949–55, for instance, Batatu has calculated that fifteen out of thirty-two senior ICP leaders were Shi'i, Batatu, *Old Social Classes*, p. 700.

[48] The term *Shu'ubiyyah* originated in 'Abbasid times denoting a movement among non-Arabs for political equality with the Arabs. It quickly acquired a negative connotation as some Arabs felt it was an attempt by Persians to gain mastery of the empire. In modern times, the term has become synonymous with anti-Arabism, primarily used against Shi'is, but also against anyone who did not sign up to the principles of Arab *qawmiyyah*, see Ofra Bengio, *Saddam's Word: Political Discourse in Iraq*, New York: Oxford University Press, 1998, pp. 103–106.

[49] Jamal 'Abd al-Nasir, 'Irhab al-Shuyu'iyyin', speech given at an anti-communist demonstration in Damascus, 12 Mar. 1959, in *Nahnu wa l-'Iraq*, p. 65.

[50] Ibid., p. 66.

[51] In a clever play with words, Nasir referred to the People's Court (*Mahkamat al-Sha'b*) as *Mahkamat al-Sabb* (the court of insults), see Jamal 'Abd al-Nasir, 'al-Hiqd al-Aswad', speech given in Damascus on 13 Mar. 1959, in *Nahnu wa l-'Iraq*, pp. 77–78. In the speech of 13 March Nasir also attacked the court and its president, Colonel Fadil 'Abbas al-Mahdawi and his 'butchers' claiming that the court's activities were a reflection of Qasim's hatred of the UAR, see 'Nasser on Peril to Arab Nationalism', *The Times*, 14 Mar. 1959.

[52] Ibid., p. 75.

shu'ubiyyun, the opportunists and the separatists'.[53] But it was the communists who above all were spectres in Nasir's view. Thus, in a speech called 'Black Hatred', delivered the following day, he declared that the aim of the Iraqi communists was to enact 'a communist Fertile Crescent' from which they would 'discharge communism' to the Arab World.[54] Finally, after having left no room for misinterpretation of his feelings about communism in a speech entitled 'We Will Exterminate the Red Dictatorship!' delivered on 14 March,[55] he resorted in another speech the next day to the old charge of communist anti-religiosity by claiming the Shawwaf revolt was launched to preserve *qawmiyyah* and religion.[56]

Following such vitriolic rhetoric, which was broadcast by UAR radio across the Arab World, it is no wonder the pan-Arabists emerged as enemies in the minds of the Iraqi communists. Writing in late 1959, *Ittihad al-Sha'b* thus declared that the Ba'th and the Istiqlal, the local Iraqi political parties most openly espousing pro-Nasirist positions, had ceased to be 'patriotic political parties' and had 'turned into gangs of plotters and murderers' who had 'put their forces entirely in the service of the imperialists and their collaborators, in the UAR.' Realising the continuously immense appeal of Arab nationalism, however, the party, trying to wrest Nasir's hegemony over it, declared that:

> Arab nationalism has no links with the plotting on the free Iraqi Republic. The aggressive activity of the UAR and their hirelings in Iraq in the name of defending "Arab nationalism" is nothing but a distortion to the concept of Arab nationalism. If the Iraqi citizens, both nationalists and others, regarded Nasser before the 14th of July a nationalist hero, that is due to the patriotic struggle which was waged by Egypt and by Nasser against imperialism and reaction. Now that Nasser had reconciled his quarrel with imperialism and dedicated his efforts to subvert the Iraqi Republic in the name of "saving Arab nationalism", this is something which ought to be grasped by the sincere nationalists.[57]

[53] 'Abd al-Nasir, 'Irhab', p. 66.

[54] 'Abd al-Nasir, 'al-Hiqd al-Aswad', p. 73.

[55] Jamal 'Abd al-Nasir, 'Sa-Naqdi 'Ala al-Diktaturiyyah al-Hamra'!', speech given at a military manoeuvre in Syria, 14 Mar. 1959, in *Nahnu wa l-'Iraq*.

[56] Jamal 'Abd al-Nasir, 'Dimuqratiyyat al-Irhab wa l-Mashaniq', speech given at a rally in Syria, 15 Mar. 1959, in *Nahnu wa l-'Iraq*, 98. The accusation of communist atheism had also been brought up during the speech on 13 March, see *The Times*, 14 Mar. 1959.

[57] 'Attitude to Nationalists', *Ittihad al-Sha'b*, no. 11, 1959, printed in English in *Iraqi Review* 1, no. 19, 7 Dec. 1959, p. 6.

While the ICP thus was careful not to explicitly declare Nasir an 'imperialist hireling', which would have been detrimental to their own cause given Nasir's image as an anti-imperialist hero in the Arab World and Iraq, they nevertheless maintained that Egypt was 'expansionist' and was playing into the hands of imperialism.[58] Nasir, on the other hand, had no such inhibitions and bluntly declared that the Iraqi communists were in league with British imperialism. He explained that because Arab nationalism was a hindrance to both—a barrier preventing imperialist schemes such as the Baghdad Pact and 'a great High Dam' acting as a bulwark against communism, the ICP had made common cause with the British to defeat it.[59] This allegation of an 'unholy alliance' between Iraqi communism and British imperialism was a theme that had predated the Mosul events in various anti-Iraqi Egyptian editorials. The conspiracy theory, for that is surely what it was, argued that once these two unlikely bedfellows had defeated Arab nationalism (read: Nasirism) they would go on to fight each other for overall control of the Middle East. To fuel this kind of reasoning the Egyptian press reported that British intelligence circles were expecting a new pro-British coup in Iraq, following which a peace agreement with Israel would be signed by Iraq, thereby paving the way for Iraq's domination of the region.[60]

At the time, the Mosul events constituted a major regional crisis between Nasir's UAR and Qasim's Iraq, which threatened to upset the power balance and possibly lead to a major conflict involving the two superpowers as well. In the colourful language of *The Times* of London, it was said to be the 'emergence of a new Middle Eastern struggle between Communism and nationalism for the loyalty of the Arab world'.[61] Thus, after five days of poisonous attacks on Qasim and the Iraqi communists delivered by Nasir in Damascus, a major anti-Iraqi demonstration was staged back in Cairo on 16 March. As many as 50,000 demonstrators were reported to have participated in the protests, in which

[58] 'There is no Disagreement or Tension Between our Republic and the U.A.R. They are Plotting and our Republic Defends Itself', editorial from *Ittihad al-Sha'b*, 15 Nov. 1959, printed in English in *Iraqi Review* 1, no. 19, 7 Dec. 1959, p. 15.

[59] Jamal 'Abd al-Nasir, 'Kunna Wahdana', speech given at a rally outside the presidential palace in Damascus, 16 Mar. 1959, in *Nahnu wa l-'Iraq*, pp. 104–105.

[60] See *The Times*, 23 Mar. 1959.

[61] Ibid.

protesters carried mock coffins decorated with Qasim's picture and miniature gallows which featured hanged rats, evidently representing the Iraqi communists.[62]

The Soviets, for their part, did their best to defuse the situation, clearly unwilling to upset either of the two sides, which were both Soviet allies. Thus, although Khrushchev described Nasir's plotting against Iraq as an 'annexation' attempt that was against the will of the people, and being quoted as saying that he was 'grieved' by Nasir's verbal attacks on Iraq over the past days, he insisted that Soviet-UAR relations would remain as before and that he had been aware of Nasir's anti-communism prior to the events.[63] Khrushchev's 'annexation' accusation was however vehemently refuted by Nasir who argued that Egypt had no need for Iraq.[64] But the Egyptian campaign against Iraqi communism continued unabated. Thus, a month after the original events in Mosul had occurred and when ordered long had been restored in the northern Iraqi city, the Egyptian press reported of the outbreak of a 'civil war' in Iraq, with widespread fighting between communists and anti-communists in al-Ramadi, al-'Anah and Jabal Sinjar. In their usual conspiratorial manner, the Egyptian newspapers also reported of a secret agreement between Moscow and Qasim and that the Soviet Union would send 'volunteers', including 2,000 Soviet Kurds, to protect the Iraqi regime.[65]

For the Iraqi communists, the new situation was extremely perilous. They had now acquired a powerful enemy in Nasir and the tide of Arab nationalism was thus thoroughly set against them. Consequently, the ICP grew increasingly threatened by Nasirism and pan-Arabism not only on the rhetorical but also on the ideological level. The party therefore started to elaborate a coherent ideological stand on Arab *qawmiyyah*. In a historical outline on Arab nationalism, the party showed its ambiguous view on the subject. Iraq, it explained in its 1960 National Charter, was part of 'the big Arab Homeland', and the Iraqi people were tied to the 'peoples of the Arab nation' historically, linguistically and by 'other common national characteristics.' Thus, accepting the basic premise of Arab nation-

[62] '50,000 in Cairo Demonstration Against General Kassem', *The Times*, 17 Mar. 1959.

[63] 'Russia Accuses Nasser of Annexation Aim', *The Times*, 17 Mar. 1959.

[64] 'Cairo Reluctant to Provoke Mr. Khrushchev Too Far', *The Times*, 23 Mar. 1959.

[65] 'Cairo Reports of Civil War in Iraq', *The Times*, 11 Apr. 1959.

alism, i.e. the existence of an 'Arab homeland' (*al-watan al-'arabi*), the party helped strengthen the ideological position of Arab nationalism by adopting its language. Neglecting the long and complex history of the region and the fact that there had been no unified 'Arab' entity since the Umayyads, if then, the party echoed al-Kawakibi and other pan-Arabist ideologues in maintaining that it was in fact 'imperialist domination' that had created 'varied economic, political and cultural conditions... in the various Arab countries.'[66] Claiming it tackled Arab unity 'on the basis of the material reality in which the Arab nation lives', the party explained that it was 'well known that thc partition ... imposed on the Arab nation' was an 'outcome of the long domination of imperialism.' Since all the Arabs' problems were caused by 'imperialism', the logical conclusion was thus that 'the Arabs in various parts of their land are faced before anything else with the task of directing their struggle for liberation from imperialism'.[67] The focus on anti-imperialism was thus key to the ideational merger of Arab nationalism with communism in ICP ideology.

Thus, from this moment onwards the Communist Party adopted the language of Arab nationalism and accommodated the pan-Arabists and Nasirists ideologically, producing its own syncretised nationalist communism, which would remain central ideationally in the decades to come.

'Abd al-Karim Qasim and the Issue of Power

Following the defeat of the Nasirites and the other nationalist forces at Mosul in 1959, the ICP became increasingly aware that it provided most of Qasim's organisational and propagandistic support. In fact, much of his popular appeal hinged on communist efforts to paint him as a true 'patriot'. Voices were therefore raised from within the party ranks for the advancement of its positions vis-à-vis the regime. The demand for a share of power was published in the editorial of *Ittihad al-Sha'b* on 28 April 1959, followed by a Central Committee proclamation the following day in the same venue.[68] The communists' position was also backed by the

[66] 'National Charter', p. 3.

[67] 'The Arab Policy in the Programme of the Communist Party', editorial from *Ittihad al-Sha'b*, 22 Jan. 1960, printed in English in *Iraqi Review* 1, no. 24, 1 Feb. 1960, p. 12.

[68] Zaki Khayri claims both 'Amer 'Abdallah and Baha' al-Din Nuri, despite belonging

Fig. 3. Members of the ICP leadership take part in the historic May Day demonstration in 1959, from which the demand for government representation was put forward. From left to right: CC-member Karim Ahmad al-Daud, former leaders of the party Zaki Khairi and Baha' al-Din Nuri, Politburo-member Muhammad Husayn Abu al-'Iss, candidate member of CC 'Abd al-Qadir Isma'il, and members of Politburo 'Amer 'Abdallah and Jamal al-Haydari.

National Democrats, who at the time was the only political party to have representation in Qasim's government.[69] Qasim for his part refused to accede to the demands.[70] On 30 April, he announced a 'freezing' of party

to the 'cautious current', participated in the writing of these editorials, Zaki Khayri, *Sada al-Sinin fi Dhakirat Shuyu'i 'Iraqi Mukhadram*, Gothenburg: Arabiska Bokstavscentret, 1996 (reprint), p. 209.

[69] The request from the NDP was published in *al-Thawrah*, a journal loosely attached to the National Democrats, on the same day as the article in *Ittihad al-Sha'b*, see 'Claim for Communists to Join Iraq Cabinet', *The Times*, 28 Apr. 1959.

[70] In Ismael's version, the ICP's ensuing brawl with Qasim was essentially a personal altercation between Salam 'Adel and Qasim. In his account, the ICP Politburo blamed the worsened situation on 'Adel. It has to be pointed out, however, that Ismael relies entirely on Yusuf and Khaled to back up this claim, and as 'Adel's wife, Thaminah Naji Yusuf is undoubtedly a biased source; see Ismael, *Rise and Fall*, p. 89. Ghanem Hamdoun, long-time ICP member and former editor of *al-Thaqafah al-Jadidah*, thought Yusuf had definitely presented a biased account that put Salam

activities in the armed forces, thereby clearly aiming at circumscribing the ICP's power and influence. The party was shocked, but following its by now familiar logic, it thought the issue could be solved through increasing 'popular pressure' on Qasim, and so the party took the demand to the streets in the historic May Day demonstration the following day,[71] which in the party's own estimation comprised more than a million people.[72]

The demand for government representation continued to be pursued by ICP-affiliated newspapers, such as *Sawt al-Ahrar* ('Voice of the Independents'), which on 4 May reiterated the original request.[73] *Ray al-'Am* ('The Opinion of the Public'), an independent newspaper edited by the famous pro-communist Iraqi poet Muhammad Mahdi al-Jawahiri, also voiced its support and demanded that the government be purged of undesirable elements—another of the ICP's key demands on Qasim.[74] On 6 May, *Ittihad al-Sha'b* again repeated the demand and Salam 'Adel was quoted as saying that the 'democratic parties' (i.e. the ICP, the NDP and the KDP) were the 'foundation-stone' of the democratic system and that they were an instrument with which to unify the people. He even said that the ICP would be willing to cooperate with the discredited Istiqlalists and the Ba'th Party, if they cleaned up their act.[75] The NDP's official organ, *al-Ahali*, was also quoted as saying that its support for ICP inclusion in the cabinet was 'not on the basis of their party programme, but on a patriotic programme dictated by the present stage of political development under the revolution.'[76]

But despite this immense media and mass campaign, Qasim could not be swayed. The communists thus found themselves in a precarious situation: should they continue to prop up a regime that, according to their own reckoning, owed much of its popular support and perhaps its very physical survival to them and yet was unwilling to recognise the balance

---

'Adel in too favourable a light, Ghanem Hamdoun, interview by author, London, 6 Feb. 2005.

[71] Mahmud, *al-Sira'*, pp. 33–34.

[72] *Ittihad al-Sha'b*, 4 May 1959, quoted in Batatu, *Old Social Classes*, p. 900. Batatu, the other hand, alleges that the figure was 'more than 300,000'.

[73] 'Iraq Communists' Demands', *The Times*, 5 May 1959.

[74] Ibid.

[75] See 'Iraq Communists' Claim Pressed', *The Times*, 7 May 1959.

[76] As quoted in 'Iraq Communists' Bid For Posts', *The Times*, 11 May 1959.

Fig. 4. Popular demonstration in support of the new Iraqi Republic, May Day 1959.

of forces in terms of government representation, or should they go it alone and leave Qasim to his fate, quietly preparing militarily for any eventualities? Voices were raised for the latter option, especially among the party's supporters within the army, who through their presence at the heart of the state's military power seem to have better understood the peculiarities of contemporary Iraqi power relations, that is, whoever controlled Baghdad and the Ministry of Defence ultimately controlled the country. Thus, later that month, Colonel Ibrahim Husayn al-Juburi and Lieutenant Colonel Khaz'al 'Ali al-Sa'di, both communist sympathisers, argued that the ICP should attempt to seize power. They were dissuaded, however, by 'Atshan Dayyul al-Azayrjawi, the secretary of the party's Military Organisation, who maintained that Qasim's popularity was too great for any such undertaking.[77] A plan for an armed communist uprising to overthrow Qasim and seize power was scheduled for 5 July, but abandoned by the leadership in the last minute.[78] Soviet pressure might have come to bear on the party as well. Senior ICP leader George Hanna Tellu, who at the time had been receiving medical treatment in

[77] Batatu, *Old Social Classes*, pp. 902–903.

[78] Mahmud, *al-Sira'*, p. 36. It might have been caused by nationalist officers' plans to overthrow Qasim and 'liquidate' the communists, which ICP discovered in early June 1959, Duglah, *Min al-Dhakirah*, pp. 59–61.

Fig. 5. Communist influence in the army. From the left: Staff Colonel Majid Muhammad Amin, in the middle, Lieutenant Colonel Fadel al-Mahdawi, and to the right, Lieutenant Colonel Wasfi Taher.

Moscow, conveyed a Soviet request to the ICP leadership not to provoke Qasim and to drop their demand for participation in the government.[79] This explanation is also backed by Mahmud who further claims that 'Amer 'Abdallah in the evening of 5 July even went to the Ministry of Defence to inform Qasim that a planned uprising against him had been on the verge of being carried out by 'some adventurers' and that the party had 'thwarted it'.[80]

Whether true or not, it is clear that the communists' decision to retreat from their positions and gradually fall in line behind Qasim was much more the outcome of an internal ideological struggle within the ICP leadership than prompted by any direct external pressures. On 23 May, the party leadership had officially dropped the demand for communist

[79] Batatu, *Old Social Classes*, p. 903. Communist veteran 'Aziz al-Hajj supports this version of events, 'Aziz al-Hajj, *Shahadah li l-Ta'rikh: Awraq fi l-Sirah al-Dhatiyyah al-Siyasiyyah*, London: al-Rafid, 2001, p. 150.

[80] Mahmud, *al-Sira'*, p. 37.

participation in Qasim's cabinet,[81] but the internal party debate continued unabated. Despite pressure from those within the party who wanted to take on Qasim, the accommodationist current within the Central Committee eventually prevailed, probably influenced by the marked change in Qasim's policy vis-à-vis the ICP. Although just a few months before having been at the mercy of communist organisations in order to put down the Mosul revolt, Qasim now began using his own foes against the communists. In late June, he granted a wide-ranging amnesty for those political activists that had been imprisoned for their activities during the Mosul crisis.[82] It is likely that this additional pressure was what swayed the Central Committee-majority to toe the line behind Qasim, although it is clear that this decision was far from popular within the ICP as a whole.

Nevertheless, from early July onwards, the party's official policy towards Qasim was one of accommodation and caution. The party paper, *Ittihad al-Sha'b*, thus explained that the ICP had not in any way been challenging the regime but had merely been 'exercising one of its elemental democratic rights', which should not 'be taken to connote a desire on its part to oppose the national government,' but was just an indication of the 'confidence' the party had 'in the leadership' of Qasim. However, it hastened to add it was 'a well known truth' that the ICP constituted '*the basic political force in the country*'.[83]

The retreat forced on the party by Qasim's refusal of ICP government representation was cemented by the disastrous events that took place in Kirkuk on 14–16 July 1959. There, ethnic violence erupted between local Kurdish and Turkmen groups, leaving many dead. This incident prompted a revision of the party's views on the 'masses', transforming them from a revolutionary to a spontaneous and potentially detrimental force in need of retraining and education. As many involved in the incident were communist sympathisers or members, it also put the party on the back foot in the power struggle with Qasim, forcing it to issue an unprecedented public self-criticism.

The ethnic set-up of Kirkuk was indeed tensional by the time of the revolution. Fiercely contested, by 1959 this erstwhile predominantly Turk-

[81] See 'Iraq Communist Hint of Struggle Ahead', *The Times*, 25 May 1959.

[82] 'Policy Reversal By Gen. Kassem', *The Times*, 27 Jun. 1959.

[83] *Ittihad al-Sha'b*, 10 Jul. 1959, quoted in Batatu, *Old Social Classes*, p. 909 (Batatu's emphasis).

men city had seen a dramatic increase of immigrant Kurds employed in the local oil industry, making their total approximately a third of the population. As ethnic divisions in the city roughly corresponded to its socio-economic stratification, that is, the wealthy merchants, the shop owners, the artisans, etc., were in the main Turkmen while the unskilled workers, the small shopkeepers and the oil workers predominantly Kurdish, this undoubtedly added to the tensional nature of intra-city relations. Following the 1958 Revolution, these tensions increasingly became political as many of the Kurds joined trade unions and the Communist Party. Throughout 1958, tensions increased and finally clashes erupted in July 1959 following the decision by Kurdish communists and KDP-members to have a single 14 July celebration, while the Turkmen were determined to stage their own. During the evening of the anniversary, the two processions clashed as they encountered each other during their routes. The following day Kurdish soldiers, claiming they had been fired upon, shelled Turkmen areas of the city with mortars. This touched off further fighting between the two sides, and order was not finally restored until 17 July when army reinforcements from Baghdad were able to disarm the Kurdish soldiers. At the time, Qasim estimated the number of dead to be seventy-nine.[84] 'What, in effect, seems to have happened', Batatu commented on the incident, 'was the bending by the Kurds of all the auxiliary organizations of the Communist party to their own ends, that is, to the pursuit of their deadly feud with their old antagonists, the Turkmen.'[85] The ICP became vulnerable to attacks due to the participation in large numbers of Kurdish low-ranking communists in the atrocities. The clashes were used by Qasim and the pan-Arabists to strike at the party, although it essentially was an ethnic conflict between the local Turkmen and Kurdish populations.

A Central Committee-report entitled 'For the Sake of Strengthening the Unity of the National Forces in Defence of the Republic and the Gains of the Revolution' set the tone for the party's retreat. The report, published in its entirety in *Ittihad al-Sha'b* on 29 August, severely self-criticised the communist bid for power. It maintained that although the party's general analysis and definition of the revolution had been correct, it had failed to 'study the likely effects' of putting pressure on Qasim, and

[84] Batatu, *Old Social Classes*, pp. 912–919.
[85] Ibid., p. 913.

had thus 'diminished the role and standing of the national government and the other national forces'. In fact, Qasim's regime had become 'the centre around which the national forces gathered.' The party admitted that while its general front theory was correct in principle, from 'a practical point of view' the demand for government participation had been wrong. Then, remarkably, the report rebuked a core tenet of its own front theory, namely the notion that 'application of pressure on the national bourgeoisie' would lead to desirable results. Although the 'mass card' was about the only tactical manoeuvre left, the report stated that the ICP's media campaign and its delivery of the demand for power amidst the huge mass demonstration on May Day, had been 'another factor that had deepened the negative effects of the situation', because it had 'slandered' the party's intentions in the views of the authorities, the bourgeoisie and the moderate forces.[86]

This stand marked a more profound revision of the ICP's core ideas on 'the masses', as it highlighted the problem of trying to control their revolutionary spirit. As previously discussed, since the Second Conference in 1956, the party had tried its best to adhere to the Soviet non-violent approach. A key element in its willingness to renounce violence was the idea of the indomitable force of the 'masses'. They, along with the strength of the socialist camp, would be able to put enough pressure on a 'loyal' government to impel it towards socialism. But the uncontrolled energy of the masses, which during the monarchy generally had been a force for good as it mainly targeted the *ancien régime*, was now a much trickier subject as the ICP had pledged to safeguard Qasim and his regime, and that was not always at the fore of the general public's thinking. 'The Iraqi people's revolutionary outbursts', the report thus explained,

> is a positive trait which at times, especially in the era of revolution, has great impact on the destruction of the old system's pillars and paralyses the enemy of the revolution, and is, as a result, a warrant for the revolution's rapid progression along the road of victory and consolidation, and this trait is deeply rooted in

[86] *Min Ajli Ta'ziz Wahdat al-Quwa al-Wataniyyah fi l-Difa' 'an al-Jumhuriyyah wa Makasib al-Thawrah*, Report of the Central Committee of the Iraqi Communist Party, mid-July 1959, originally published in *Ittihad al-Sha'b*, 29 Aug. 1959, reprinted in Yusuf and Khaled, *Salam 'Adel*, 2, pp. 515–516. For excerpts of the self-criticism in English, see 'Iraq Communist Confession of Errors', *The Times*, 4 Aug. 1959.

the history of the Iraqi people. During the course of long epochs the people was exposed to the most repulsive forms of oppression and despotism, at the hands of conquerors and tyrants, but it had a real and violent response in numerous strong revolutions and uprisings, the majority of which became immersed in blood and were crushed with voracity and ferocity. As a result, through the generations the souls of the masses acquired a spirit [*ruh*] that was a combination of [the desire for] revenge on the reactionary forces and the striving for freedom. Because of the excessive methods of governing with injustice and arbitrary reactionary laws, the masses in the past used to attempt to solve their problems in a violent way and breach the law in a spontaneous way. During the course of long epochs of terror and servitude, a fierce revolutionary spirit crystallised in the heart of society under the pressure of the stupendous resentment and the long repression that was accumulated day after day, and when it was solved on the Day of Deliverance [*yawm al-khalas*], on the morning of the fourteenth of July, this spirit found a relief, and then the outpour of the volcano gushed out.[87]

This innate Iraqi revolutionary 'spirit', however, paid little attention to the party's affirmations that the country was in the midst of a 'national-democratic revolution', and that the masses therefore, 'objectively', ought to have no interest in rebelling. This spirit, which throughout the party's history had been conceived as fundamentally good, and which in its own reckoning was the 'warrant' for the revolution's rapid progression and ultimately the very backbone of the national front theory, was now a nuisance that would require a long time and a continuous educational effort to solve.[88]

The party, although willing to take on much of the blame for Kirkuk, explained that in reality *it* had been the 'least influential in preventing the cases of torturing prisoners', because it had never been part of the government.[89] Much later, when the pendulum temporarily had swung back again for Qasim after a failed Ba'thi attempt on his life on 7 October 1959, he exonerated the ICP from most of the blame for Kirkuk. Instead, when he was discharged from hospital in early December, he accused, in a marathon six-hour speech, in equal measure the Ba'th Party, 'imperialism', 'old racial feuds', and 'the extremist groups whether from the left or

[87] *Min Ajli Ta'ziz*, p. 523.
[88] Ibid., p. 524.
[89] Ibid.

the right who are prepossessed by blind fanaticism', and adjusted the casualty figure to only thirty-one dead.[90]

The public self-criticism issued by the ICP leadership was unique. No other Iraqi political force had ever admitted to mistakes so frankly and so openly. Throughout the autumn of 1959, the party was pushed further and further to the back not only by the relentless attacks of the nationalists, but now also by their 'patriotic' ally, Qasim.[91] For the communists the tactic of going public was well in keeping with their ideological analysis of post-revolutionary Iraq: 'contradictions' within the 'national classes of the people', that is 'the workers, the peasants, the petty bourgeoisie (artisans, professionals, small farmers and intelligentsia), the middle bourgeoisie, i.e. the anti-imperialist and anti-feudal bourgeoisie',[92] should be resolved in a peaceful manner, and antagonism ought to be reserved for 'enemies of the revolution'. 'In our opinion', the party thus explained, 'everyone who upholds his erroneous concepts and stands and who cannot view the others except through the mistakes which they have committed, proves that he is far from the spirit of modesty and of being a pupil of the people. Everyone who fails as a pupil cannot succeed as a teacher.' Accordingly, the ICP leadership argued that its 'acknowledgement' of mistakes was 'nothing but a manifestation of being pupils of the revolution'.[93] Others, however, were not as willing 'pupils of the revolution', but were more intent on bending it to their own advantage. The public self-criticism thus appears as the single most damaging event that overtook the party during the Qasim years, and it is all the more ironic that the communists brought it upon themselves as a result of ideological conviction.

[90] 'Premier States Policy for the Republic' *Iraqi Review* 1, no. 20, 23 Dec. 1959, p. 3. See also 'Kassem's Return', *The Times*, 5 Dec. 1959.

[91] The case of the People's Resistance Force serves as an illustration of the party's dwindling fortunes at this point. Its dramatic expansion, which from Aug. 1958 to May 1959 had gone from 11,000 to 25,000 members, prompted Qasim on 24 May 1959 to circumscribe its powers severely, prohibiting it from making arrests or house searches without prior clearance from the military Governor-General, Batatu, *Old Social Classes*, pp. 894–895; 905.

[92] 'National Charter', p. 3.

[93] 'In Order To Let the Patriotic Forces be Able to Contribute in a Better Way to the Consolidation of the Country's Stab', editorial from *Ittihad al-Sha'b*, 2 Dec. 1959, printed in English in *Iraqi Review* 1, no. 20, 23 Dec. 1959, p. 18.

Legality, Patriotism and Regime Solidarity

During the winter of 1959–60, the ICP's ideological categorisation of Qasim as 'progressive' and as representing 'national bourgeois' leadership of the revolution was tested to the limit by Qasim's manipulation and political scheming. Promising political liberalisation and licensing of political parties, yet continuously refusing the ICP to benefit from such developments, Qasim forced the ICP leaders to adapt their theories creatively to the changing political situation. This episode thus serves as a striking example of the elasticity of communist ideology at this point.

As mentioned before, throughout the first year of the revolution, Qasim met a significant number of communist demands, at least partially. During this revolutionary honeymoon, the ICP had created a popular hero out of Qasim, through a continuous propagandistic effort employing epithets such as *al-Za'im* ('The Leader') when referring to him in public and calling him 'a great patriotic fighter'.[94] However, since presenting their demand for government representation in April-May 1959 and increasingly following the Kirkuk affair in July, the communists slowly began to realise that their initial reading of Qasim had been too optimistic. This insight was further imprinted on their minds in early 1960 when Qasim refused to grant the ICP legal status. Thus, the fundamental irony of the period was that the party believed itself to be (and in all probability was) the strongest political force in the country and realised that Qasim was very much reliant on its support in order to preserve himself in power. Yet, due to its continuous ideological framing of his regime as a 'patriotic government' the ICP would inescapably link the government, and the person of Qasim himself, to the fate of the nascent Republic, thus forcing itself to protect the regime in order to 'safeguard' the Republic.

Qasim decided to meet one of the communists' key demands—democratisation of the political system and granting of civil liberties—on the very day the Kirkuk incident broke out, 14 July 1959, thus giving the 'cautious current' in the ICP leadership ever more substance to its position. The legalisation of political parties and ensuing general elections, scheduled for January 1960, was an event that irrevocably drove a wedge between the party and Qasim, eventually forcing the communists to re-evaluate the regime. Before the showdown that took place between Qasim

[94] 'Attitude to Nationalists', p. 6.

and the ICP during the period of January—March 1960, the party explained that:

> the existence of numerous political parties of various ideologies and political tendencies is something inevitable in a class society. That is because every social class has its distinct ideology and opinions which sprang from their material interests and which reflect those interests. Therefore, every social class is in need for its own political organisation.[95]

Following that logic, the ICP submitted an application for a party licence on 9 January 1960.[96] In a crafty move, however, Qasim encouraged long-time communist dissident Daud al-Sayegh to put in his own application for a makeshift organisation with the same name. While al-Sayegh's application had been received much later than the ICP's, to say nothing of the fact that he came nowhere near fulfilling the numerical demands for a licence, Qasim nevertheless issued it to him. Although Qasim had already double-crossed the ICP only half a year earlier during the Kirkuk incident, it failed to recognise Qasim's scheming hand behind the move. Instead, the party leadership put all the blame on al-Sayegh and his followers, whom they thought were 'a worthless insignificant clique qualitatively and numerically',[97] while the party made it clear that it did 'not demand the patriotic government to combat those who are trying to split the Communist Party... by rejecting the requests of those parties for licences.'[98]

Ideologically tested to the limit by Qasim, the ICP showed some remarkable creativity in its theory on democracy. Despite having argued

[95] 'The Unity of The Party is the Loftiest Principle, Marxism Leninism Does Not Permit Any Factional Activity Against the Communist Party', *Ittihad al-Sha'b*, 4 Dec. 1959, printed in English in *Iraqi Review* 1, no. 20, 23 Dec. 1959, p. 11.

[96] See application letter to the Minister of the Interior, 'Iraqi C.P. Applies for Licence', *Iraqi Review* 1, no. 22, 18 Jan. 1960, p. 2. Such was the faith put in Qasim that the list conveying the 'founding members' of the 'new' party contained several high ranking communists, including First Secretary Salam 'Adel, Zaki Khayri, 'Aziz al-Shaykh, 'Amer 'Abdallah, and Muhammad Husayn Abu al-'Iss. The other political groups that applied for a licence were the NDP, the KDP and Daud al-Sayegh's dissident communist faction. See 'Four Groups Make Application Under New Law', *The Times*, 11 Jan. 1960.

[97] 'Dawood As-Saigh and the Communist Movement in Iraq', editorial from *Ittihad al-Sha'b*, 12 Jan. 1960, printed in English in *Iraqi Review* 1, no. 23, 25 Jan. 1960, p. 10.

[98] 'Views on Opportunist Clique', *Iraqi Review* 1, no. 23, 25 Jan. 1960, p. 6.

for the inevitability of numerous political parties in a class society only a month before, Politburo member and most senior ideologue 'Amer 'Abdallah now explained that such rights 'only applies to the social strata of the bourgeois classes which are heterogeneous in their composition in contrast to the working class which is of homogenous class coposition [sic] and consequently can have no more than one party which expresses its homogenous and similar interests and ideas.'[99] In other words, in a country ethnically divided between Arab and Kurd, Turkmen and Assyrian, and religiously fragmented between Sunni and Shi'i, Fayli and Yazidi, Nestorian, Chaldean and Jew, 'Abdallah argued that a 'homogenous' working class existed, and that democracy as a result was only for the 'bourgeois' classes!

Instead of trying to analyse the motives behind Qasim's refusal of a licence, the party spent all its energy on drumming up a campaign against al-Sayegh, whose 'party' was stillborn at any rate. In its efforts to placate Qasim, the ICP agreed to remove the word 'revolutionary' from its National Charter, and downplayed its history of revolutionary struggle. In its reply to the Ministry of the Interior's objections to their licence application, they explained that:

> Marxism-Leninism is a scientific theory that deals with the general laws of the development of societies. And in view of the fact that Marxism-Leninism has been proved in practice to be the most true and advanced of all theories of the science of social development, various progressive forces in the world have taken it as a guide and made use of its ideas.[100]

In other words, the party was reassuring Qasim that its previously revolutionary ideology was now merely a 'scientific' tool with which to analyse social affairs. But again he refused a licence with the pretext that an 'Iraqi Communist Party' already existed, which prompted the party to stubbornly resubmit their application, but this time for the name 'Ittihad al-Sha'b' instead. In a Kafkaesque masterpiece, Qasim's Interior Minister replied that such a name change was 'legally impossible inasmuch as the name is considered a part of the inner rules of the party as is clearly stated in art. 2 of the Law of Associations. The alteration of the name, therefore,

[99] Ibid., p. 2.

[100] 'Reply to the Minister's Letter', 6 Feb. 1960, *Iraqi Review* 1, no. 25, 24 Feb. 1960, pp. 4–5.

after the application for founding the party amounts to changing the inner rules of the party which is against the rule.'[101] Instead, on 9 February, Daud al-Sayegh's insignificant faction was formally licenced by Qasim.[102]

Only too late, and after much public humiliation, did the ICP leadership realise that Qasim never had intended for them to be licenced, just as he never intended for them to be given seats in the government. In the midst of the process, Qasim even had the party begging on its knees. 'We are, after all,' Zaki Khayri pleaded, 'a part of this nation—not to mention the glorious past of our Party with its ideology, struggle and caders [sic]—and we are simply asking for a ligitimate [sic] right to form a party.'[103]

The Kurdish Question

Along with Arab unity, the 'Kurdish question' was the key issue facing the ICP during the Qasim years. Initially, as we have seen, the party focused most of its energy on Arab unity, but over time, the deteriorating relationship between the Kurdish nationalists and Qasim made the Kurdish issue more important. Following the logic of ideologically construing the 1958 Revolution as the 'revolution of the people', and giving additional evidence of the elasticity of the theory of 'national-democratic revolution', it was further stretched to be 'the revolution of Arabs and Kurds' as well. Similarly, the ICP tried to accommodate Kurdish nationalism ideologically by infusing it with notions of progressive anti-imperialism, following the same pattern as its ideological accommodation of Arab nationalism. However, as war broke out in 1961 between Qasim's regime and the Kurdish nationalists, both of whom had been defined as worthy of support from an ideological perspective, the ICP cautiously sided with the Kurds due to their previous fallout with Qasim.

Before the revolution, the ICP had cooperated with the Kurdistan Democratic Party (KDP) and had tried to make it join the Front of National Union, but the resistance of the Ba'th Party and the Istiqlal had

101 'Ministry of the Interior, Letter no. 671', 22 Feb. 1960, printed in English in *Iraqi Review* 1, no. 26, 9 Mar. 1960, p. 3.

102 See 'Parties Reappear in Iraq', *The Times*, 10 Feb. 1960.

103 'Comrade Zeki Khairie Inteviewed [sic] by Itthad [sic] al-Shaab', *Iraqi Review* 1, no. 25, 24 Feb. 1960, p. 3.

eventually put an end to those ambitions. After the revolution, cooperation deepened and on 1 September 1958 the ICP leadership presented its *Mashru' Mithaq li l-Jabhah al-Wataniyyah fi Kurdistan* ('Plan for the Charter of the National Front in Kurdistan') to the leaders of the KDP, and after deliberations they signed it on 10 November. The new charter stressed the importance of safeguarding the Republic, by now the communists' main slogan, strengthening the 'brotherhood' between Arabs and Kurds, and implementing the Agrarian Reform Law. It also called for a democratic constitution and, crucially, recognition of the rights of the Kurdish people, including the right to decide its own fate. At the same time, however, this right was circumscribed as the charter called for combating 'separatist ideas' nourished by imperialists and reactionaries aiming at separating Iraqi Kurdistan from the rest of Iraq. Instead, it called for the Kurds' 'self-administrative rights' to be legislated incorporating a unified administrative area for Iraqi Kurdistan, and the legislation of the Kurdish people's cultural rights.[104]

The ICP's stand on the Kurdish question was complicated and contradictory. Kurdish nationalism, as indeed Arab nationalism, ultimately rested on assumptions of ethnic homogeneity, which for a communist party undoubtedly were perilous conceptions. Like Arab nationalism, the struggle of the 'Kurdish nation' therefore needed to be framed within a general *Weltanschauung* of anti-imperialist struggle. Thus, in the communist view, 'imperialism', as with Arab nationalism, was to blame for the division of the 'Kurdish nation'. Due to the similar historical situations of both Arabs and Kurds, that is, having been 'subjected to the injustices of the Ottoman domination and the evils of the extinct imperialist-royal regime', a 'brotherhood' had evolved between the two peoples. In this the party's ideologically tinged mythology, the 14 July Revolution was nothing short of 'the revolution of the Arabs and Kurds and all the sons of the fraternal nationalities in the one fatherland.' At the same time, however, the party warned Kurdish nationalists that only 'under the reign of a liberated system' could their rights be exercised, and although ICP's historic leader, Fahad, had pledged the right for the Kurds to 'decide their own fate', including the option of choosing separation once liberated from imperialism, no such concrete measures were now forthcoming from the party. In fact, the ICP stated that it 'denounces ... all the chauvinist ten-

[104] Sbahi, *'Uqud min Ta'rikh*, pp. 500–501.

dencies and the separatist calls which prepossess some of the Kurdish chauvinists.'[105] The premise of allowing the Kurds to decide their own fate thus rested on the same historically preconditioned grounds as the position the party had acquired vis-à-vis 'the masses', that is, as long as they embarked on the path chosen by the party the Kurds received its support, but should they choose a path contradictory to its aims, they would have to be 're-educated' before being able to make their own choices.

While the KDP, the principal political force in Kurdistan along with the communists, had signed ICP's charter in November 1958, relations between them eventually deteriorated due to events on the ground. After the revolution, many Kurdish *aghas* and tribal leaders who opposed the Agrarian Reform Law and the general direction of the new regime, had fled to Iran, and had there been provided with arms and money by the Shah, Mohammad Reza Pahlavi.[106] Pressured by militant Arab nationalists from one direction and by conservative Kurdish *aghas* aiming at reversing the effects of the revolution from the other, the KDP was moving away from the 'political' struggle and became increasingly immersed in power struggles based on primordial loyalties and ethnic ties. Following the 1958 Revolution, Mulla Mustafa Barzani, who was invited back from his exile in the Soviet Union by Qasim, tried to assert his influence over Iraq's Kurdish population, to the detriment of the Iraqist wing of the KDP led by Ibrahim Ahmad. Qasim was keen on using Mulla Mustafa as a counterweight to the pan-Arabists (who had been putting out feelers to Ahmad), and therefore put his political weight behind Barzani, providing him with one of Nuri al-Sa'id's old residences in Baghdad, a car and a generous monthly allowance. With the Kirkuk events of July 1959, Mulla Mustafa struck against communist influence within the KDP and the Kurdish nationalist movement in general. Already ten days before the events he had ousted pro-ICP elements from the KDP Politburo, and following the incident itself he ejected ICP sympathiser Hamzah 'Abdallah as well. By August, Mulla Mustafa's actions had precipitated an open conflict between the ICP and Kurdish tribesmen in Iraqi Kurdistan.

105 'The National Rights of the Kurdish People in the Programme of the ICP', editorial from *Ittihad al-Sha'b*, 21 Jan. 1960, printed in English in *Iraqi Review* 1, no. 24, 1 Feb. 1960, p. 11.

106 Sbahi, *'Uqud min Ta'rikh*, pp. 502–3.

The ICP, for its part, reacted to these developments by directing more of the party's attention towards the Kurdish issue. Thus, in late 1960, Party Secretary Salam 'Adel forwarded a proposal to the Politburo arguing that the party needed to mobilise politically and organisationally to counter these developments. To this effect, he proposed that the ICP should reconfirm its slogan of autonomy for Iraqi Kurdistan and that a central committee for its Kurdish branch should be set up. He also suggested the branch should be renamed *al-Hizb al-Shuyu'i li Kurdistan al-'Iraq* ('The Communist Party of Iraqi Kurdistan'). Yet, due to the internal party struggle between Salam 'Adel and other members of the Politburo which was at its height at this moment,[107] the proposals met with resistance. Thus, the reorganisation of the Kurdistan branch was only partially adopted and the reaffirmation of autonomy for Kurdistan was voted down and not adopted until 1962 when war between Barzani and Qasim already had broken out.[108]

Mulla Mustafa's cooperation with Qasim soon broke down, as the latter was unhappy with KDP demands for autonomy. As a result, Qasim tried to ostracise Barzani by withdrawing his monetary support and by supplying Kurdish tribal rivals with arms and money.[109] From spring 1961, the political situation in northern Iraq deteriorated rapidly. On 30 May, the ICP issued a statement calling on the 'national forces' to be vigilant against the 'schemes of imperialism', and warned that the government was preparing for military action against the Barzanists. The tone vis-à-vis the Qasim regime had markedly changed. 'The popular masses, and all the national forces', the statement read,

> are increasingly becoming convinced, day after day, that the protracted [period] called "the emergency period" and the pressing into an order of individual dictatorship, is bringing with it an increase of tragedies and hardships on the sons of the people, and oppresses more and more their most elementary rights and democratic liberties, and threatens in a continuing way national independence.[110]

Throughout the summer, the crisis deepened, and on 22 August, the party issued another manifesto warning the population about the situation in Iraqi Kurdistan. It detailed the scheming activities of foreign oil

[107] See next section of this chapter.

[108] Sbahi, *'Uqud min Ta'rikh*, p. 506.

[109] McDowall, *History of the Kurds*, pp. 302–308.

[110] ICP Manifesto, 30 May 1961, quoted in Sbahi, *'Uqud min Ta'rikh*, p. 508.

companies and western diplomats in the area, and criticised the government for its erroneous policy, which, according to the ICP, was trying to accommodate the feudalist *aghas* at the expense of the progressive peasants' movement and the Barzanists, whom they by now had accepted as representatives of the Kurdish national movement despite earlier disagreements. The population was called upon to defend the Barzanists, 'the righteous sons of the Iraqi people', by calling on the government to stop military preparations against them.[111]

The Kurdish revolt that then broke out and which lasted until 1963 initially started among large tribal landowners and *aghas* who were disgruntled by the Agrarian Reform Law and therefore refused to pay tax. The rebellion quickly gained the support also of their subject tribal populations. 'In striking testimony to the strength of tribal loyalties', David McDowall commented on this development, 'their followers were insufficiently aware of the social and economic issues at stake to recognize that they were supporting the very class that exploited them, or that they stood to benefit from land reform.'[112] As Qasim ventured to subdue the rebellion, Barzani was able to strike at rival tribes, who by now had lost their monetary support from the regime. When in September 1961 the army in a retaliatory raid indiscriminately launched an air strike on Barzan, Mulla Mustafa's region, this brought him and his followers into the war, and when the KDP's offices were closed down later the same month, it too joined the revolt and became an ally of Barzani. Through training by Kurdish officers who deserted from the Iraqi army to the rebellion, the KDP formed a new fighting force, the *peshmergah* ('those who face death'), within its areas. Qasim, for his part, did not want such an escalation and was clearly reluctant to continue the seemingly pointless fighting further. Instead, he offered amnesties to the rebels in November 1961 and again in March 1962. But the rebellion was gaining momentum while Qasim became increasingly isolated due to his erstwhile manipulations.[113]

As the war broke out in September 1961, the ICP issued a long statement calling on 'the masses' to fight the government's 'national oppression' in Iraqi Kurdistan and for a democratic solution to the problem.[114]

[111] ICP Manifesto, 22 Aug. 1961, quoted in Sbahi, *'Uqud min Ta'rikh*, pp. 508–9.

[112] McDowall, *History of the Kurds*, p. 309.

[113] Ibid., pp. 308–311.

From spring 1962, the party concentrated its attention on the Kurdish issue and in March, it finally adopted Salam 'Adel's previous proposal of Kurdish autonomy. 'Adel, who at the time was in Moscow, then began to lobby leaders of international communist parties and heads of socialist states for support for the Kurdish cause and to take a stand against the war.[115] The Kurdish war thus marked the final breakdown of relations between the communists and Qasim, and as they openly came out in support of Barzani and against Qasim, thousands of ICP members and supporters were thrown into jail.[116]

Ideological Struggle and Qasim's Downfall

As we have seen, within the ICP there was an intense ideological struggle over the issue of power. The struggle was for the most part contained within the upper echelons of the party leadership, usually within the Politburo and the Central Committee. The clash came to a head at the Central Committee meeting of July 1959 where loyalty to the Qasim regime was decided. At around the same time a group consisting of Zaki Khayri, 'Amer 'Abdallah, Muhammad Husayn Abu al-'Iss and Baha' al-Din Nuri, incensed over what they perceived as Salam 'Adel's 'leftist' deviation, decided to remove him from the party Secretariat and replace him with Hadi Hashem al-A'zami. Salam 'Adel prepared a report outlining the reasons behind his past decisions. Despite this, and despite the rallying to his side of Jamal al-Haydari, Khayri's group accused him of having taken a stance against the world communist movement and internationalism. Under pressure from these senior communists Salam 'Adel eventually caved in and withdrew his report, quoting 'internationalist discipline' as the reason. Salam 'Adel's submissiveness did not help him, though, as the Extended Meeting decided to send him, Jamal al-Haydari and others to Moscow, and that the new Politburo was to be made up of Zaki Khayri, 'Amer 'Abdallah and Baha' al-Din Nuri—the so-called 'Bloc of Three'.[117] Much of the struggle occurred subtly and within the Polit-

[114] Sbahi, *'Uqud min Ta'rikh*, p. 512.

[115] Ibid., pp. 512–513.

[116] Ibid., p. 513.

[117] Mahmud, *al-Sira'*, pp. 39–40. This episode is naturally contentious. For example, according to Saleh Mahdi Duglah, Central Committee-member at the time, the

Fig. 6. Members of the ICP delegation to the Twenty-First CPSU Congress in 1959 in conversation with Soviet communists. At the far right, CC-member Saleh Mahdi Duglah, second from the right, First Secretary Husayn Ahmad al-Radi and third from the right, Politburo-member Jamal al-Haydari.

buro. Duglah, for instance, recalls how at the time he was not even sure there was a 'bloc inimical to the party', because its members had no 'personal relations' and 'between them they did not hold unified or joint political or ideological convictions'.[118]

The ICP leadership's internal struggle worsened as the party became immersed in the gradually escalating ideological struggle on the world level between the Communist Party of the Soviet Union (CPSU) and the Communist Party of China (CPC). The Chinese had quietly been

July meeting simply decided to send people to Moscow for 'party studies', including himself, Jamal al-Haydari, Hadi Hashem al-A'zami, 'Aziz al-Hajj, and Sharif al-Shaykh, but crucially omitting Salam 'Adel. As he remembers it, there was a proposal by Baha' al-Din Nuri to remove Salam 'Adel from the Secretariat and replace him with Hadi Hashem, but during the voting it received only Nuri's support, Duglah, *Min al-Dhakirah*, p. 62; 78. In Ismael's version, what he calls the 'Clique of Four' (he also includes Muhammad Husayn Abu al-'Iss) reprimanded Salam 'Adel and constituted themselves as a 'Secretariat' to 'assist' him, Ismael, *Rise and Fall*, p. 96; 101.

[118] Duglah, *Min al-Dhakirah*, pp. 76–77.

resisting the new direction taken by the Soviets after their Twentieth Congress back in 1956, but had sought to resolve the issues in a 'comradely manner' without going public with their criticisms. However, in April 1960 the CPC decided the lull was over, and in a harshly damning article entitled 'Long Live Leninism' it rebuked much of CPSU's new ideological outlook.[119] The ICP published the entire article in serialised form in *Ittihad al-Sha'b* throughout May 1960. In June 1960, Khrushchev openly attacked the CPC. Later, in September, the ICP leadership met to study the new world situation. The meeting ultimately decided to support the Soviets, but had almost to resort to voting as seven out of fifteen Central Committee members were against the decision. In November, at the 'International Meeting of Communist and Workers Parties' held in Moscow, the ICP came to play an important role in the struggle between the CPSU and the CPC. The Chinese communists proposed the ICP delegation as a member of the body set up to draft the meeting statement. The Soviet communists, not certain whether absolute support was forthcoming from the Iraqis, suggested instead that the leader of the Syrian Communists, Khaled Bakdash, be elected, and then put pressure on the Iraqi delegation to withdraw its candidacy, which it eventually did. The ICP delegation, which consisted of the exiled Salam 'Adel and Jamal al-Haydari, along with Baha' al-Din Nuri, was pressured by the Soviets to openly attack the CPC in its speech so as to sway those communist parties that had not yet made up their minds in the ongoing international struggle. Thus, both Nuri and al-Haydari criticised the Chinese and the Albanians (who had sided with the CPC) in their speeches.[120]

The internal party struggle, on the other hand, did not entirely reflect the struggle on the world level between the CPSU and the CPC. It reflected more the personal traits and dispositions of the individual leaders. For instance, Zaki Khayri, the leader of the 'Bloc of Three' and the oldest of the party leaders, whose political and ideological inclinations in Duglah's reckoning were 'a non-homogenous hodgepodge' which 'at times conflicted between the right and the left',[121] in the midst of this controversy drafted an internal document called *Masa'il fi l-Thawrah—Mus-*

[119] Communist Party of China, *Long Live Leninism*, *n.p.*: Foreign Languages Press, 1960.

[120] Mahmud, *al-Sira'*, pp. 47–48.

[121] Duglah, *Min al-Dhakirah*, p. 77.

sawadah Bahth fi Stratijiyyat al-Thawrah al-'Iraqiyyah wa Taktikiha ('Questions on the Revolution—A Draft for the Study of the Strategy of the Iraqi Revolution and Its Tactics'). In it, he called for the adoption of the Chinese slogan of 'People's Democracy', and for the seizure of power in the appropriate circumstances in a non-defined future.[122] Meanwhile, in October 1961, Salam 'Adel, whose tendency Duglah described as being 'to the left'[123] attended the Twenty-Second CPSU Congress as the official ICP representative. There he gave a speech highly critical of the CPC.[124] Another ideological contradiction was the allegedly 'rightist' 'Bloc of Three', which more or less took control of the Politburo through its July 1959 'coup'. While decisively pro-Soviet in its inclinations, it nevertheless decided at that very congregation to send a highflying delegation on an official visit to China.[125]

The Twenty-Second CPSU Congress was pivotal for the ICP's ideological course during this period. It adopted a new CPSU programme, which among other things exchanged the principle of the 'dictatorship of the proletariat' with the idea of 'the state of all classes', an idea that fitted in well with the ICP's conception of its 'own' revolution as one of 'all classes'. A month later, the Iraqi communists met to discuss the new Soviet programme. At the meeting the new programme was described as 'a second Communist Manifesto or a Communist Manifesto for the contemporary era', and the meeting majority decided to undertake a wide education campaign of all ICP members in light of the new document. Thus, in mid-November the whole party witnessed a re-training campaign informed by the decisions of the Twenty-Second and the Twentieth congresses.[126]

In September 1962, Salam 'Adel, Jamal al-Haydari and the other exiles returned from abroad, and an Extended Meeting of the Central Committee the same month discussed their previous conduct. It was only during the preceding summer that the issue of a bloc had become known outside the Politburo. After intense discussions, all three members of the bloc that had opposed Salam 'Adel's leadership were ordered to issue writ-

122 Mahmud, *al-Sira'*, p. 51.

123 Duglah, *Min al-Dhakirah*, pp. 77–78.

124 Mahmud, *al-Sira'*, pp. 56–57.

125 The delegation consisted of Hadi Hashem, Jamal al-Haydari, Saleh Duglah and Muhammad Husayn Abu al-'Iss, Duglah, *Min al-Dhakirah*, p. 62.

126 Mahmud, *al-Sira'*, pp. 57–59.

Fig. 7. ICP First Secretary, Husayn Ahmad al-Radi (Salam 'Adel), delivering a speech at the Twenty-Second Congress of the Communist Party of the Soviet Union in October 1961.

ten self-criticisms. Zaki Khayri's and Muhammad Husayn Abu al-'Iss's self-criticisms were distributed among the members of the Central Committee for perusal, and they were both subsequently told to redo their self-criticisms more 'profoundly'.[127] 'Amer 'Abdallah and Baha' al-Din Nuri were removed from their duties, had their memberships frozen and were exiled to Moscow, while Zaki Khayri was sent to work in the mid-Euphrates.[128] But the leadership of the party had by now become ardent supporters of the Soviet line and throughout the autumn of 1962 when the country was immersed in devastating crises, it spent most of its propagandistic effort on rallying support for the Soviets on the international arena instead of paying attention to the internal situation.[129]

[127] Duglah, *Min al-Dhakirah*, p. 79.
[128] Mahmud, *al-Sira'*, p. 63.
[129] Ibid., pp. 64–65.

It would have been wise for the ICP leadership to centre more of its attention on the domestic political scene, for during 1962 the Ba'thists, along with their nationalist allies, had busily been preparing the overthrow of the Qasim regime. Organising what they termed a 'Nationalist Front' (bearing close resemblance to ICP's 'national front'), they had brought together nationalist officers, former members of the Istiqlal Party, students, teachers and other members of professional associations. Importantly they had also nestled their way into the army, despite Qasim's watchfulness. The communists, for their part, were aware of the ongoing plotting. By virtue of their influence in the army, the communists had been able to uncover the Ba'thist plans well in advance of their execution and had publicly warned Qasim already on 3 January 1963, urging him to 'purge' the army and release political prisoners and generally give the ICP the space of political manoeuvre he had granted the party at Mosul in 1959.[130] But besides calling on the 'masses' to be 'vigilant', the ICP leadership took few practical steps to prepare for the coming clash, thus showing that despite temporarily challenged in preceding years, the idea of moving beyond the mere 'supervision' of a 'patriotic' regime was just not on the agenda.

Instead, on 8 February 1963, the Ba'thists and their allies struck. The ICP resisted with what little resources they had at their disposal, but the Ba'th Party had made sure their incipient move was to wipe out the communists' trump card—Brigadier Jalal al-Awqati, chief of the Iraqi Air Force and a card-carrying ICP member. The next victim was Qasim himself, who following a summary 'trial' was executed by the plotters. For some days the communists managed to hold out in parts of Baghdad, and in Basra until 12 February, but eventually they yielded to the onslaught of the Ba'thi-controlled armed forces.[131] The nationalist victory, which according to senior ICP leader Saleh Mahdi Duglah cost the lives of some 5,000 people,[132] initiated a 'seemingly unending year of horror'.[133] The surviving communists fled to Iraqi Kurdistan or abroad, where throughout 1963 they tried to lie as low as possible.

130 Batatu, *Old Social Classes*, pp. 967–972.

131 See 'Kassim Fought to the Last Round', *The Times*, 11 Feb. 1963. The new nationalist regime had officially made it its policy to 'crush' the communists, see 'Iraq Communists Hunted Out By New Regime', *The Times*, 18 Feb. 1963.

132 *al-Akhbar*, 27 Oct. 1963, quoted in Batatu, *Old Social Classes*, p. 985.

133 Batatu, *Old Social Classes*, p. 985.

4

'NON-CAPITALIST' DEVELOPMENT, 'ARAB SOCIALISM' AND ARMED REBELLION DURING THE REIGN OF THE 'AREFS, 1963–1968

Political Developments, 1963–68

In February 1963, 'Abd al-Karim Qasim was removed from power in a violent coup carried out by his former ally, 'Abd al-Salam 'Aref, who joined forces with the Ba'th Party. Following the tempestuous end to the Qasim era, Iraq witnessed a short but sanguinary period of nationalist rule. The country became immersed in violent strife from February to November, when the Ba'thist plotters themselves were betrayed by 'Aref. He ended the worst excesses and atrocities and gradually brought the country back to normality. Initiating a rapprochement with Cairo, Moscow and the Kurds, his methods were markedly different from those of the Ba'thists, but he was no friend of the communists. Throughout his rule and that of his brother, 'Abd al-Rahman, who succeeded him after his abrupt death in a helicopter accident in April 1966, thousands of communists and their supporters remained in jail and the party had to stay clandestine.

Discarding the Ba'thist National Guards, 'Aref set up the so-called Republican Guard, an elite military unit designed to protect the President. He also purged his new government of prominent Ba'thists, such as former Vice-President Ahmad Hasan al-Bakr and the Minister of Defence, Hardan al-Tikriti. While 'Aref by this point had lost his erstwhile passion for union with Nasir's Egypt, others within his close entourage remained ideologically committed to such a course. As the core of the criticism emanating from the 'Aref and Iraqi Nasirist camps during the Qasim period had centred on the issue of union, it would have been detrimental to 'Aref's interests at this point to publicly rebuke the idea. Thus, in 1964 and 1965 a series of unity negotiations took place between Iraq and Egypt. None, however, led to any palpable results. Frustration with 'Aref's policies led the Nasirist Commander of the Air Force, 'Aref 'Abd al-Razzaq, to attempt a coup in 1965. But the plot was discovered, and al-Razzaq and his associates had to flee the country.[1]

'Abd al-Salam 'Aref's older brother, 'Abd al-Rahman, took over the presidency in 1966 following the death of his brother, but he was of a weaker disposition than his predecessor. Rivalries now surfaced among the military officers who constituted the basic support of the regime. 'Aref 'Abd al-Razzaq attempted yet another coup but senior officers rallied around the President and thwarted it. Having lost what little credibility in terms of vocal support of pan-Arabism and opposition to Zionism it held before, the regime was finally de-legitimised in the eyes of the general public after its disastrous encounter with Israel in the Six-Day War of 1967. It was merely a matter of time before some other constellation of officers would attempt another coup, and indeed, on 17 July 1968, the 'Aref regime was finally overthrown by a combination of Ba'thists and military officers.

For the ICP, the Qasim period had ended with disaster. Though putting up brave (or foolhardy, depending on the point of view) resistance against the February coup, scores of its cells, committees and organisations were crushed by the Ba'thist National Guards, many of whom saw the occasion as an opportunity to enact revenge on the communists for the 1959 Mosul events.[2] On 3 July 1963, ICP rank-and-file members in Baghdad launched an armed uprising in Rashid military camp. Cut off from the leadership and acting in isolation from other party organisations, however, the undertaking eventually failed, prompting a ferocious reply from the Ba'thists who began a new drive to round up and execute communists.[3] Eventually Muhammad Saleh al-'Abli and Jamal al-Hay-

1 Farouk-Sluglett and Sluglett, *Iraq Since 1958*, pp. 93–97. See also 'Iraq Coup Attempt "Foiled by President's Brother"', *The Times*, 18 Sept. 1965.

2 See ch. 3.

3 See 'Iraq Crushes A "Communist Plot"', *The Times*, 4 Jul. 1963. For a more comprehensive treatment of the attempted uprising, see 'Ali Karim Sa'id, *al-'Iraq—al-Birriyyah al-Musallahah: Harakat Hasan Sari' wa Qitar al-Mawt 1963*, Beirut: al-Furat, 2002. Even prior to this event, ICP members and supporters had continued

Fig. 8. Three victims of Ba'thist terror. Standing to the left, CC-member Muhammad Saleh al-'Abli, standing to the right, Politburo-member Jamal al-Haydari, and sitting, First Secretary Husayn Ahmad al-Radi (Salam 'Adel).

---

to be rounded up and executed intermittently. Thus, for instance, on 12 March *The Times* reported that twenty-five communists had been executed and on 23 June a further twenty-eight, see '25 More Executed in Iraq', *The Times*, 12 Mar. 1963; 'Iraq Execution of 28 Communists', *The Times*, 24 Jun. 1963.

Fig. 9. Muhammad Husayn Abu l-'Iss. One of the ICP leaders that were murdered by the Ba'thists during the coup of February 1963.

dari, who, after First Secretary Salam 'Adel's capture and lethal torture in March, had led the remnants of the party, were also apprehended and executed.[4] After this incident, the few communist leaders remaining in the country nearly all resided in Iraqi Kurdistan. Most, however, had made their way to Eastern Europe or the Soviet Union. All in all, the Ba'thists got their hands on twelve Central Committee members, eight of which were eventually killed.[5] 'Aref's November counter-coup thus came as a welcome respite for the party.

The various exiled leaders, most of whom were living in either Prague or Moscow, began to meet regularly in the so-called Committee of the Organisation Abroad (COA), initially headed by 'Aziz al-Hajj.[6] Until 1967, it constituted a semi-official alternative leadership to the internal leadership in Iraq. In August 1964, the ICP managed to return to some sort of organisational normality as the COA met in Prague and elected an up-to-date Central Committee and Politburo. The sanctions that had been in place on Baha' al-Din Nuri, 'Amer 'Abdallah and Thabit Habib al-'Ani since 1962 were now lifted and they were allowed to take part as full members. Those who had issued the sanctions in the first place now agreed there had been 'no genuine bloc' and that the sanctions were 'unjust and groundless'.[7] Not only were they rehabilitated, but Nuri and

[4] Mahmud, *al-Sira'*, p. 70.

[5] Those who died at the hands of the Ba'thists were: Salam 'Adel (Husayn Ahmad al-Radi), Jamal al-Haydari, Muhammad Saleh al-'Abli, Muhammad Husayn Abu l-'Iss, George Hanna Tellu, 'Abd al-Rahim Sharif, Hamzah Salman and Nafi' Yunes. Zaki Khayri and Baqer Ibrahim al-Musawi hid in the Mid-Euphrates region, whereas 'Aziz Muhammad and 'Umar 'Ali al-Shaykh secreted themselves in Iraqi Kurdistan. Of those captured by the Ba'thists, only Saleh Mahdi Duglah was able to escape, Duglah, *Min al-Dhakirah*, pp. 103–104; For a more exhaustive list of the party's 'martyrs', see *Shuhada' al-Hizb, Shuhada' al-Watan 1934–1963*, Beirut: Dar al-Kunuz al-Adabiyyah, 2001.

[6] Ismael, on the other hand, claims the COA was headed by 'Abd al-Salam al-Nasiri, and even goes as far as claiming he had become the '*de facto* leader' of the whole ICP, Ismael, *Rise and Fall*, p. 117.

[7] Baha' al-Din Nuri, *Mudhakkirat Baha' al-Din Nuri: Sikritir al-Lajnah al-Markaziyyah li l-Hizb al-Shuyu'i al-'Iraqi*, London: Dar al-Hikmah, 2001, p. 313. Again, Ismael presents a deviating account. Rather than a collective decision, he claims that al-Nasiri singlehandedly lifted the sanction. Providing no references to back up his claim, he argues that al-Nasiri 'without consultation with the Central Committee… rehabilitated' the above persons. Interestingly, for the passages where Ismael does

'Abdallah were also elected to the new Politburo.[8] 'Aziz Muhammad, a previous member of the Politburo and secretary of the party's Kurdistan branch, was elected new First Secretary to replace the martyred Salam 'Adel. The meeting also decided a 'switch' of leaders residing abroad should take place. Thus, 'Aziz Muhammad, Baqer Ibrahim and Karim Ahmad al-Daud were sent to Moscow for party studies, while Zaki Khayri went to Prague to replace 'Aziz al-Hajj as the ICP's representative on the editorial board of *Problems of Peace and Socialism*, while those abroad went back to Iraq.[9]

Analysing the Ba'th Party

During the latter stages of the Qasim period, the Ba'th Party had emerged as a major political force in Iraq, threatening the ICP ideologically with its blend of anti-communism and nationalist Arab Socialism. True to their class-based ideological approach, the communists categorised the Ba'th as a 'petty bourgeois' political party. However, as the Iraqi Ba'th became involved in political acts leading to the deaths of many communists during 1963, ICP analyses increasingly described it as a 'fascist' organisation.

These changes of ideological perception were closely related to events on the ground, where in early 1963 not only the Iraqi Ba'th but also its Syrian counterpart had been able to seize power through military coups. The new Ba'thist regimes in Iraq and Syria began unity talks with Nasir's Egypt, which despite differences of opinion resulted in an agreement on 17 April. But there was little love lost between the Ba'thists and Nasir. At the time, the Iraqi Ba'th was led by the anti-Nasirist 'Ali Saleh al-Sa'di, and that proved to be a major obstacle to the rapprochement. During the summer and autumn of 1963, a gradual fallout thus occurred

---

provide references, these are exclusively 'Aziz al-Hajj, i.e. al-Nasiri's political rival, Ismael, *Rise and Fall*, p. 119.

8 The other members elected to the Politburo were Baqer Ibrahim al-Musawi, 'Umar al-Shaykh, 'Aziz Muhammad and 'Abd al-Salam al-Nasiri. Because Zaki Khayri explicitly had confessed to forming a 'bloc' in his self-criticism, 'Aziz Muhammad decided that Khayri, who incidentally was absent from the meeting, would need a 'transition period' before returning to the Politburo, Nuri, *Mudhakkirat*, p. 314.

9 Ibid., p. 315.

between Nasir and the Iraqi and Syrian regimes over the nature of the proposed unification, eventually leading to a complete revocation of the agreement. Following the Sixth Ba'thist National Convention, held in Damascus between 5 October and 23 October, tensions between pro- and anti-Nasirist forces within the Iraqi Ba'th came to the surface and in November led to outright fighting between the two sides.[10] As the two factions were busy fighting each other, 'Aref seized his opportunity and arrested the National Command on 18 November and took control of the government.[11]

The Ba'th Party was a complex and contradictory organisation with many competing tendencies and personalities. Its ideology, insofar as it had any unified outlook, had been shaped by its two founders, Michel 'Aflaq and Salah al-Din al-Baytar. Their experience as students at the Sorbonne in the 1930s when, in their view, French Leftism betrayed the Syrian cause had been pivotal in establishing anti-communism as one of the Ba'th Party's main foundational principles. Having both been attracted to communism early on, they had put much hope in the leftist front government that came to power in France in 1936. But as the new government was reluctant to pursue a markedly different Syrian policy, 'Aflaq and al-Baytar turned against communism and the 'imperialist nature' of Western socialism. From then on, they began formulating the ideas that later shaped the future Ba'th Party—ideas that were vehemently anti-Western and staunchly Arab nationalist in essence.[12] In the Ba'thist view, communism was a Western concept linked with 'imperialism' whose ultimate aim was to annihilate the national aspirations of the Arabs. The Ba'th Party therefore tried to present itself as a 'Third Way'—a genuine Arab way—in between capitalism and communism. While not rejecting the ultimate utopian aims of communism, the Ba'thists argued that because the Arab world was still dominated by feudal conditions, it was not ready to adopt communist ideology. Ba'thist ideology also rejected the communist focus on classes and class struggle. For the Ba'thists, 'Arab Socialism' was not of one class but for the whole 'people'. To them, social-

[10] 'Trouble Flares in Baghdad As Factions Struggle', *The Times*, 14 Nov. 1963

[11] Abu Jaber, *Arab Ba'th*, pp. 68–83. See also 'President Arif Seizes Power in Iraq', *The Times*, 19 Nov. 1963.

[12] Abu Jaber, *Arab Ba'th*, pp. 11–12. For examples of 'Aflaq's views, see Michel 'Aflaq, *Fi Sabil al-Ba'th*, Beirut: Dar al-Tali'ah li l-Taba'ah wa l-Nashr, 1974.

ism meant the economic and political liberation of man, arguing that communist economic determinism distorted the spiritual values of the Arabs. Rather than being the inevitable outcome of class struggle, socialism would be brought about when a majority of the population was convinced it represented a moral and just society.[13]

Unsurprisingly, considering the treatment meted out to communists by the Ba'thist National Guards, communist views on the Ba'th Party were harsh and unrelenting following the February 1963 coup. Some efforts at keeping analyses within traditional ideological frameworks could be discerned but generally the brutality showed by the Ba'th Party throughout 1963 made the ICP characterise the Ba'th as a 'fascist' organisation. A meeting of Arab communist parties held in the offices of *Problems of Peace and Socialism* in Prague during the summer of 1963 characteristically attempted a conventional class-based analysis. 'The leadership of this [Ba'th] Party', they wrote, 'consists in the main of representatives of anti-communist petty-bourgeois elements.' Stressing its anti-communist character further, they underlined how its formation after World War II had been 'in opposition to the Communist movement.' Implicitly describing the Ba'th Party's blend of nationalism and socialism as a sort of fascism, they also argued that it had 'absorbed all that has been ultra-reactionary both in Arab history and the Right-wing Socialist movement in the West.'[14]

'Aziz al-Hajj, who during this period was the ICP's representative on the editorial board of *Problems of Peace and Socialism*, did not stop at describing the Ba'thists as anti-communists but, writing at the height of Ba'thi anti-communist purges in 1963, called them a 'gang of counter-revolutionaries',[15] although framing his denunciation within a more traditional class-based analysis. 'From the beginning', he wrote,

> the party has been violently anti-communist, and has propounded a theory of national assimilation of all the people of the Arab world. [...] Baath drew its strength from the petty-bourgeoisie, recruiting members among students, intellectuals and servicemen. It had no real base among the workers, and its contact

[13] Abu Jaber, *Arab Ba'th*, pp. 103–109.

[14] 'The Present Stage of the National-Liberation Movement of the Arab Peoples', *World Marxist Review* 6, no. 10, Oct. 1963, p. 72.

[15] Aziz el-Haj, 'The Current Situation in Iraq', *World Marxist Review* 6, no. 11, Nov. 1963, p. 34.

with the peasants was even weaker. As it took the way of plotting and provocation, it was joined by large numbers of Nuri Said supporters, feudalists and reactionary officers. [...] Baath policy is a betrayal of the July 14 revolution; it is a policy of renouncing national independence and positive neutrality, exacerbating the already tense situation in the Middle East, and imposing fascist terror in this whole area.[16]

In this manner, the Iraqi communists resorted to an ideological safety valve that automatically categorised inexplicable and complex regional political phenomena as directed by 'imperialism', a *pis aller* that since has been utilised many times. The party tried to deny the existence of a Ba'thist ideology by describing the Ba'thists as an eclectic mix of thugs and anti-communists. It is clear, however, that although Ba'thi ideology may be difficult to pinpoint, the Ba'th Party did certainly act from an ideological basis of Arab nationalism. One of the reasons its ideology appears illusive is because of 'Aflaq's avowed intention to remain aloof from theory. In his view, abstract thinking and theorising would deprive reality of its essence. Arab nationalism, according to 'Aflaq, was not the product of thought but precipitated thought. While thus discarding theorising, 'Aflaq distinguished his ideology from Western socialism, and by asseverating the party's focus on pragmatism rather than abstractness, he wanted to show that the new ideology was indigenous to the Arab world.[17]

Yet, despite al-Hajj's acknowledgement of the complex set-up of the Ba'th Party—its being a melting pot of all social forces inimical to the ICP and the existence of an enunciated Ba'thi theory of assimilation—he nevertheless did his utmost to deprive them of any historical or political agency of their own. Theirs was the policy of 'plotting and provocation' and the imposition of 'fascist terror', a communist euphemism for incomprehensible political acts falling outside the normal framework of analysis. Thus, writing in May 1964, *Tariq al-Sha'b* referred to the episode as the 'period of the Ba'thist killing regime',[18] and in another article in the same issue, 'Ali Saleh al-Sa'di, the Iraqi Ba'th leader, was described as 'an Iraqi offspring of Hitler'.[19]

[16] Ibid., p. 37.

[17] Kaylani, 'Syrian Ba'th', p. 5; Abu Jaber, *Arab Ba'th*, pp. 97–102.

[18] 'al-Hurriyyah li l-Mu'taqilin wa l-Sujuna' al-Siyasiyyin', *Tariq al-Sha'b* 21, no. 1, May 1964.

[19] 'Min Nashriyat al-Hizb', *Tariq al-Sha'b* 21, no. 1, May 1964.

Getting Enmeshed in the Kurdish Question

During the period from the Ba'thist coup in 1963 until the overthrow of 'Abd al-Rahman 'Aref in 1968, the Kurdish areas became the ICP's main operational sphere inside Iraq due to the repression it suffered elsewhere. Thus, from having been a relatively peripheral question in the preceding era, the Kurdish problem now took centre stage for the party. The main features of its new policy was a focus on democracy as a political demand for Iraqi Kurdistan. But at the same time the subordinated relations with Kurdish nationalist leader Mulla Mustafa Barzani eventually forced the party to readjust its ideological analysis of him and eventually settle for playing second fiddle to his party, the KDP.

Since its founding in the 1930s, the ICP had been an instrumental force in Iraqi Kurdistan, but had made sure to stay clear of the quagmiry arena of Kurdish infighting. Following the February 1963 coup, however, the communists were drawn into Kurdish politics in a more direct manner. Fleeing the terror of Arab Iraq, they sought refuge in KDP-controlled parts of Iraqi Kurdistan. In areas pertaining to Mulla Mustafa Barzani cooperation proceeded smoothly; there the communists were allowed to retain their weapons and were given places to gather and set up camp. In areas controlled by a leftwing KDP faction under the leadership of Ibrahim Ahmad and Jalal Talabani, however, they were not allowed to carry arms, and in more than one place they were attacked, in a few places with deadly outcome.[20]

The war between the Kurdish nationalists and the Iraqi state,[21] which had begun already during the later Qasim years, forced the ICP to deal with the Kurdish question more comprehensively. In March 1962, the party's Central Committee had analysed the problem, and in November 1963, 'Aziz al-Hajj, writing in *Problems of Peace and Socialism*, expanded on its position at length. The ICP's policy on the Kurdish issue, he explained, was based on a number of premises. Firstly, that 'Imperialism divided Kurdistan and encouraged and is still encouraging persecution of the Kurds. Hence imperialism is the first and main enemy of the Kurdish people', a statement showing a clear ahistorical simplification of the issue.

[20] These fatal attacks took place in Bamu province, where among others communist 'Ali al-'Askari was killed with his own gun, Nuri, *Mudhakkirat*, pp. 348–349.

[21] See ch. 3.

Secondly, it was argued that the 'Kurdish question is a component part of the national question of the peoples of Iraq, Iran and Turkey, and the Kurdish national-liberation struggle is part and parcel of the national struggle waged by all these peoples against imperialism and reaction and for a national-democratic regime.' In other words, the ICP thus argued that the Kurds, like Arabs, Turks, and other peoples of the region, were suffering from oppression from 'imperialism' and that it therefore was in their interest to ally with these peoples against it. However, the third point was more complicated as it admitted that the 'Kurdish question has its peculiar aspects despite the fact that it is part of the national question … because the Kurds suffer from national oppression … The Kurds in Iraq are part of the divided Kurdish nation.'[22]

Syncretising core ideas of Kurdish nationalist ideology, the ICP thus argued that the Kurds living in Iraq in fact were part of an imagined greater 'Kurdish nation'. The third point was also problematic as it acknowledged that Kurds suffered oppression not only from 'imperialism' but also from the Arab majority in the country, an issue that on the face of it would justify the Kurds taking up arms against the Arab regime in Baghdad. Not necessarily so, because:

> the problem of the Kurdish nationality is organically linked with the cause of democracy for the Arab people; that organic unity of the two causes within the borders of one and the same state, Iraq, is so firm that neither can be solved in isolation from the other. The ordeal suffered by the Kurds is part of the ordeal of the Iraqi people. […] The solution of the Kurdish national problem is part of the solution of the democratic issue in Iraq. […] At present this can only mean turning Arab-Kurd unity into a democratic unity, a matter which can be achieved by granting autonomy to Iraqi Kurdistan within the framework of a united Iraqi republic …[23]

In the same manner as the ICP previously had argued, with considerable success, that Arabs and Kurds were linked in their struggle against foreign domination and thus had been instrumental in fostering a distinct anti-imperialist Iraqist nationalism, they were now trying to use the same sets of arguments on the much more complicated issue of internal ethnic relations. The overall aim, of course, was to keep the Kurdish national

[22] el-Haj, 'Current Situation', p. 40.

[23] Statement of the ICP Central Committee, Mar. 1962, quoted in el-Haj, 'Current Situation', p. 40.

movement within the framework of the Iraqi state. The key to the party's thinking was thus the linking of 'democracy' with the idea of the Iraqi Kurdish 'nation'—a link they argued was 'organic'. Yet, at the same time, the Kurds were imagined to be part of a larger 'Kurdish nation'.[24] This, undoubtedly, was the inherent problem in communist thinking. The danger, therefore, should 'democracy' prevail in Iraq, was that the Kurds might opt to 'rejoin' their 'brethren' in the imagined entity of greater Kurdistan.

The Ba'thi coup brought about an emotional response from the ICP, who, somewhat exaggeratedly, claimed the 'principal aim' of the coup had been 'to destroy the Communist party ... in the Arab regions in order ... to launch an armed attack on Kurdistan.' Accordingly, the war itself was described as 'racist' and 'genocidal'. In the same perfunctory manner, the Kurdish response was seen as 'a struggle for liberation from the rule of the fascist Ba'athists—the henchmen of imperialism—for a national-democratic government which would guarantee Kurdish autonomy.'[25] In reality, of course, the forces driving these two sides into armed conflict were more complex. Nevertheless, when the new 'Aref regime signed a peace agreement with Mulla Mustafa Barzani on 10 February 1964, and especially as this was backed by Moscow, the ICP leadership supported the move although there were those in their own party who wanted the Kurdish armed struggle to continue in order to overthrow the regime in Baghdad.[26] The leftwing KDP-faction led by Ibrahim Ahmad and Jalal Talabani, however, criticised Mulla Mustafa's concessions as the agreement had failed to mention the issue of self-administration and autonomy. But just as Qasim before him, 'Aref put his force behind Mulla Mustafa, providing him with arms and money, thereby enabling him to sideline his critics. Rallying the conservative elements of Kurdish society behind him, Mulla Mustafa represented a completely different ideological and socio-political force than the avowed leftists within the Ahmad-Talabani faction.

[24] Using Kurdish nationalist language, the ICP spoke of 'Kurdistan, the homeland of the Kurds', ICP delegate at 1963 Arab meeting, 'Present Stage', p. 66. Similarly, 'Aziz al-Hajj, himself a Fayli Kurd, used terms such as the 'divided Kurdish nation', which, in his view, was 'distinguished by its common language, land, historical heritage and its common aspiration to live in freedom', Aziz al-Hajj, 'Support the Just Struggle of the Kurdish People!', *World Marxist Review* 9, no. 4, Apr. 1966, p. 46.

[25] Iraqi delegate at the Arab communist meeting in 1963, 'Present Stage', p. 67.

[26] Mahmud, *al-Sira'*, p. 78.

But since the 1961 uprising that faction had unreservedly backed Barzani and described him as the leader of the 'Kurdish nation'.[27]

At this point, the ICP in earnest began arguing for democracy as a solution to the Kurdish problem. However, to prevent the Kurds from opting for separation should democratic rights be granted, it made sure to condition democracy organisationally in the form of autonomy. 'Autonomy for Iraqi Kurdistan', 'Aziz al-Hajj explained in April 1966, 'is conceived as an administrative territory whose affairs should be in the hands of an elected legislative body which, in turn, would elect an executive body responsible to the people. National autonomy is in the interests not only of the Kurdish people, it is also in the interests of the people of Iraq.'[28] Due to the oppression Kurds suffered at the hands of the Arab administration in Baghdad, the ICP argued that they primarily needed autonomy as a precondition to democracy. 'Democracy will be meaningless, mere nonsense for the Kurdish people', the party had argued in its March 1962 Statement, 'unless they are guaranteed the real possibility of enjoying their national rights and managing their own affairs. This can be achieved only through autonomy.'[29] Later, when the party leadership had been forced to assume a more radical stance, it clung to this demand for autonomy but linked it to the demand for the overthrow of the regime, which by then had become the party leadership's watchword. 'The Communist Party of Iraq', 'Aziz al-Hajj thus wrote,

> true to the principles of proletarian internationalism and recognising the principle of complete self-determination for the whole divided Kurdish nation, fully supports this demand for autonomy and regards it as an elementary and just right. At the same time it is the considered view of the Iraqi Communists that a democratic solution of the Kurdish problem is impossible unless the present reactionary regime is overthrown.[30]

Continuing to echo the language of Arab and Kurdish nationalism, when war broke out again in 1965 the ICP argued that it harmed the interests of the 'Arab nation' and used the anti-imperialist character of Kurdish nationalism to try once again to patch up the relationship with

[27] McDowall, *History of the Kurds*, pp. 315–316.

[28] al-Hajj, 'Support!', p. 46.

[29] Report of Central Committee of the ICP, Mar. 1962, quoted in al-Hajj, 'Support!', p. 46.

[30] al-Hajj, 'Support!', p. 46.

Baghdad. 'It is in no way in the interest of the Arab nation', a party manifesto published in *Tariq al-Sha'b* read, 'to launch an unjust war against the Kurdish people which at all times have been and continues to be a loyal ally to the Arab liberation movement in the struggle against colonialism and reaction'.[31] As a further sign of its deluded view of the war, clouded by its ideological viewing of it through the prism of anti-imperialist struggle, the party argued the war was fomented by imperialism against the 'Arab liberation movement'. 'The frantic activity that the circles from CENTO,[32] the oil companies, and the agencies of Zionism and reaction have undertaken to incite war in Kurdistan', the manifesto claimed, 'is, however, part of a broad imperialist plan hatched against the Arab liberation movement and its successful progressive course.'[33]

Over time, however, as the party became increasingly enmeshed in the internal strife afflicting the Kurdish nationalist movement, its ideological understanding of events was accordingly challenged by facts on the ground. The tribal areas of northern Iraq were more prone to influences of patrimonialism and less susceptible to ideological politics; in Iraqi Kurdistan, politics was overshadowed by the indomitable figure of Mulla Mustafa Barzani. Despite his initially narrow tribal support base, by now he had grown into a living embodiment of Kurdish nationalism, and, as such, the ICP was in no position to disregard him. The Ahmad-Talabani faction had unsuccessfully tried to challenge his authority in April 1964, when they convened a KDP Congress that condemned Barzani. Mulla Mustafa, however, replied by convening his own congress in July where representatives of their faction were arrested. He set up a new leadership and ousted most of the old one. Some days later, he amassed a large force of *peshmergahs* and forced Ahmad and Talabani, together with their approximately 4,000 supporters, into Iran.[34] With Mulla Mustafa's new omnipotent position, the ICP was also coerced into subordination. Thus, when Baha' al-Din Nuri in early 1966 was sent to Iraqi Kurdistan to be Secretary of the party's *Iqlim* ('region'), he found himself forced to pay

31 Manifesto of the Iraqi Communist Party, 'La Tal'abu bi l-Nar ya Hukam Baghdad, Shabh al-Harb al-Ahliyyah Yukhayyim 'Ala Ard al-'Iraq', *Tariq al-Sha'b* 21, no. 5, Mar. 1965, p. 1.

32 The Central Treaty Organisation, i.e. the Baghdad Pact.

33 'La Tal'abu bi l-Nar', p. 4.

34 McDowall, *History of the Kurds*, pp. 316–317.

Mulla Mustafa a courtesy visit to inform him of the new arrangements. At this meeting, Barzani simply instructed Nuri that he wanted Soviet aid in his fight against the regime and he made it clear that he saw Nuri and the ICP as errand boys of the Soviets, expecting them to deliver the message to their masters.[35]

Another factor adding to the impression that power politics now took precedence over ideological politics was the party's position on the aforementioned Ahmad-Talabani faction. On the face of it, Ibrahim Ahmad's group represented a 'progressive' wing of the KDP, while, on the other hand, it was clear Mulla Mustafa had feudalist-tribalist inclinations. Yet, the party not only denounced the faction, it actually commissioned its *Fedayeen* fighters, who since Nuri's arrival in early 1966 had been attached to Barzani's leadership in the regions of Balik, Qarah Dagh, Garmiyan and Bahandinan, to combat it. But characteristically of the ICP, it maintained its ideologically-tinged assessment of the faction as being a 'nationalist organisation walking along an erroneous path' trying to persuade it to return to the Barzani camp.[36] This incensed Mulla Mustafa, however, who asserted much pressure on the ICP to denounce the faction as 'treacherous donkeys'. At another meeting between Barzani and Nuri in December 1966, Mulla Mustafa shocked his visitor by demanding that the communists kill Ibrahim Ahmad and Jalal Talabani. When Nuri rejected the order, Barzani threatened to demolish the ICP's Kurdish branch and to hunt down and kill all communists in Iraqi Kurdistan.[37] While never carried out, these threats nevertheless illustrate the party's quandary after having become immersed in local Kurdish tribal politics.[38]

Yet, despite its succumbing to Barzani's power politics, the ICP never abandoned ideology as a framework for understanding Kurdish politics. Thus in the summer of 1966, the *Iqlim* wrote an 'appraisal leaflet' discussing Mulla Mustafa's person, treating his 'ideological composition', 'class affiliation' and 'capabilities'. The resulting assessment described him as a 'representative of the Kurdish bourgeoisie', from the 'wing that carries a mixture of tribal-peasant mentalities and the mentality of the intellectuals

[35] Nuri, *Mudhakkirat*, pp. 334–342.

[36] Ibid., pp. 349–351.

[37] Ibid., pp. 352–354.

[38] Such was the ICP's respect for Barzani that in early 1967 it decided to replace Nuri as Secretary of the *Iqlim* because Barzani was angry with him following their brawl, ibid., p. 364.

of the bygone era', and that he relied on 'tribal methods'. But despite these scathing remarks he was nevertheless confirmed as a 'patriotic and national leader' (*za'im watani wa qawmi*) who served his people.[39]

This assessment epitomises the party's ambivalent position towards Barzani. On the one hand he was a representative of the 'Kurdish bourgeoisie' while at the same time carrying a 'tribal-peasant' mentality and relying on 'tribal methods'. In this manner, Mulla Mustafa's all-encompassing figure forced the ICP to readjust its theories in order to ideologically understand and categorise him. Thus, much the same way as Qasim ideologically had been construed as a representative of the 'national bourgeoisie', Barzani was now construed as a representative of the 'Kurdish bourgeoisie'. By ideologically accommodating and putting the weight of the party behind him, the communists unavoidably strengthened his position in Iraqi Kurdistan to the point where they could no longer seriously challenge his authority. Thus, although having been among the strongest political forces in the Kurdish areas since the dawn of ideological politics following World War II, the ICP now surrendered its positions in the belief that doing so would favour the Kurdish 'national liberation' movement. What it in reality did, was to force the communists to play a secondary role in the Kurdish areas over the coming decades.

Neo-Colonialism, National Liberation and the Petty Bourgeoisie

The period under study marked a dramatic shift in the ICP's views on the Iraqi 'bourgeoisie' and its role in the revolution. The previously optimistic stance was modified and a more hesitant mood could be discerned within the leadership of the party. Thus, it was now argued that parts of the so-called 'national bourgeoisie' would side with 'imperialism' at crucial junctures. This development was explained by the new notion of 'neo-colonialism', whereby imperialism, especially in its US variety, was argued to have assumed more aggressive policies towards the Third World.

For Iraq, the new idea, as discussed above, was used by the ICP to analyse the Ba'thist ascendency to power, describing the Ba'thists as imperialist puppets. Equally, the development of a new Soviet theory maintaining that newly independent states in the Third World could by-pass capital-

[39] Ibid., p. 344.

ism and reach socialism through a 'non-capitalist path' allowed ideologically for the circumventing of the 'national bourgeoisie'. Thus, as the 'national bourgeoisie' was said to side with 'imperialism', this opened up for the potential national leadership of the so-called 'petty bourgeoisie'. As this class was perceived to be closer to the communists ideologically and socio-economically, the 'social struggle' was argued to sharpen as these so-called 'revolutionary democrats' seized control of the 'national-democratic' state.

Accordingly, the nationalist coup of February 1963 was interpreted as having been 'engineered with the active participation of the US imperialists' and was seen as 'one of the links' in the US 'policy of neo-colonialism.'[40] The key to this 'policy', according to the communists, was the Iraqi oil reserves. 'Oil is not simply a question of national wealth which is being plundered and squandered', 'Aziz al-Hajj thus wrote,

> it is also, and this is even more dangerous, a question of an imperialist administrative apparatus established by the oil companies inside the country. This apparatus has always interfered in our domestic and external affairs, has encouraged plots and worked to prevent any genuine economic or social advancement. Oil in Iraq and throughout the Middle East, besides being cheap and bringing in fabulous profits for foreign companies, is indispensable to the imperialists for the realisation of their war designs.[41]

'Neo-colonialism' was a new Soviet idea about the nature of imperialism in the post-colonial era formulated as a response to the national bourgeoisie's perceived siding with imperialism after attaining independence in countries such as Iraq. The theory explained how 'imperialism' tried to 're-colonise' the Third World after its attainment of formal independence, and how this new US-led phenomenon differed from the old raw Western European colonialism in that it was mainly characterised by indirect economic domination rather than direct imperial control. 'In carrying out its policy of neo-colonialism in the Arab East,' the Arab communists thus explained,

> US imperialism relies not so much on the feudal chiefs and the pro-imperialist bourgeoisie as on the new social strata of the national bourgeoisie and part of the intelligentsia who subscribe to slogans of nationalism, Arab unity and even social-

[40] 'Present Stage', p. 63.
[41] el-Haj, 'Current Situation', pp. 40–41.

ism. The neo-colonialists, while pretending to sympathise with the liberation movement of the Arab peoples, seek to direct this movement into anti-democratic channels, towards agreement with imperialism.[42]

For these reasons, neo-colonialism was seen as 'the main danger to the Arab peoples'. Among its detrimental traits was its operating in 'a disguised form', that it capitalised on Arab nationalism and thus was 'disorienting the people', and, perhaps worst of all, much like the communists themselves, neo-colonialism 'relies on the new social classes and sections, on the new ideological and political groupings'. Due to the sharpened domestic struggle neo-colonialism was said to give rise to, the 'struggle against neo-colonialism inevitably merges with the struggle against the reactionary bourgeoisie and the feudal chiefs, assuming the character of a bitter class struggle.'[43]

Faced with this neo-colonialist challenge, which in the communists' view diverted the national bourgeoisie in an anti-democratic direction and towards collaboration with imperialism, Soviet theoreticians developed the notion of 'non-capitalist development' in the early 1960s. The idea was clearly designed to accommodate Third World regimes leaning towards the 'socialist camp' in the ongoing Cold War in which the Soviets and the Americans were outbidding each other to receive the crucial support of newly independent regimes and equally to entice such regimes into further commitments. The theory modified the historically-determinist stages of feudalism, capitalism and socialism in the progression towards communism, as it added a new category in between the feudalist and capitalist stages, which potentially could replace the capitalist stage altogether.[44]

By theoretically establishing that radical Third World regimes emerging from feudalism could take a different route than capitalism, Soviet theoreticians argued that 'objectively' they were heading for socialism without passing through the capitalist stage. That way, by awarding a regime the recognition of 'non-capitalist' development, the Soviets hoped to incorporate it into its sphere of influence. The communist parties in

[42] 'Present Stage', p. 63.

[43] Ibid., p. 63.

[44] For the conceptual evolution of this theory, see Esmail Hosseinzadeh, *Soviet Non-Capitalist Development: The Case of Nasser's Egypt*, New York: Praeger, 1989, pp. 7–65.

the Arab East were quick to adopt the new notions. 'After political independence ...', they argued at their 1963 meeting,

> power in most of the Arab countries passed into the hands either of the national bourgeoisie or the petty bourgeoisie, or of the pro-imperialist bourgeoisie who are closely linked with the feudal chiefs. Two paths are open to these countries: the capitalist or the non-capitalist path. The working class and its Communist Party stand, naturally, for the non-capitalist way. The new sovereign states can take the non-capitalist way provided a united national front is established based on the alliance of the working class and the peasantry and which will also include the national bourgeoisie.[45]

'Aziz al-Hajj went even further in his description of the wonders of 'non-capitalist development' and how thanks to it Third World liberation had turned into an integral part of the 'world revolution'. In an article written together with Fu'ad Nassar of the Jordanian Communist Party, he explained that:

> the majority of the former colonies, even though they have rid themselves of the political rule of imperialism, still remain within the orbit of capitalist economy. In these countries the question of what road to take poses itself with growing urgency as the revolutionary anti-imperialist movement grows. The deepening of national-liberation revolution in a number of countries leads to a situation in which these countries advance with seven-league strides in the socio-economic reshaping of society, passing over from semi-feudal and semi-capitalist, and in some cases from primitive tribal formations, to non-capitalist lines, ultimately leading to socialism. [Thus,] the national-liberation movement has grown from a "reserve" of the socialist revolution, into one of the vital components of the world revolutionary process.[46]

The possibility for emerging countries to choose between 'capitalist' and 'non-capitalist' development upon independence meant that there was no longer an absolute necessity for the 'national bourgeoisie' to lead the country through a stage of national capitalist development. This line of thinking corresponded well with the feeling that the bourgeoisie inevitably would move into duplicitous cooperation with imperialism. In contradiction to the generally favourable analysis of the national bourgeoisie during the Qasim period, the communists were now arguing, 'the national

[45] 'Present Stage', pp. 73–74.

[46] Fuad Nassar and Aziz al-Hajj, 'The National-Liberation Movement and the World Revolutionary Process', *World Marxist Review* 7, no. 3, Mar. 1964, p. 9.

bourgeoisie, because of its dual nature, is incapable of solving the new problems that arise on the day after winning independence.' This, of course, was explained in class terms by the strain brought upon the 'national bourgeoisie' during the class struggle, something that made it yield to imperialist pressure, and thus 'a part of the national bourgeoisie (and at times sections of the small bourgeoisie) succumbs to imperialist propaganda which seeks to frighten the peoples of the newly-emerged countries with the bogey of communism, and claims that it is in their interests to come to terms with imperialism, alleging that this would guarantee their sovereignty.'[47] Instead, it was argued, other classes and strata, such as the 'petty bourgeoisie', could take up the helm of the country. 'We do not look upon the national-democratic revolution in the contemporary circumstances on the basis of the classical criteria alone', the ICP thus argued in *Tariq al-Sha'b* in 1965,

> and we are not ignorant of the new characteristics it has gained or is gaining. We resolutely refute the idea that talks about the necessity of a bourgeois power as a precondition for the implementation of our national-democratic revolution's present tasks, and at the same time we refute the idea of expelling the national bourgeoisie as a whole from the ranks of the anti-imperialist forces under the pretence that its role has ended.[48]

Yet, the communist recipe of a wide social front directed against 'imperialism' to reach socialism remained the same. 'The question of solidarity and the front between the anti-imperialist forces continues to preserve itself with all vigour in our country', the ICP thus argued, 'and following on that, the best [form of] government for the radical implementation of the democratic tasks and the paving of the way for Iraq's coming progression towards socialism is a coalition government [*sultah i'tilafiyyah*] in which all the anti-imperialist and anti-reactionary forces are represented.'[49]

Nevertheless, the perceived increasingly social content of the political struggle did mark a significant change in the communist view of the post-colonial state and the role played by the so-called 'petty bourgeoisie' in it. The new idea was summed up in the concept of 'national democracy', a

[47] 'Present Stage', pp. 63–64.

[48] 'al-Ishtirakiyyah wa Siyasat al-Hukm al-Rahin', *Tariq al-Sha'b* 21, no. 5, Mar. 1965.

[49] Ibid.

notion first established at the Conference of Communist and Workers' Parties in Moscow in 1960. Within the new 'national democratic' state, a gradual transition to a society in which socialist production relations predominated was said to take place. Within such a development, the 'petty bourgeoisie' was seen as playing a key role as an instrument of transition. As more and more 'petty bourgeois' parties and regimes began using socialist rhetoric and implemented state capitalist policies, these were categorised as 'revolutionary democrats' which gradually moved closer to 'Scientific Socialism', i.e. socialism of the Marxist-Leninist variety.[50] As we shall see, this idea of a heightened internal struggle with an ever more pronounced social content was well in keeping with developments within the theory of non-capitalist development. Increasingly, proponents of that theory argued regimes following 'non-capitalist' paths had also started to implement socialist tasks.

A Non-Capitalist Path to Rapprochement with Nasir

At the centre of the communist re-evaluation of politics in the Middle East was the re-conceptualisation of Jamal 'Abd al-Nasir. Pivotal for this development was Soviet foreign policy and its expansionist programme for the Middle East. For the ICP, the re-visioning of Nasir, transforming him from foe to friend, is particularly informative. Despite having labelled him anti-democratic and implicitly arguing that he served the interests of imperialism during the struggles of early 1959, the impact of new ideas emanating from the Soviet Union was at this point stronger than local concerns on the ground. In other words, although the Iraqi communists undoubtedly were better aware of and understood Arab affairs more profoundly, their policy on Nasir and his regime—their own neighbour—was dictated by theoreticians in faraway Moscow. Importantly, however, the ideational metamorphosis that allowed for the re-conceptualisation was without exception justified ideologically.

Relations between the Soviet Union and Nasir's Egypt had at best been lukewarm during the preceding years, with Khrushchev publicly criticising Nasir's anti-communism at the Twenty-First CPSU Congress in 1959,[51]

[50] Tareq Y. Ismael, *The Communist Movement in the Arab World*, London: Routledge, 2005, p. 49.

[51] John R. Swanson, 'The Soviet Union and the Arab World: Revolutionary Progress

and reaching a nadir at the time of the breakup of the UAR in 1961. However, as Nasir's public rhetoric turned more socialist and Egypt initiated a nationalisation programme in the early 1960s as well as adopting its 1962 National Charter, relations slowly thawed. Since the Chinese were also courting the Egyptians, with a high-level visit by Premier Chou En-lai in late 1963, rapprochement seemed ever more crucial for the Soviet leaders. Thus, in November 1963, *Pravda* recognised for the first time that Egypt had entered the 'non-capitalist path', although retaining the caveat that Nasir's continued maltreatment of the Egyptian communists constituted an obstacle to progress.[52] A month later, it was explained that the nationalisation measures introduced by Nasir indeed afforded Egypt the basis for 'non-capitalist development' but that they were a 'revolution from above' and as such needed to be accompanied by far-reaching democratisation on the ground.[53] Correspondingly, Nasir's rhetoric was further radicalised during the months leading up to Khrushchev's visit to Egypt, repeatedly attacking 'imperialism' and 'neo-colonialism'. During the visit, starting on 9 May and lasting for sixteen days, Nasir enthusiastically declared that Egypt was 'building socialism'. While not willing to grant Egypt such prominence, Khrushchev nevertheless conceded that Egypt had 'embarked upon the path of socialist construction'.[54]

Ideologically, Khrushchev thus removed the old Marxist-Leninist tenet that stipulated 'socialism' as a distinct phase led by the communist party. Instead, a new precept arguing that socialism could be reached in a myriad of ways was introduced. As a result, violent revolutions were no longer seen as essential prerequisites for reaching the desired objective, a revision that, as we have seen, went back to the Twentieth CPSU Congress in 1956. 'What are the basic features of the national-liberation movement at the present stage?', 'Aziz al-Hajj and Fu'ad Nassar had thus asked in an article in *Problems of Peace and Socialism* in early 1964 presenting the 'new-old' non-violent vision. 'Firstly', they replied,

---

through Dependence on Local Elites', *The Western Political Quarterly* 27, no. 4, Dec. 1974, p. 647.

52 I. Beliaev, *Pravda*, 26 Nov. 1963, as quoted in Oles M. Smolansky, *The Soviet Union and the Arab East under Khrushchev*, Lewisburg, PA: Bucknell University Press, 1974, p. 214.

53 G. Mirskii, 'The Changing Arab East', *New Times*, 15 Jan. 1964, quoted in Smolansky, *Arab East*, p. 214.

54 Smolansky, *Arab East*, pp. 263–273.

the movement, having outgrown the national boundaries, has acquired an all-embracing, global character. It is no longer directed against any one colonial power but against the *entire colonial system*. [...] Secondly, the distinctive feature of the present phase of the national-liberation movement is the remarkable diversity of the forms and methods of the struggle, depending on the conditions in the particular country, on the alignment of class and political forces in the country, on the level of its socio-economic development and of the mass action. It would be wrong therefore, to regard the armed struggle as the only revolutionary form, and to write off all other forms as "reformism and capitulation". Each people chooses the ways and means best suited for solving the problems confronting it.[55]

To the Soviets, these notions were particularly beneficial since they allowed them to penetrate a region in which they had hitherto had little or no influence. Thus, recognising heterodox Arab ways of 'reaching socialism' increased Soviet popularity among the 'radical' Arab regimes. The price paid for such inroads in terms of political influence was, of course, an abandonment of ideological monopoly. Nevertheless, if the toll of their extended influence was the dissolution of local communist parties, as happened in Egypt and Algeria, it seemed a price the Soviets were willing to pay. For the Arab communists on the ground, however, the theory ought to have appeared much less appealing since in effect it removed their fundamental raison d'être, albeit with the idealistic promise of a socialist future. It is therefore surprising to find that the leaders of the ICP, a party renowned for its militancy and unrelenting struggle during three decades, would welcome these ideas with an overwhelming majority and make them the new platform of the party's policy.[56]

Initially, however, the ICP leadership expressed some doubts about the socialist nature of Nasir's regime. While conceding that Egypt's 1962 National Charter was 'written under the influence of socialism', its delegate to the 1963 Arab communist meeting nevertheless argued that the charter did 'not speak of the abolition of the exploitation of man by man'. He further maintained that while many of the measures undertaken by Egypt were 'progressive inasmuch as they promote the country's industrial development and the expansion of the state sector' they did not 'do away with the roots of capitalist exploitation.'[57] This was well in keeping with

[55] Nassar and al-Hajj, 'National-Liberation Movement', p. 8 (original emphasis).
[56] See 'Ajinah, *Ikhtiyar al-Mutajaddad*, 88; Nuri, *Mudhakkirat*, pp. 312–313.
[57] 'Present Stage', p. 73.

Soviet misgivings about the charter expressed at the time of its publication. The Soviet press had commented that although the charter did show that 'transformations' had taken place in Egypt since the 1952 revolution, it also demonstrated apparent 'contradictions' as, for instance, the charter insisted on the inherent harmony of Islam and Arab Socialism and also because it rejected the Marxist-Leninist notion of the 'dictatorship of the proletariat'. Finally, Soviet media questioned what kind of socialism could be built if the 'true socialists' were all incarcerated.[58]

By the time of Khrushchev's Egypt visit, however, such misgivings had been brushed aside. Thus, in a thoroughly pro-Nasirite article on the front page of *Tariq al-Sha'b*, the ICP leadership welcomed Khrushchev to Egypt, 'the land of decisive struggle against imperialism' and 'the land of the revolution on the banks of the Nile'. Arab-Soviet friendship, the article maintained, was 'a decisive precondition' for the victory of every struggle for 'freedom and peace and for the sake of thorough progress towards a happy life and a better future.'[59] Although the re-evaluation of Nasir had been a long time coming, closely corresponding to the penetration of the theory of non-capitalist development among Arab communist leaders, the seal of the transformation was brought about at a meeting of Arab communist parties in late April 1964 which Khrushchev had called upon to publish the statement he would bring to Cairo the following month.[60] 'The Communists in our countries', the meeting statement, which was published in the Beirut daily *al-Akhbar* on 7 June 1964, consequently stated,

> are of the opinion that the higher national [*qawmi*] interests of the Arab nation [*al-ummah al-'Arabiyyah*] and its liberation and democratic movement requires the securing of all the necessary preconditions for cooperation of the national forces within every Arab country, and the rapprochement and cooperation between all the national and democratic forces and currents and the working class progressive movements for the sake of rebuilding society on a socialist foundation in the Arab world. For that reason, it is necessary, and imperative, that all the national forces in the Arab liberation movement on the governmental and popular levels abandon views of caution, doubt and antipathy vis-à-vis each other

[58] V. Maeskii, *Pravda*, 19 Jul. 1962, as quoted in Smolansky, *Arab East*, pp. 211–212.

[59] 'Ahlan bi Sadiq al-'Arab fi Ard al-'Arab, al-Sadaqah al-'Arabiyyah—al-Sufiyatiyyah Tatatawwar wa Tazdawhar', *Tariq al-Sha'b* 21, no. 1, May 1964, p. 1; 7.

[60] Mahmud, *al-Sira'*, p. 75.

and undertake the necessary steps and endeavour to bring closer the trust and realise the desired cooperation between them…[61]

Rethinking Arab Unity

At this juncture, the new theories of 'revolutionary democracy' and 'non-capitalist development' had been firmly incorporated into ICP ideology. These theoretical changes thus allowed the ICP to accommodate Nasir, in accordance with the new Soviet assessment of the Egyptian leader and his regime. The previous objection to Nasir's political system because of its anti-democratic nature was now brushed aside as the Iraqi communists argued that Nasir's system in fact represented a new form of democracy—a 'revolutionary democracy', or a 'democracy of the Arab toilers'. As Nasir adopted the language of class and argued that the Arab unity he sought was that of Arab workers and peasants, this meant that ideologically the ICP could now justify supporting Nasir and his version of Arab unity.

Fully adopting the language of pan-Arab nationalism, the 1963 meeting of Arab communists had argued that 'Arab unity, as a movement aimed at uniting the Arab peoples reflects the conditions that have taken shape in the Arab countries; it is not the outcome of transient circumstances or of the desires of one class or party.'[62] The communists thus argued, somewhat uncharacteristically for adherents of rigid class-based historical materialism, that 'Arab unity' was of historical transcendence, transgressing the narrow interests of its constituent actors—it was a historical necessity. 'The progressive aspect of Arab unity', the statement continued, 'is that it is spearheaded against imperialism and feudalism. This aspect, approved by the people, is supported by all the democratic forces in the Arab countries.'[63] Yet, contradictory, the communists also acknowledged that those actually leading the drive for this unity—the 'Arab bourgeoisie'—were appropriating the movement for the benefit of their own 'class interests'. The statement thus explained that Arab unity's

[61] *al-Akhbar*, 7 Jun. 1964, quoted in Mahmud, *al-Sira'*, p. 76. For an alternative translation, omitting the phrase 'for the sake of rebuilding society on a socialist foundation in the Arab world', see Ismael, *Communist Movement*, p. 55.

[62] 'Present Stage', p. 69.

[63] Ibid.

'reactionary aspect is manifested in the desire of the Arab bourgeoisie to subordinate the liberation movement to its narrow class interests. The bourgeoisie is not waging a resolute struggle for the complete abolition of colonialism and for uprooting the survivals of feudalism; its ultimate aim is to win political power.'[64]

To solve this apparent contradiction, the communists argued that there were two discernable 'trends' within the movement for Arab unity—one 'bourgeois-nationalist' and another 'revolutionary-democratic'. The position towards the former was one of hostility as to the communists it was based on 'anti-communism' and attacks on democracy, 'a nationalist-chauvinist ideology', 'isolation of the Arab peoples from the socialist camp', and 'reconciliation with imperialism'. The 'bourgeois-nationalist' trend did however have some redeeming features as it was said to be 'reluctant to break completely with the socialist camp because of the advantageous relationship', and was therefore 'constantly manoeuvring between the socialist camp and imperialism.' The 'revolutionary-democratic' trend, on the other hand, was said to be resting on a democratic foundation, according to the communists. The importance of democracy as a precondition for unity, nay its being an 'indispensable condition', was firmly stressed despite the fact that no system even remotely resembling 'democracy' ever existed in any of the regimes construed to be 'revolutionary democratic'. Thus, notwithstanding all ado about the indispensability of democracy, the 'Arab bourgeoisie' was perceived to be 'incapable of achieving the unity of the peoples on a democratic foundation'. Despite this apparent contradiction, it was thought that 'in the course of the deepening of the national-democratic revolution, of the emergence of the state of national democracy in which an important role will be played by the working class in alliance with the peasantry and all working people, the slogan of Arab unity can be realised.'[65] The increased role of workers and peasants in the revolutionary democratic regimes was thus key to the new thinking. In Egypt, for instance, Nasir had announced a new electoral law guaranteeing at least half of the seats in the National Assembly to workers and peasants.[66]

The reassessment of Arab unity was accordingly intimately linked with this reconceptualisation of Nasir and the Egyptian system as socialist.

[64] Ibid.

[65] Ibid., pp. 70–72.

[66] Smolansky, *Arab East*, p. 269.

The changing characterisation of Nasir's regime allowed the ICP to argue for a qualitatively different definition of 'democracy'. Nasir, it was said, thus represented the interests of the toiling masses, and so, *ipso facto*, his system was 'revolutionary democratic'. This line of thinking was a direct result of an ideological row that had erupted between Khrushchev, Nasir and Iraqi President 'Abd al-Salam 'Aref during Khrushchev's visit to Egypt in May 1964. Incensed by 'Aref's insistence on the ethnically exclusivist nature of Arab unity expressed in his religiously-tinged speech at Aswan on 16 May, in which he thanked God for being Arab, Khrushchev berated what he saw as Arab chauvinism. If ethnicity was the criteria for unity, Khrushchev argued, he and his Soviet technicians might as well leave. He did not intend to assist the Arabs 'in general', he said, instead insisting that Arab unity was a class issue and that it should be modified to mean the 'fraternal unification of all Arab toilers'.[67] To rebut Khrushchev's contentions, Nasir felt obliged to explain in a speech in Cairo on 20 May that Arab unity was not a 'racist slogan' but a reflection of a 'deep historical reality'. The Arabs, he argued, had always formed a single 'nation', characterised by a 'unity of material existence, a single conscience, and a single world view', arguing, in a manner familiar to the traditions of Arab nationalism, that the divisions existing in the Arab world were a creation of 'imperialism'. In the end, he maintained, unity would be based on 'freedom and socialism',[68] adding, 'the national society which the Arab masses have built will have no room for the oppressive fief or capital'.[69]

Accepting Nasir's attempt to smooth over the differences, which in reality were of a fundamental nature, Khrushchev ideologically opened up for the ensuing re-evaluation of Arab unity among Arab communists. Indeed, the ICP soon picked up Nasir's arguments. 'The treatment of Arab unity', *Tariq al-Sha'b* contended,

> on the basis of its being in essence a unity of Arab toilers, not a unity of reactionary rulers and exploitative classes, and the confirmation by President Jamal 'Abd al-Nasir that it is not a racist unity but the unity of the working people, acquires for the Arab unity movement a new progressive warranty whose nature it is to be raised to the utmost level of the notions of this movement in the

[67] *Pravda*, 18 May 1964, as quoted in Smolansky, *Arab East*, pp. 275–277.
[68] *Pravda*, 21 May 1964, as quoted in Smolansky, *Arab East*, p. 277.
[69] *al-Ahram*, 21 May 1964, as quoted in Ismael, *Communist Movement*, p. 48.

eyes of millions among the toiling Arab masses and creating of it a real mass movement.[70]

Upon Khrushchev's return to Moscow, having been impressed by his host, he also declared in a televised speech that Nasir's anti-communism definitely was a thing of the past.[71] The last obstacle to a communist reassessment of Nasir had thus been removed. 'The announcement of President 'Abd al-Nasir that the combating of the communist movement in Egypt is the legacy of the past', an ICP statement in *Tariq al-Sha'b* in July 1964 consequently read, 'is an important thing that gives evidence to a significant development in the objective contemplation of the progressive political forces in society and in the more comprehending treatment of the notion of the forces of the working people and its role in the realisation of the progressive programme which Egypt progresses towards.'[72] This rapprochement with Nasir may appear extraordinary considering his active involvement in the downfall of the Qasim regime, which opened up for the ensuing large-scale nationalist killing of communists. But Nasir's erstwhile ferocious anti-communism was now decisively downplayed by the Iraqi communists to transform him from foe to friend in accordance with the new Soviet ideas.

Later, at the meeting of the ICP's *Lajnat Tanzim al-Kharij* ('The Committe for the Organisation Abroad', COA), which was held in Prague in August 1964, the new Soviet ideological endorsement of Nasir led the party leadership to discard its previous demand for democratisation—its 'indispensable condition'—as a precondition for Arab unity. 'It is erroneous ...', the report of the meeting thus declared,

that Communists should continue to cling to political democracy as a condition for the support of any Arab unity. The question of democracy, including the issue of party life, can be solved within the course of the operation of unity itself with mass struggle, persuasion, and the persistent influence of the socialist camp upon the Arab leaders themselves.[73]

70 'Hawla l-Ittifaq al-Ula al-Mubram bayna l-Jumhuriyyah al-'Iraqiyyah wa l-Jumhuriyyah al-'Arabiyyah al-Mutahhidah', *Tariq al-Sha'b* 21, no. 1, Jul. 1964, pp. 1–2.

71 Smolansky, *Arab East*, p. 282.

72 'Hawla l-Ittifaq', p. 2.

73 Unpublished report of the August meeting, quoted in Batatu, *Old Social Classes*, p. 1037.

In other words, the old line of supporting mass pressure on the 'national bourgeoisie', which had proved to be a disaster during the crucial Qasim years, was now back in fashion.

But the party's pro-Nasirism did not end there. Even the most fundamental internationalist objection to an 'Arab' union based on imagined notions of common descent, culture and language, as Khrushchev implicitly expressed at Aswan, was now removed in communist writings on the topic. Arguing against the notion that unity was implicitly based on ideas of Arab superiority, which was obvious in much Arab nationalist theorising on the subject, the ICP, controversially, argued that Nasir's unity was nothing of the sort. 'The traditional Arab example and the successful requirements of the Arabs' issue', wrote *Tariq al-Sha'b*, thus taking Nasir's words at face value,

> are in contradistinction to the inclination towards narrow national fanaticism, superiority tendencies and hatred of peoples. And it is true as President 'Abd al-Nasir said that the unity which the Arabs seek is not a racist unity. The establishment of the unity on this basis necessarily requires the granting of rights to the peoples that co-exist with the Arabs, especially the fraternal Kurdish people, which requires the granting of its national [*qawmi*] rights...[74]

Thus, heavily influenced by Khrushchev's implicit acceptance of these ideas, the ICP leadership wholly adopted the new notion of Arab unity as the unity of Arab toilers. This way, fundamental principles of its own ideology were overridden by the nationalist desire to achieve unity. What the ICP therefore actually did was to alter the fundamental principle of class-based internationalism to accommodate the principle of ethnicity-based nationalism, thereby trying to fuse two seemingly irreconcilable tenets.

The August Line

The meeting of ICP leaders that took place in Prague in August 1964 was crucial for the development of the party's ideology over the years to come. With overwhelming majority the meeting adopted the new theories of non-capitalist development and revolutionary democracy, and with the backdrop of the nationalisation programme that had been initi-

[74] 'Hawla l-Ittifaq', p. 3.

ated by the 'Aref regime the month before, it decided that the new theories were also applicable on Iraq. Thus, in a divisive move, the ICP leadership that was living abroad decided to support a regime back home that had incarcerated thousands of communists and leftists and whose conservative social policies were in clear contradiction to communist ideology.

Two months before the August meeting, in June 1964, another meeting of ICP leaders working in the COA had met in Moscow. This meeting constituted the ideological preamble to the line adopted in August. It was led by 'Abd al-Salam al-Nasiri, who in Baha' al-Din Nuri's recollection was 'at all times rightwing in his disposition'.[75] Those present at the meeting[76] engaged in a lively discussion of the Soviet thesis that 'petty bourgeois' regimes could be impelled towards socialism along the path of non-capitalist development under the impact of the 'world socialist system'. Since international relations are the decisive variable in this kind of vision, its logical continuation was the notion of the dispensability of the communist party itself. 'Previously', the meeting thus stated,

> the road towards the dictatorship of the proletariat was the conquest of power by the working class and its political party. Yet, in this age it is possible that it can be brought forth in other forms. It is possible that it comes about ... in a gradual form in the composition and nature of the national-democratic power..., and this kind of gradual development does not require the existence of a revolutionary party of the working class at the helm of the regime.[77]

The notion of the redundancy of the communist party had already been implicitly acknowledged in pro-Khrushchevite ideas emanating from Arab communist parties prior to the meeting. For instance, in a clear exposition of historical determinism the statement of the 1963 meeting of Arab communist parties had explained that the 'progressiveness' of Arab governments should be given 'every support' because it was 'the outcome of the nation-wide liberation struggle, a result of the spread of the ideas of democracy and socialism among the people, of the growing

[75] Nuri, *Mudhakkirat*, . 312.

[76] The attendees were 'Abd al-Salam al-Nasiri, Husayn Sultan, Dr. Nazihah al-Dulaymi, Ara Khajadur, 'Amer 'Abdallah, Baha' al-Din Nuri, Rahim 'Ajinah, Nuri 'Abd al-Razzaq, Thaminah Naji Yusuf (Salam 'Adel's wife) and 'Aziz al-'Ajinah, al-Ikhtiyar al-Mutajaddad, p. 88.

[77] Political Report of June 1964 meeting, quoted in Mahmud, *al-Sira'*, p. 80.

prestige of the socialist countries.' The communists, for their part, should do 'all in their power to reinforce these aspects of the political line of the ruling circles of the newly-independent states'.[78] Despite the apparent feebleness of some of these leaders' attachment to socialism and in some cases (e.g. 'Aref) the apparent contradiction with their pronounced moral philosophies, the Arab communists nevertheless thought the spread of 'socialism' in itself was a thing of good. 'As a result of the successes won by world socialism', the 1963 meeting had argued,

> socialist ideas are becoming increasingly popular among the masses, a fact which is compelling statesmen and public personalities in the Arab countries to speak of socialism as a perspective in the national and social advance of the young sovereign states. [...] There is no denying that the ideas of so-called "Arab socialism" have exerted their influence on students, intellectuals and also a large section of the peasantry. [...] Another positive feature of "Arab socialism" is that the word "socialism" has gained currency in the Arab East.[79]

Rather than realising that Arab leaders, with Nasir at the fore, were appropriating the communists' own prime ideological weapon in the battle for the hearts and minds of the Arab 'masses', the communists interpreted this fondness for 'socialism' as further proof of the soundness of their theory of non-capitalist development, in which the historical development of societies 'naturally' would swirl towards socialism.

With these ideological developments as a backdrop, the COA met in Prague in August 1964. The new line adopted with overwhelming majority by this meeting, arguing that like Egypt, Iraq under 'Aref was following a non-capitalist path to socialism, is known as *Khatt Ab* ('The August Line'). The main feature of the meeting was the adoption of a political report based on the updated theory of non-capitalist development. The report itself was very much a repetition of previous Khrushchevite formulations whose underlying assumption was the international communist movement's qualitative leap rendering previously held theories on the necessity of revolutionary stages in Third World liberation superfluous. The sheer impact of the 'socialist camp', together with the extended hand of 'socialist aid' would break down and transform even the fiercest regime. Consequently, the report stated the following:

[78] 'Present Stage', p. 64.

[79] Ibid., pp. 72–73.

Under the impact of the dictatorship of the proletariat's international system and by relying on complete assistance, in some Arab countries forms of political systems have been realised that take into account the importance of relying on the unity of the progressive forces in the nation [*ummah*], and the partnership of workers and peasants in the economic administration, and the riches of labour, and in directing the leadership of society and the state.[80]

This 'progressive' feature was seen as the decisive criterion for communist support. On the other hand, the party's bitter experience of struggle against Nasir was now seen as a thing of the past as the qualitative leap the 'Arab liberation movement' had gone through meant such fatal experiences could be curbed or avoided at this instant. The report thus continued:

Notwithstanding the nature of the present rulers as regards their past, their political shape and the anti-communist and anti-democratic ideology of some of them, the verdict on their previous course of action cannot be reached in isolation… from the arrogant influence of Cairo's policies, and that which is new and revolutionary in the Arab liberation movement, which demonstrates a powerful reply to the influences of Egypt.[81]

In addition, Nasir's abandoning of anti-democratic policies further helped the new assessment of him as a 'revolutionary democrat'.[82]

While the theory of revolutionary democratic regimes that would transform the non-capitalist path into socialist development seemed to resonate fairly well with developments in Nasir's Egypt, the idea of 'socialist' transformation in Iraq appeared harder to construe. Not only was the new President, 'Abd al-Salam 'Aref, a publicly devout Muslim but his regime had incarcerated thousands of communists and their supporters. Thus, earlier in the year the ICP had cautioned 'Aref that the Iraqi people would not judge regimes 'on slogans, government programmes, their constitutions or the statements of their leaders' but on 'the palpable results of their policies and measures'. It further warned that the regime's foreign policy had not been 'harmonious' with the aims of the people, which should follow 'an independent national policy in opposition to imperialism', nor had the

80 Political Report of August 1964 meeting, quoted in Mahmud, *al-Sira'*, p. 83

81 Ibid., p. 84.

82 Upon Khrushchev's visit to Egypt in May 1964, Nasir undertook a wholesale release of communist prisoners as a concession to the Soviets, Beinin, *Red Flag*, p. 210.

regime entered 'a frank and firm policy of Arab solidarity, especially with the UAR, Algeria and Yemen'.[83] But despite its caution, the only real danger the ICP leadership saw was 'the existence of broad reactionary influence within the present government.'[84]

A 'coordination agreement' between Iraq and Egypt, agreed upon in late May 1964, signalled the party's final convincing that 'Aref's Iraq had entered the non-capitalist path towards socialism. 'The conditions in the United Arab Republic', *Tariq al-Sha'b* proclaimed,

> develop in a direction that necessarily will find its match in Iraq as well. If not, it is not possible for any union between the two countries.... The official policy of the United Arab Republic, which starts from the confirmation of its considering of the interests and the role of the toilers in the socio-economic transformations and in the organisation of the affairs of society and the state, is the policy that up until now comprises, albeit incompletely, the necessary progressions for the journey upon the path of non-capitalist development and the realisation of the programme of transformations and reforms of a socialist nature.[85]

The benefits of Iraqi-Egyptian cooperation and eventual unity would not be limited to mere 'socialist transformations' and reforms, in the party's view, but would also entail more directly palpable consequences, as the unity 'with necessity' would 'merit' the readjustment of the Iraqi regime's 'general policy on a basis that takes what is progressive and positive in the policy of the United Arab Republic'. Surprisingly, to the Iraqi communist leaders, that meant ending states of emergency, political oppression, military rule, granting of political liberties, and 'transferring the country to a situation of democracy and free parliamentary and constitutional life'.[86]

In mid-July, the Iraqi regime undertook a series of measures that on the surface resembled those adopted by Egypt. Having reached an agreement in May to form a Joint Presidential Council with Egypt, the regime further pursued its Nasirist policies on 14 July when it announced a nationalisation of all banks and insurance companies, thirty-two other

[83] 'Min Ajli Ilhaq al-Hazimah bi Quwa al-Isti'mar wa l-Raj'iyyah fi al-'Iraq, Yanbaghi an Tatahaqqaq Wahdat Jami' al-Quwa al-Wataniyyah al-Dimuqratiyyah wa l-Qawmiyyin al-Taqaddumiyyin', *Tariq al-Sha'b* 21, no. 1, May 1964, p. 2.

[84] Ibid.

[85] Ibid.

[86] Ibid.

large companies, the establishment of a profit-sharing scheme for workers and the promise of worker representation on the boards of these companies. Additionally, it formed an Iraqi branch of the Egyptian Arab Socialist Union, which, however, attracted little enthusiasm.[87] The nationalisation removed the ICP leadership's last concern, and it now came out wholly in favour of the regime. In a statement that was reprinted three times and distributed throughout Iraq, the party fully backed the 'Aref regime, calling its nationalisation programmes 'historical measures' that would make 'it possible to impel the country along the path of non-capitalist development', claiming these measures were 'a return to the 14 July Revolution's vigour and its revolutionary impact' and that they would 'without a doubt help to attract the popular masses around them anew'.[88]

The political line adopted by the August meeting was thus not a sudden or abrupt change of outlook but corresponded to profound transformations that had occurred in the party's ideology over the past year. Consequently, its adoption was a formality. Twelve out of fourteen present at the meeting voted in favour of it; only 'Aziz al-Hajj, who was known for his 'leftwing' positions, was clearly against it while Ara Khajadur was vacillating between support and opposition.[89]

Later on, when the August Line had been denounced as a 'rightwing' deviationist line and had been singled out by the party opposition as the single most damaging policy adopted by the leadership during this period, the leaders that had been involved in the adoption of the new line were keen to distance themselves from it. Thus, in memoirs written long after the events, they have tried to readjust their own involvement and assert that although they were parties to the adopted line, in reality they opposed it and worked for its amendment after its adoption. Rahim 'Ajinah, for instance, asserted that the problem was the lack of 'ideological struggle' within the party leadership at the time, that 'leading members ... did not express their being opposed to the presented ideas by way of ideological struggle in accordance with the compliable party principles, but instead with disassociation from all measures and taking resort to personal attacks.'[90] Baha' al-Din Nuri, who together with 'Abd al-Salam al-Nasiri and 'Amer 'Abdallah probably was the new line's most ardent

[87] Batatu, *Old Social Classes*, p. 1031.
[88] Jul. 1964 ICP statement, quoted in Mahmud, *al-Sira'*, p. 81.
[89] Nuri, *Mudhakkirat*, pp. 313–314.
[90] 'Ajinah, *Ikhtiyar al-Mutajaddad*, p. 87

supporter, claimed that upon returning to Baghdad in December he worked for its amendment.[91] It is clear, however, that the theoretical foundation of the August Line, that is, the notion of non-capitalist development leading to socialism, was never in doubt for these ICP leaders. Thus, when Baha' al-Din Nuri in his memoirs asserted that the August Line was a 'huge error', it was only that theory's stretching to include the 'dictatorial system of 'Abd al-Salam 'Aref' that he reacted against, not the theory itself. Accordingly, his assessment stated that it had been wrong to proclaim that the 'Aref regime had been 'developing into a progressive system heading towards socialism, *as was the case of 'Abd al-Nasir's system in Egypt*'.[92] He thus vindicated the theory as such.

From the vantage point of eastern Europe and with the guiding light of Soviet theory these measures might have seemed like a gift from above at a time when the Iraqi communists had little possibility of making an impact on the ground, but for the party organisations inside Iraq, which steadily were rebuilding their battered structures, the regime's claim to be constructing 'socialism' whilst continuing its fierce repression of communists appeared preposterously hollow. Thus, most party organisations in Iraq opposed the statement.[93] The adoption of the August Line consequently stands out as one of the most clear-cut examples in the party's history of its leaders trying to impose theory on an irreconcilable reality.

Grass Roots Opposition Leads to 'Decisive Action'

The exiled ICP leadership's adoption of the unpopular August Line caused an ideological split in the party. For many lower ranking party members who had remained in Iraq after the 1963 coup, it was proof the party leadership was losing touch with Iraqi realities after excessive periods spent in the relative comfort of socialist Eastern Europe.

Since the formulation of the August Line and its meticulous propagation among party members by means of the Bulgarian-based radio station *Sawt al-Sha'b al-'Iraqi* ('Voice of the Iraqi People') and international and domestic communist print media, a growing rift between the accommodationist foreign-based leadership and the party base in Iraq emerged

[91] Nuri, *Mudhakkirat*, pp. 317–320.
[92] Ibid., p. 313 (added emphasis).
[93] 'Ajinah, *Ikhtiyar al-Mutajaddad*, p. 88.

and grew increasingly wider.[94] At first, rank-and-file opposition took peaceful form, but later it became more fierce. Following the August meeting, members in Iraq began resigning from the party en masse. The resignations, which according to a later internal party publication amounted to as much as 50 per cent in Baghdad, 25 per cent in the South and similar figures in the mid-Euphrates region, were unprecedented in the party's history; not even during the height of Ba'thi terror in 1963 had resignations reached these kind of figures.[95] Opposition was greatest in the prisons where the notion of a 'socialist' regime seemed the hardest to accommodate with realities. The students' movement was also generally a fierce opponent of the new ideas, following a well-known pattern of juvenile radicalism. Some workers' organisations, e.g. in the textile, soda and shoe industries, also actively voiced their discontent with the party's official line. Soon dissatisfaction spread to Iraqi Kurdistan.[96] A group advocating armed action, which called itself *al-Lajnah al-Thawriyyah* ('The Revolutionary Committee'), was also formed.[97]

Soon the party leadership realised their own positions were at stake and that they would be forced to revise the pro-Soviet appraisal of the regime or risk a party rebellion. By this time, Baha' al-Din Nuri had become the deputy leader of the party in the interior as First Secretary 'Aziz Muhammad had been sent abroad. Nuri, who had been one of the staunchest supporters of the August Line and who in December 1964 had published an article under his party name 'Munir Ahmad' in *Problems of Peace and Socialism* presenting his full support of the new Khrushchevite line, now sensed danger and began trimming his sails according to the new winds blowing in the party. In his memoirs, Nuri apologetically claims the article, which had been commissioned by the Politburo, was mishandled by the Russian editor of the journal who when translating it inserted his own opinions.[98] Nevertheless, in February 1965 he presented a proposal for the revision of the August Line to the party's 'Leadership

[94] Mahmud, *al-Sira'*, pp. 93–94.

[95] Internal Publication of *Lajnat al-Tanzim al-Markazi* ('The Central Organisation Committee'), 10 Sept. 1965, quoted in Mahmud, *al-Sira'*, p. 92; Ismael, *Rise and Fall*, p. 130.

[96] Mahmud, *al-Sira'*, p. 92.

[97] Ismael, *Rise and Fall*, pp. 131–132; Nuri, *Mudhakkirat*, pp. 323–324.

[98] Nuri, *Mudhakkirat*, p. 315.

Centre' (*al-Markaz al-Qiyadi*),[99] which it agreed to. A draft document with the new proposed line was then sent to the various party organisations for discussion, and finally a committee was set up to study the opinions of the more than 150 party members that had taken part in the discussions.[100] According to Mahmud, the document met with fierce opposition and rejection by the party organisations and even by some members of the leadership.[101]

To resolve ideological differences, Nuri called a Central Committee meeting, which took place in Baghdad on 18 April 1965. This was the first time it had met in Baghdad since the February 1963 coup. Continuing for four days, the meeting witnessed intense ideological struggle brought about by the leadership's accommodationist line and the party base's increasingly radicalised views. All in all, twenty-five party members took part; hence the session is remembered as the 'Meeting of Twenty-Five'.[102] The meeting officially declared the August Line to have been wrong policy and set out to reconstitute the party leadership. Remarkably, it filled the function of a party conference, although representatives from both mid-level and central leaderships were absent. It reexamined the status of all present Central Committee-members. Even more astonishing was the decision to add new members to the Central Committee from among the mid-level leaders present at the meeting. A list of sixteen names was drawn up, twelve of whom were finally elected: six of the old Central Committee-members and six new ones.[103] Central Committee members abroad, however, retained their memberships without being put through this procedure.[104] By adopting these measures, the party leadership was temporarily able to get back in the driving seat, but it was clear it had been forced to go to extraordinary lengths and adopt extrajudicial methods to do so.

[99] At this point, the Central Committee was not referred to as such due to its incomplete nature.

[100] Nuri, *Mudhakkirat*, p. 320.

[101] Mahmud, *al-Sira'*, p. 94.

[102] Out of the twenty-five, only seven were CC-members: Baha' al-Din Nuri, Ara Khajadur, 'Abd al-Salam al-Nasiri, 'Amer 'Abdallah, Nasir 'Abud, Saleh Mahdi Duglah and Husayn Sultan, Nuri, *Mudhakkirat*, pp. 320–328.

[103] Out of the seven Central Committee members only Nasir 'Abud failed to get re-elected. The six new members were: Shaker Mahmud, Kazem al-Saffar, Majid 'Abd al-Rida, Kazem Farhud, Ibrahim Ilyas and Kazem Jawwad, Ibid., pp. 329–330.

[104] Duglah, *Min al-Dhakirah*, p. 151.

Discussions at the meeting were primarily centred on two key questions: should the party raise the slogan of overthrowing the government and was there another socio-political force in the country capable of supporting socialism. The radical opposition argued that there was no such Iraqi force and that the party therefore should venture for power itself, while the conservative leadership favoured political cooperation along the lines of its traditional national front theory. However, due to the incorporation of many recalcitrant mid-level cadres, the meeting was overwhelmingly radical in its inclination.

The idea of 'decisive action' (*'amal hasem*) to solve the predicament of the party, that is, in more unadorned terms, to launch a traditional military coup d'état against the regime, had started to gain currency within the party. The idea seems to have originated among communist officers in the Iraqi army who, following the Ba'thi coup and persecution of the ICP, had been dismissed from the army and had sought refuge in Iraqi Kurdistan. There they had begun a campaign to convince the party leadership that their capabilities ought to be utilised. In distinction to the Qasim period, however, it was now stressed that any party activity in the armed forces needed to be linked directly with a comprehensive military and civilian plan to bring about change. The idea had the support of some cadres on the regional level but was strongly opposed by members of the Central Committee, especially Baha' al-Din Nuri and 'Abd al-Salam al-Nasiri.

The intellectual origins of the decisive action line were distinctively militaristic. Its proponents argued that the army was but one institution among many that could be utilised for political purposes, not only by the nationalists and the Ba'thists but also by the communists themselves. The idea, needless to say, was clearly elitist in nature and was far from anything ever contemplated by the party before. It circumscribed the hard and prolonged work to win the consent of the general population—the 'masses'—which erstwhile always had been a key component in communist thinking. But the militarist supporters of decisive action argued that the military was key to bringing about change in the country. They thus went on to try to win over officers, non-commissioned officers and soldiers, who were to be organised in an 'assault movement' (*harakah li l-inqidad*) that would strike against the regime, being supported by the party's civilian organisations and its supporters.[105]

[105] Duglah, *Min al-Dhakirah*, pp. 150–153.

The meeting adopted the new idea with a great majority. It was decided that to implement the new line, the party would set up armed formations of civilian communists who would support the communist officers at the time of the coup—these measures were known as the 'Husayn Plan' (*Khatt Husayn*).[106] The only people to voice any real objection to the plan were Baha' al-Din Nuri and 'Abd al-Salam al-Nasiri, both members of the party's Politburo. They claimed the meeting lacked legality and that there had been no majority of Central Committee members. Both offered to resign because of the decision, but that action was rejected by the meeting.[107]

While it was clear to anyone at the time that the party's *de facto* leader in Iraq, Baha' al-Din Nuri, was thoroughly against the militarist line and had been an active supporter of the August Line, in his memoirs he nevertheless claims he only opposed the idea because it was not serious enough, because the party had no adequate organisation in the army to carry out such a task. As a matter of fact, Nuri claims, he supported the idea in principle as a 'way to reach power in a country devoid of democracy and [where] the language of violence persists', that is, where violence was 'the prevailing and crucial force.'[108] Other old-timers who rode the revolutionary wave at the time included 'Amer 'Abdallah, Zaki Khayri and 'Aziz al-Hajj. For the latter two, however, the decision to switch sides seems to have been influenced by a desire to gain the upper hand in the party, with both men considering themselves destined to be party leaders.

Few in the party leadership had any real commitment to the ideas of overthrowing the government through violent means, but the pressure from below was too great and the adoption of the August Line had been too blunt for them to take a principled discussion in the face of a country brutalised by years of military dictatorships. Presenting the leadership's officially spun version of events, the pseudonym 'Nadji', writing in *Problems of Peace and Socialism*, thus explained the following:

> Noteworthy... is that during the past year, the political line of our Party was debated not only by its members but also by many non-members. It can be said that the political line is the product not only of the wisdom of the Central Committee but also of the consciousness of all Communists and revolutionaries who

[106] Nuri, *Mudhakkirat*, p. 329.
[107] Duglah, *Min al-Dhakirah*, p. 151.
[108] Nuri, *Mudhakkirat*, p. 328.

have passed through the trials of the 1958–59 democratic revolution, through the ordeals of the Kassem military dictatorship, the Baathist counter-revolutionary regime and the present militarist regime. Our Party has emerged from these ordeals closely united.[109]

In reality, of course, wide cracks were appearing in the fabric of the party. The statement should also be read as an admission that the leadership at this juncture was forced to amend its own policy due to pressure from outside the party. In other words, public opinion was so thoroughly set against the party's original accommodationist line that it had little choice but to change it. 'Nadji' also implicitly acknowledged the aloofness of the Central Committee from the rest of the party and promised that in the 'future Party functionaries and rank and file will have a bigger say in determining the attitude of the party and formulating its policy.'[110]

Meanwhile, the Soviets were not comfortable with the ICP's adoption of a slogan calling for the overthrow of a regime they were supporting. Moscow therefore put pressure on ICP leaders residing in Eastern Europe to change the new line. 'Voice of the Iraqi People' thus began to broadcast a long series of translated Soviet speeches that openly supported the ideas of the August Line as regards the superfluousness of the dictatorship of the proletariat, the dispensability of the working class's leading role, the 'socialist' orientation of Nasir's Egypt and support for the 'Aref regime.[111]

The decision of the April 'Meeting of Twenty-Five' to adopt the 'decisive action' line as official policy created widespread enthusiasm among rank-and-file members, with some even independently starting to search for weapons with which to carry out the plan.[112] As regards the ICP leaders abroad, their about-face was complete. In a very short period they went, in the words of Mahmud, from being 'missionaries of 'Aref's socialism to being philosophers of the revolutionary military coup'.[113]

The new make-up of the interior leadership and its radical slogan of 'decisive action', designed to appease internal opposition and allow the

109 Nadji, 'The Situation in Iraq and the Position of the Communist Party', *World Marxist Review* 8, no. 6, Jun. 1965, p. 58.

110 Ibid.

111 Mahmud, *al-Sira'*, p. 94.

112 Nuri, *Mudhakkirat*, p. 331.

113 Mahmud, *al-Sira'*, p. 95.

old leaders to recapture the momentum, actually provided the impetus for the radical sections' further advancement of their positions over the following two years. The Baghdad Regional Committee (BRC) was at the centre of this development. The gradual fallout between an institutionalised old guard leadership and radicalised youngsters in the party base also presented an opportunity for two of the party's veterans, 'Aziz al-Hajj and Zaki Khayri, to launch an opposition against the leadership on which they themselves had their own designs. 'Aziz al-Hajj had voiced his opposition to the new line already at the actual August meeting and had soon thereafter begun distributing a leaflet criticising the line together with Ara Khajadur, Nuri 'Abd al-Razzaq, Majid 'Abd al-Rida and Mahdi al-Hafez.[114] Despite their differences, al-Hajj and Khayri cooperated in opposing the party leadership, represented by 'Aziz Muhammad, Baha' al-Din Nuri and others.

At a meeting in September, it was decided to implement the decisive action and actually carry out the coup. But either the ICP leaders had not learnt their lesson from recent Iraqi history or they were just not sincere in their intentions to see the coup through, for in a stupendously feeble-minded move they decided to break the first rule of clandestine plotting and went public with a statement announcing their new policy of seeking the violent overthrow of the regime. 'We, like none of the other social forces', the statement declared, 'head in a direction of increasing our special possibilities and the undertaking of decisive revolutionary action in order to overthrow the regime with a military undertaking and with the support of the party organisations and the mass organisations.'[115]

After the meeting, the Central Committee also wrote to the Politburo requesting their consent to carry out the coup. While none in the Politburo favoured such an action, they found themselves powerless to do anything but call for an extended meeting to discuss the matter thoroughly.[116] The enlarged meeting, which took place in October, discussed

[114] Though the leaflet was anonymous, merely signed 'a group of communists' (*lafif min al-shuyu'iyyin*), Baha' al-Din Nuri asserts al-Hajj was behind it, Nuri, *Mudhakkirat*, p. 316. In Feb. 1965, al-Hajj also criticised the theoretical basis of the August Line in a pamphlet issued in Prague entitled 'On Non-Capitalist Development in Iraq: Personal Comments' (*Hawla l-Tatawwur Ghayr al-Ra'smali fi l-'Iraq: Mulahazat Shakhsiyyah*), Ismael, *Rise and Fall*, p. 129.

[115] Communiqué of Sept. 1965 meeting, quoted in Mahmud, *al-Sira'*, p. 95.

[116] Mahmud, *al-Sira'*, pp. 94–95.

the issue of military action from a wide range of perspectives. According to Batatu, there were no less than six resolutions.[117] At this juncture, it was clear the party's organisational meeting procedures were as hurried and flustered as the ideological outlook of its leadership. The dual nature of the organisational set-up, with half of the leadership abroad and half at home, was of course to blame. At this crucial moment, when the accommodationist leadership were being forced into assuming radical positions, First Secretary 'Aziz Muhammad was living abroad inadequately informed about vital events in the interior. Thus, when the COA met in November to discuss the findings of the October meeting, he complained he had not received the minutes of the meeting and did not know the details.[118] In reality, the exterior leadership had become powerless to influence events in Iraq. Although they deplored the actions of the new 'Central Committee' in the interior, with Zaki Khayri calling it a 'coup',[119] there was little they could do but to seal its decisions and try to keep the lid on.

Refuting 'Aref's Arab Socialism

The radical mood swing within the party and its repercussions on the leadership also took concrete shape in the form of a public change of policy vis-à-vis the 'Aref regime. From having hailed the measures implemented by 'Aref in July 1964 as resembling those of Nasir's Egypt and thus opening up the possibility of a 'non-capitalist' path to socialism also for Iraq, the party gradually adopted a more cautious line towards the regime which eventually developed into open hostility—a development that closely corresponded to the internal ideological struggle outlined above. Crucially, however, the changing policy on 'Aref was due to pressure from the party base, so the theory of non-capitalist development leading to socialism consequently remained unchallenged.

[117] Batatu, *Old Social Classes*, p. 1046. Batatu erroneously asserts (p. 1045) that this was the 'Meeting of 25'. Ismael, too, repeats the same contention, without providing references, Ismael, *Rise and Fall*, p. 139. However, Nuri's statement that the meeting took place in April 1965 has been confirmed by veteran communist 'Adel Haba, *pers. comm.* with author, 2 Aug. 2007.

[118] Batatu, *Old Social Classes*, p. 1048. See pp. 1045–1061 for more details of the Oct. and Nov. meetings.

[119] Ibid., p. 1060.

The regime's claim to be 'Arab socialist' now became the ICP leadership's main ideological sticking point, although the same leaders had argued before that such a rhetorical use of 'socialism' was salubrious as it popularised the idea and contributed to the dissemination of a socialist Zeitgeist. With the radicalisation of the party's stand, however, it was clear that allowing 'Aref to unopposed portray himself and his regime as socialist ran counter to the party's interests, because if the regime was socialist the ICP's new policy of overthrowing it would be hard to justify ideologically. In the above-cited seminal article entitled *al-Ishtirakiyyah wa Siyasat al-Hukm al-Rahin* ('Socialism and the Policy of the Present Regime'), published in *Tariq al-Sha'b* in March 1965, the party leadership thus spelt out its new, harder line:

> The official information apparatuses (radio, television, the press, the assemblies, etc.), dedicate their efforts to presenting the existing system as if it was a socialist system…, or as if Iraq really was living through the stage of transition from capitalism to socialism. We communists would have desired, if these claims were consistent with reality, if the banner of socialism was fluttering above the earth of the beloved homeland, that the toiling Iraqi masses should really aspire to socialism and support every step that is taken towards it, but this does not exist. Unfortunately, the socialist system and the system of the present regime and its practical policy are not brought together.[120]

Yet again, the party leadership thus did a volte-face. Its previously dropped demand for democratic liberties as the 'inevitable precondition' for Arab unity and consequently for embarking on the 'non-capitalist' path was now reiterated. 'The socialist path, especially in a country that has endured terror and despotism for centuries as is the case in Iraq', they accordingly argued, 'means the granting of democratic liberties to the workers and peasants and the whole people, and allowing them to participate in the freedom to organise in parties and trade unions and the freedom to strike, meet and demonstrate.'[121] Stressing the importance of fighting neo-colonialism and specifically its interests in Iraqi oil, the article then went on to invalidate the regime's claim to being socialist as it had failed to stand up to the 'imperialist companies'. 'The socialist path means successful serious work', it stated,

[120] 'Ishtirakiyyah'.
[121] Ibid.

in order to liquidate the ideological, political and economic positions of colonialism, for the sake of completing economic and political national liberation. This question gains great importance, especially in a country like Iraq where, contrary to some other Arab countries, the controlled economic sector (oil) continues to be seized by the imperialist companies, and [where] this sector continues to be the fundamental source of income for the state's budget. And until now, what oil rights have the senior officials extracted since 8 February, or since 18 November? None![122]

It was thus clear that the issue of oil occupied a central position in the reasoning and theorising of the Iraqi communist leaders, something that at a later stage would provide the ideological basis for cooperation with the Ba'th Party following its nationalisation of the Iraqi oil industry in 1972.[123]

While not opposed to the regime's development plans, the party leadership stressed that 'socialist construction' demanded a planned economy according to 'scientific programmes', but the regime's measures would not allow for 'the liberation from the serious errors' of past development programmes, and it did 'not allow for the planning of economic development on peaceful scientific grounds'. In fact, the ICP argued, the only thing underpinning the regime's claim to socialism was its nationalisation programme, and that, although commendable, was not enough. 'If we discounted the "socialist" formulations and propaganda dedicated to the embellishment of the current regime, [which] do not rely on palpable realities', the article thus argued,

then the nationalisation measures that were assumed in July 1964 are the only pretence that the partisans of this regime can bring forward as evidence for its "socialism". We support the nationalisation of the capital of the imperialists and their helpers among the big capitalists with regard to the interests of national capital, but nationalisation alone—in isolation from the regime's set-up, its procedure, and from the particular circumstances of the prevailing relations of production in society—does not earn the regime, whoever it is, a socialist nature.[124]

Putting the final nail in the regime's coffin, the article concluded that its 'principal steps' were 'not in keeping with the demands of socialist construction'—that in fact what it was carrying out was 'non-socialist

122 Ibid.
123 See ch. 5.
124 'Ishtirakiyyah'.

construction'. On top of that, the state apparatus, it claimed, was 'full of reactionaries' and people 'full of hatred towards every progress and socialism'. The article continued in the same scathing manner:

> Many of the regime's partisans justify all the vile actions and the states of emergency under the pretence that Iraq is living through a "period of transition", [but] this is a disproved pretence—firstly—because the present regime is not socialist, neither in its set-up nor in its policy, and—secondly—because there is no justification, even if Iraq had been in a period of transition to socialism neither to continue military rule and states of emergency nor to stifle liberties and detain thousands of patriots in prison and combat communism as an ideology and a system, neither is there any justification for procrastination vis-à-vis the legitimate demands of the Kurds nor for neglecting to expropriate Iraq's oil rights and implement agrarian reform, etc. The so-called "period of transition" was used by Qasim and then the Ba'th leaders, and is used today as well, as an excuse to justify the states of emergency and the rule of military dictatorship and to justify monopolisation of the regime by small groups that do not have trust in the possibility of remaining in power in case democratic methods were employed in the administration of the country.[125]

The article also ventured to disprove Arab nationalist leaders' ideological claim to be representing a new form of socialism—'Arab socialism'. Although a few years earlier ICP leaders, as we have seen, were receptive towards this sort of Arab nationalist rhetoric, they now realised it undermined their own claim to ideological hegemony. 'There is no [such thing] as "European", "Asian" or "Arab Socialism", and no "Christian" or "Islamic [Socialism]"', it was therefore now argued, 'there is but one socialism—Scientific Socialism—that has been victorious in some countries and will be victorious in the rest of the world's countries.'[126]

But however acrimoniously the ICP leadership may appear to have been castigating the 'Aref regime on this occasion, it was nevertheless clear that the ideological foundation, the theoretical particularity that had allowed the glorification of the regime in the August Line, namely the notion of a 'non-capitalist' path to socialism, remained unaffected. It was only the brusqueness of the 'Aref regime, coupled with the relentless pressure of the party base that had made the leadership question its characterisation of the regime, but the theory itself remained incontrovertible.

[125] Ibid.
[126] Ibid.

Thus, the same article that had thoroughly vitiated the 'Aref regime would nevertheless conclude in the following conciliatory manner:

We Communists do not consider the struggle for socialism to depend on us alone in the present historical conditions. We look with optimism at the phenomenon of social groups and new political organisations and personalities adopting progressive socialist ideas and orientations. The revolution in a number of previously colonised countries—including Algeria and the UAR—has gone beyond the framework of political liberation and has taken up the implementation of great social transformations that have obtained the slogan of socialism, which the non-communist leaders of these countries call for to a progressive and positive level, and before them a horizon welcoming the non-capitalist development and the progression towards socialism has opened up. The adoption by some new socio-political groups of a number of—gradually increasing—the economic and philosophical notions which we alone have been calling for in the past, is a great victory for Marxism-Leninism and a proof of its correctness and the definiteness of its [ultimate] victory.[127]

In other words, countries like Egypt and Algeria, which resembled Iraq to a large extent with their state capitalist economies and corporatist political organisation and which claimed to be Arab socialist although the local communist parties had been forced to dissolve, constituted 'a great victory for Marxism-Leninism', while the 'Aref regime in Iraq did not. In this way, the April 1965 meeting that abolished the August Line and which took up the call for the overthrow of the regime, at the same time also uncritically gave its support to Algeria and Egypt. The meeting statement thus declared its appreciation of:

the role played by the governments of the UAR and Algeria in the Arab world and on the international arena in support of world peace, the national-liberation movement and the struggle to abolish the strongholds of colonialism. The Iraqi Communist Party regards the success and important social changes in these countries as a victory for the working people of the entire Arab world. It calls for close co-operation of all the patriotic forces of Iraq and the UAR leaders. While it welcomes any constructive criticism from other patriotic forces as a positive instrument conducive to mutual co-operation, the Party regards as equally legitimate constructive criticism of the UAR leaders, for example, for their incorrect attitude to the national-liberation movement of the people of Iraq, in particular, for the support they are still rendering the present dictatorial Aref regime.[128]

[127] Ibid.

[128] Nadji, 'Situation in Iraq', p. 59.

As further proof that the ICP leadership's changed position on the 'Aref regime was not brought about by ideological opposition but by pressure from below, we may quote the party's appeal for cooperation conveyed in the above-cited article of March 1965. In it, the party said it would 'ally with anyone who calls himself a socialist and links his talk with actions irrespective of his ideological differences with us.'[129] Despite the harsh words, it is clear there was no real *ideological* objection to 'Arab Socialism'—the problem was the 'Aref regime itself. Thus, rejecting its own rigid definition of 'socialism' earlier in the same article, the ICP leaders did a U-turn and declared that their way might not be the only path to socialism. 'We believe', they declared, 'in multiple and varying ways of transition to socialism: we reject ready-made "characterisations" and rigid notions in defining Iraq's road towards socialism, we are completely prepared to discuss and exchange views with anyone for whom the creation of better ways for Iraq's progression towards socialism is important.'[130]

The impression that the rejection of the 'Aref regime was conditioned by pressures from the party base rather than based on a critical assessment of the theory of 'non-capitalist development' was further strengthened later on when 'Aziz al-Hajj lambasted the 'Aref dictatorship' and its continuing subjection of 'patriots to spiritual and moral torture, to murder Communists and democrats' and his scathing criticism of how the regime was pursuing its 'criminal policy of genocide' in Iraqi Kurdistan,[131] and when the ICP later characterised it as a 'servile stooge of the imperialists ... betraying the basic national interests' and that it was 'a regime of treason'.[132]

The Issue of 'Political Violence' and the Split of the Party

These contradictory ideological positions which, as we have seen, were caused more by internal opposition within the party than disagreements within the leadership, eventually caused a decisive organisational split of the party in 1966–67. Three different groups came to be involved in a

[129] 'Ishtirakiyyah'.

[130] Ibid.

[131] Aziz al-Hajj, 'Their Heroism Illuminates the Path to Victory', *World Marxist Review* 8, no. 10, Oct. 1965, p. 57.

[132] Statement of the ICP in February 1966, as quoted in al-Hajj, 'Support!', p. 46.

detrimental power struggle to obtain the leadership of the ICP and thus be able to steer the party in a new direction. These three contending groups were the old-timers in the old leadership, the Baghdad Regional Committee (BRC) and a new group of radicalised youths calling themselves the 'Cadre Faction'. At the heart of the ideological differences was the issue of how to attain power. The fight centred on the issue of whether to utilise 'political violence' to seize power or if the party should continue the well-established practise of non-violence favoured by the old leadership. Both the BRC and the Cadre group advocated the former. The problem posed by this issue represented a radical challenge to the party's old theory of gradual, non-violent 'national-democratic' revolution led by 'revolutionary democrats', which had progressively been adopted over the preceding years.[133] Though initially having been forced to adopt the idea of a military coup, the old leadership resisted political violence with such vehemence that in the end the issue actually destroyed the organisational cohesion of the party.

In early 1967, internal party contradictions reached a breaking point as 'Aziz al-Hajj, followed by Zaki Khayri, returned to Iraq. The existence of contending party centres vying for the adherence of the rank-and-file had launched the leadership into a state of paralysis. To break this state of affairs it decided to form a new Politburo incorporating both Khayri and al-Hajj, who since his return from abroad had formed a working alliance with the BRC radicals. This allowed for the return of a semblance of authority and the new Politburo meted out token disciplinary measures to some of the Baghdad members that had been involved in the open criticism of the leadership.[134]

However, the makeshift alliance between Khayri and al-Hajj eventually broke down and Khayri moved over to the 'August Line group', i.e. those ICP leaders who publicly had been forced to renounce the August Line but privately still adhered to it, such as Baha' al-Din Nuri and 'Abd al-Salam al-Nasiri. At the same time, al-Hajj dropped his caution and openly threw himself in the arms of the Baghdad organisation. In an

[133] See Chapters 2 and 3, as well as the earlier sections of this chapter.

[134] In addition to Khayri and al-Hajj, the new Politburo consisted of Party Secretary 'Aziz Muhammad and Baha' al-Din Nuri, Mahmud, *al-Sira'*, p. 108. According to Ismael, sections of the BRC were disbanded and cadres removed to other places during these disciplinary measures. Ismael, however, does not provide any documentary evidence to prove this, Ismael, *Rise and Fall*, p. 143.

extraordinary turn of events, 'Aziz al-Hajj, who throughout the summer of 1967 had been meeting weekly with Zaki Khayri and Baha' al-Din Nuri in the new Politburo, tried to 'arrest' his fellow comrades in an attempt that can only be labelled an internal coup. It then transpired that al-Hajj had formed an alliance with BRC leaders whilst a member of the Politburo. On 17 September, former First Secretary and member of the old leadership, Baha' al-Din Nuri, was kidnapped by four armed youths from the Baghdad organisation. Initially planning to kidnap all the old ICP leaders, the plotters only additionally successfully managed to grab Zaki Khayri. The plan failed as Nuri managed to escape the day after. On 19 September, the ICP leadership condemned and expelled the plotters from the party.[135] When Zaki Khayri after some twenty days in captivity managed to escape, he sent a letter to all party members denouncing the splitting action of his former ally, 'Aziz al-Hajj. Then, in yet another extraordinary development in this saga of coups, plots and counter-coups, the ICP leadership had 'Aziz al-Hajj 'arrested' through its special security official, Shawkat Khaznadar. However, they did let him go after just one night's imprisonment.[136]

In an emergency meeting on 3 October, Kazem Jawwad, the BRC leader, proposed to dissolve the Central Committee as a way of resolving the leadership crisis and form a new tripartite committee consisting of 'Aziz al-Hajj and two others from outside the existing Central Committee, a proposal that gained majority support. Members of the party old guard, like 'Amer 'Abdallah, 'Abd al-Salam al-Nasiri, Saleh Mahdi Duglah and Baqer Ibrahim resigned to pave way for the new leadership. Baha' al-Din Nuri, however, who was acting leader of the meeting as 'Aziz Muhammad, the Party Secretary, was abroad and the deputy leader, Zaki Khayri, was detained by the plotters, refused to resign and was supported in this position by Karim Ahmad al-Daud, Thabet Habib al-'Ani and Ara Khajadur. Eventually this made others retreat from their positions and after having agreed to the demand of convening a party congress within the shortest time span possible the meeting ended with the very fragile cohesion of the old leadership.[137]

135 Nuri, *Mudhakkirat*, pp. 367–376.

136 Ibid., pp. 382–384. See also Khaznadar's memoirs: Shawkat Khaznadar, *Safar wa Mahattat: al-Hizb al-Shuyu'i al-'Iraqi... Ru'yah min al-Dakhil*, Beirut: Dar al-Kunuz al-Adabiyyah, 2005.

137 Nuri, *Mudhakkirat*, pp. 378–379.

Having failed the coup attempt, the Baghdad leaders instead decided to turn to the radicalised rank-and-file members and get them to join the splitting faction. Thus, on the day of the kidnapping, 'the Emergency Meeting of Advanced Cadres' went public and announced the dismissal of the Central Committee instructing the party base to cut its relations with the old leadership.[138] However, although the splitters had the support of the vast majority of the Baghdad organisation, including some of its leaders, and the backing of several *Muhafazahs*, most notably the Sulaymaniyyah *Muhafazah*, out of the fourteen people forming the BRC only four decided to go with the splitters, and only one ('Aziz al-Hajj) from the Central Committee.[139]

On 26 September, another group made itself known as 'A Detachment of the Party's Cadres' (*Fariq min Kawader al-Hizb*).[140] It criticised the Central Committee, holding it responsible for the deepening of the crisis, while also criticising the leaders of the Baghdad organisation who, it claimed, were of the same 'revisionist' make as the Central Committee members but who had made a U-turn when sensing the opposition in the party base. It also raised the slogan of armed popular struggle to overthrow the regime and establish a people's democratic regime.[141]

In the minds of the opposition, the events of September 1967 had constituted a 'purging revolt' (*intifadat al-tathir*). Their new temporary leadership drew much rank-and-file support. In Baghdad, more than half of all organisations adhered to the new leadership, in the Kurdistan Branch the majority, and Basra and al-Kut pledged their allegiance as well. In the political prisons of the regime thousands of prisoners

[138] For excerpts of the meeting statement, see Ismael, *Rise and Fall*, p. 147. Ismael (p. 148) also accepts al-Hajj's version of events that the meeting first decided to 'cleanse' the party, and then initiated the 'coup'. Note that Mahmud claims the kidnapping took place on 12 Sept., Mahmud, *al-Sira'*, pp. 119–121.

[139] Nuri, *Mudhakkirat*, pp. 377–378. The four people in the BRC joining the splitters were: Husayn Jawwad al-Gumar, Malik Mansur, 'Abd al-Hamid al-Safi and Khadr Salman. Kazem al-Saffar was also with the splitters but was at this moment in prison. By the time of the split, Baqer Ibrahim had been expelled from the BRC leadership. Following that incident Kazem Jawwad had been commissioned *mas'ul* of the BRC leadership, Ibrahim, *Mudhakkirat*, pp. 142–145.

[140] Therefore, this faction is known as the 'Cadre Faction'.

[141] Mahmud, *al-Sira'*, pp. 122–123. For a lengthy quote from its statement, see Ismael, *Rise and Fall*, pp. 150–151.

adhered to the new leadership's ideas of an uprising to overthrow the regime.[142]

However, before the breakaway of the dissident organisations in 1967, the old leadership tried to accommodate the opposition by radicalising its own message. Seizing the prevailing sentiments in their organisation and the predicament of the old leadership, the BRC tried to capitalise on the situation. The Baghdad organisation was a body functioning in a capital that had witnessed much violence and rapid change over preceding years, and, as such, was especially prone to radicalism and, some would say, extremism. In 1966, it launched a covert campaign against the leadership. Calling the 'decisive action' line an 'opportunist slogan', the BRC argued for its replacement by their own watchword of an 'armed popular uprising' (*al-intifadah al-sha'biyyah al-musallahah*). In essence, this idea, which was clearly Guevarist in origin, argued that an initial 'spark' by the army would 'create the fire' that would ignite the 'revolution'.[143] The coating of the proposal was undoubtedly intended to portray the idea as more radical than the official line. In June 1966, the BRC revealed its intention of challenging the leadership for overall control by issuing an openly critical communiqué. Proposing the Baghdad organisation as the new centre alongside the Central Committee, the BRC organised a series of demonstrations to underline its point. Baqer Ibrahim, who on the eve of the split was *mas'ul* of the BRC, claims the splitters' demands were to make seizure of power the party's main task, to ensure the ICP would be independent of the Soviet Union, to revise the party position on Arab nationalism and Arab unity, and that it should reassert violence as the struggle method of the party.[144]

Powerless as the old leadership was, the only reply it could muster was a counter-communiqué published in August which criticised the BRC. Instead, in a sudden turn of events, the Central Committee, trying to outdo Baghdad in radicalism, accused them of stalling implementation of the 'decisive action' plan. In a document entitled *al-Inqilab al-'Askari*

[142] Mahmud, *al-Sira'*, p. 125. Zaki Khayri later admitted that the old leadership at this point was able to keep 'no more than ten per cent' of its pre-split membership, Ismael interview with Khayri, 15 Mar. 1987, as quoted in Ismael, *Rise and Fall*, p. 159.

[143] Mahmud, *al-Sira'*, p. 104.

[144] Ibrahim, *Mudhakkirat*, p. 142.

huwa Intifadah Sha'biyyah Mutabbaqah 'ala Zuruf Biladina ('The Military Coup is a Popular Uprising Applied to the Conditions of Our Country'), distributed among party organisations in 1967, the Central Committee transgressed the position of the April 1965 meeting and claimed that the 'military coup is a popular uprising ... and it can become the inception of the era of social revolution' and that the 'situation in our country prescribes a military undertaking, and not necessarily a mass undertaking'.[145]

Nevertheless, when Israel attacked Egypt and thus initiated what was to become known as the Six-Day War on 5 June 1967, this set in motion the final stage of the process that eventually led to the party's split into separate factions. The Politburo, represented by Baha' al-Din Nuri, Zaki Khayri and 'Aziz al-Hajj[146] met to decide the party's position on the war. In traditional fashion, it condemned Zionism and called for a united Arab struggle against Israel and imperialism, and, on Khayri's initiative, it raised the slogan of a 'national defence government' (*hukumat difa' watani*) as an alternative to 'Aref's regime in order for the country to more effectively fight Israel.[147] Thus, in reality, the Politburo, at a time when the regime was at its weakest, effectively revoked its policy of overthrowing it, instead seemingly arguing for a similar militarist regime able more effectively to carry out foreign policies akin to those of the present one. 'Despite the fact that the government of 'Abd al-Rahman 'Aref was lightweight and incapable of taking part in the war against Israel', Nuri's later assessment of the regime's involvement in the war thus read, 'its position during the war was not bad. It rendered palpable political and military support to Egypt and Syria.'[148] Following the leadership's questionable position on the war, the last semblance of unity broke down and the rank-and-file began to organise oppositional activity inside the party.

[145] Mahmud, *al-Sira'*, pp. 105–106. Ismael, on the other hand, castigating the Central Committee, argues the document in fact stated that the military coup was *not* a 'popular uprising'. In his version, the Central Committee was actually criticising the BRC for 'adventurism'. However, as frequently happens in Ismael's account, there is no documentation to back up the claim, Ismael, *Rise and Fall*, p. 143.

[146] 'Aziz Muhammad was abroad.

[147] Nuri, *Mudhakkirat*, pp. 364–365. This, as may be recalled, was the same name the pan-Arabist officers of the Rashid 'Ali al-Gaylani movement used to describe their government in 1941, see ch. 1.

[148] Ibid., p. 365.

The following month, the leader of the Cadre Faction, Khaled Ahmad Zaki (Comrade Zafer), sent a critical memorandum to the Central Committee. An adherent of Fahad's old Marxist-Leninist ideology, Zaki castigated the party's 'revisionist' line, which, he argued, it had followed since its subordination to Qasim in 1959. 'Our Party has suffered from rightist views and policies', he wrote,

> since the beginning of the fifties—i.e. after the stage of comrade Fahad's leadership—and since mid-1959 they started to crystallise, but were completed in a clearly characterised and defined rightist revisionist line in June-August 1964. This current deviated from Marxism-Leninism not only in questions of tactics, but also in strategy. We are here not concerned with discussing and refuting this liquidationist current, but we are bent on showing that despite the passing of two and a half years since the attempt to alter it, until now there has been no serious uncovering of its ideological efforts and their objective and subjective causes, and there has been no unrestricted self-criticism, and the party has not educated its members of those dangerous errors ...[149]

As a remedy to this situation, Zaki proposed a plan involving the 'freezing or removal' of everyone involved in the formulation of the August Line, the 'inoculation of new revolutionary elements', the creation of a new leading body with members that had actively opposed the August Line, and the convening of a national congress.[150]

While not envisioning itself as a separate entity, the Cadre Faction had begun independently to prepare for armed struggle since its 30 June meeting. In the southern Marshes, the mid-Euphrates countryside and Iraqi Kurdistan it had set up armed contingents under its command. Although small in size compared to the mainstream party and especially compared to the following of Baghdad with its more populist rhetoric, it nevertheless gained some influence among grassroots party organisations, e.g. in the two Baghdad districts Madinat al-Thawrah and Madinat al-Shu'lah, among officers and intellectuals and in the peasant organisations of al-'Amarah, al-Gharraf and the mid-Euphrates.[151]

In the midst of the new leadership's growing importance, the Cadre Faction, which since its appearance had severely criticised those very leaders, now themselves did a U-turn and opened up for negotiations with

[149] Memorandum of 30 June 1967, quoted in Mahmud, *al-Sira'*, pp. 114–115.

[150] Mahmud, *al-Sira'*, p. 116.

[151] Ibid., p. 124.

Baghdad. After tense deliberations, it eventually decided to join forces with the BRC.[152] This followed a failed attempt in July by Baghdad to induce the Central Committee's support against the Cadre Faction, whom they thought were infringing on their part of the opposition as it had gained significant support among students. After that, 'Aziz al-Hajj, who had become Baghdad's unofficial leader, had turned to the Cadre Faction to enlist their support for his planned coup against the Central Committee, an invitation they had turned down.[153] Following discussions, the Cadre Faction eventually decided to join forces with the Baghdad organisation and form what was to be known as *al-Hizb al-Shuyu'i al-'Iraqi—al-Qiyadah al-Markaziyyah* ('The Iraqi Communist Party—Central Command').[154]

The Central Command adopted the line of armed struggle following discussion of a document presented to the meeting entitled 'The Tactical Plan' (*al-Khittah al-Taktikiyyah*),[155] a document that was based on Zaki's ideas. Criticising the Central Committee's military coup line, he had put forward his own idea of a 'popular armed uprising', which in inclination resembled Maoist ideas. 'Firstly', he wrote, refuting the military coup, 'it does not enjoy wide popular support ... and secondly, all the senior leaders of the army and the other officers (are associated) with various wings of the anti-communist, anti-working class and anti-Kurdish nationalism camp'. He also discarded the possibility of using the army as a vehicle for revolutionary change. 'The army as an apparatus in a capitalist-feudalist state', he wrote, 'cannot (in essence) be a neutral installation, nay it is a principal class tool in oppressing the working class and the revolutionary movement ... And the final solution can only come through the dissolution of the army as "an apparatus" and its retraining on new revolutionary grounds...' Instead, he argued, what was needed was a people's war on the Chinese model.[156]

[152] Mahmud, *al-Sira'*, pp. 125–126.

[153] Ibid., pp. 117–119.

[154] The meeting, which Ismael terms the 'party conference', took place on 2 Jan. 1968; see Ismael, *Rise and Fall*, pp. 151–152. Ismael (p. 97) rightly argues that the name could be translated 'Central Leadership' rather than 'Central Command'. However, to indicate clearly that the group represented a separate organisation, the latter designation has been chosen in this study.

[155] Ibid., p. 126.

[156] Khaled Ahmad Zaki's memo of 1967, quoted in Mahmud, *al-Sira'*, pp. 106–108.

On 28 May 1968, the armed uprising, led by Zaki, was announced. The new organisation's 'Communiqué no. 1' reported a successful attack on a police unit in the southern Marshes. However, the armed uprising had alarmed the authorities, who dispatched a whole army brigade of about 700 soldiers to deal with the insurgents. Thus, only two days after the initiation of the uprising a major confrontation with the army took place on 30 May. The clashes, which soon developed into an unevenly matched manhunt was over within a week. The toll was heavy on the Central Command: of the eight insurgents, three, including Zaki, were killed in battle, three surrendered and the remaining two were wounded and eventually apprehended.[157]

To make matters worse for the Central Command radicals, within two months of their announced armed uprising, the Ba'thists launched their 17–30 July coups overthrowing the 'Aref regime. As its predecessor in 1963, the new Ba'thi regime made anti-communism and the thwarting of the revolt its main initial task. The Central Command leader, 'Aziz al-Hajj, was eventually captured by Ba'thi police in February 1969.[158] Following his breakdown and consequent revelation of all essential party secrets the back of the new organisation was broken within a month, with the arrest of Politburo members Kazem al-Saffar, Matti Hindi Hindu, 'Abd al-Hamid al-Safi and Ahmad Mahmud al-Hallaq, and also Central Committee members Saleh Rida al-'Askari, Sami Ahmad 'Abbas, Malik Mansur, Ghazi Antoine, Khudayr 'Abbas al-Zubaydi and Peter Yusuf. With al-Hajj's appearance on Baghdad TV on 3 April 1969 attacking the Central Command and denouncing the ICP and the world communist movement, a service for which he received recognition as the Ba'thist regime's permanent representative at UNESCO in Paris, the final blow to the Central Command experiment was struck.[159] Those of his comrades that did not end up in the infamous Qasr al-Nihayah torture centre made their way to Iraqi Kurdistan. Most that had followed the Central Command eventually rejoined the mainstream ICP, while others, led by Ibrahim

[157] Ismael, *Rise and Fall*, pp. 153–154.

[158] Mahmud, *al-Sira'*, pp. 127–129.

[159] Though Ismael tries to exonerate al-Hajj by claiming his public denunciation of former comrades and revealing of party secrets was actually an attempt to 'ensure its survival' and 'alleviate the Ba'thist wrath', it is probably closer to the truth to assert that al-Hajj was more bent on saving his own skin. For Ismael's assertion, see Ismael, *Rise and Fall*, p. 221.

Fig. 10. Members of the Central Command leadership after being captured by the authorities. Standing from right to left: Kazem Rida al-Saffar, Politburo-member and second-in-command after 'Aziz al-Hajj, Central Committee-members Malik Mansur and Peter Yusuf, followed by Saleh Rida al-'Askari, CC-member and *Mas'ul* (Comrade-in-charge) of the Party's *Jihaz al-Siddami* ('strike force', i.e. section charged with party security), unnamed members of which are seated in the front row on the floor. Seated in the middle row, from left to right: 'Aziz al-Hajj, Secretary of the Central Command, next to him is Talal Salman, a reporter from al-Sayyad Magazine conducting an interview with al-Hajj, then follows Khudayr 'Abbas al-Zubaydi, member of the Central Committee and lastly Ahmad Khadr al-Safi, member of the Politburo.

al-'Alawi (Najm Mahmud) continued the organisation's activities, convening a meeting in August 1969 which elected a new leadership, and in 1974 what it called the Third Conference of the Iraqi Communist Party, but in terms of real impact on the Iraqi political scene it had played its role.[160]

[160] al-Kharsan, *Safahat min Ta'rikh*, pp. 249–253. For an alternative reading of the significance of this organisation following its failed armed uprising, see Ismael, *Rise and Fall*, ch. 5, pp. 204–263.

Meanwhile, the old guard had held its Third Conference in late December 1967 in Iraqi Kurdistan. The conference lasted for several days and had fifty-seven delegates. Since it was held in KDP heartland, the ICP had to ask Mulla Mustafa Barzani for permission. Noteworthy was the return from abroad of Party Secretary 'Aziz Muhammad, who throughout the internal crisis had been notoriously missing from developments in the country. Incredibly, this detachment from events on the ground, a characteristic not normally associated with a leader of a political party, was rewarded and Muhammad was re-elected as Party Secretary because he had remained outside the internal struggles. A report assessing the party's policy over the period 1956–1967, which confirmed that all the members of the old guard with the exception of 'Aziz al-Hajj and the partial exception of Ara Khajadur had been responsible for the August Line, was adopted. But with the radical opposition having broken away there was no longer any need to keep up appearances and so the tactic of the military coup was dropped. Unsurprisingly, the splitters were also condemned. The party's focus, the conference instead decided, should be on the 'daily mass struggle', and the struggle to establish a 'transitory coalition government' that would implement urgent demands such as democratic liberties in order to usher in the secondary strategic objective, namely the 'revolutionary democratic republic' under the leadership of the working class.[161]

The Third Conference's assessments and the ensuing policies would come to determine much of the party's actions in the decade to come, the decade of Ba'thi consolidation of power.

[161] Nuri, *Mudhakkirat*, pp. 385–386; Khayri, *Dhakirat*, pp. 286–287; Duglah, *Min al-Dhakirah*, pp. 153–154.

[illegible]

[illegible]

[illegible]

5

NATIONALISM, PATRIOTISM AND 'PROGRESSIVENESS' IN THE ERA OF BA'THI CONSOLIDATION OF STATE POWER, 1968–1979

Political Developments, 1968–1979

Seizing power from a miniscule social support base, the Ba'th Party which in successive coups on 17 and 30 July 1968 outmanoeuvred its army rivals,[1] tenaciously sought to consolidate its influence. This it did by skilful manipulation of the other political forces in the country—the Kurdish nationalists and the communists—and by initially relying on the aid of the Soviet Union. Interchangeably, the Ba'th moved towards rapprochement with one party while repressing the other; thus, at first, it sought dialogue with the KDP while launching a police campaign against the ICP. After 1971, it moved close to the Soviet Union, and as a result, its suppression of the communists eased—to the detriment of the Kurds. The Ba'thi regime nationalised Iraq's oil resources in 1972, which along with the Soviet-Ba'thi rapprochement swayed the ICP to establish a national front with the Ba'thists in July 1973, something that prompted a dramatic deterioration of relations with the Kurds for both parties. After escalating its attacks on the ICP—both verbally and physically—throughout 1973–74, the Kurdish nationalists launched a rebellion against the state in 1974–75. Taking the side of the regime, the ICP supported the state's brutal suppression of the uprising. Having subdued the Kurdish nationalist movement, the Ba'th once again moved away from both the

[1] 'Another Coup in Iraq', *The Times*, 18 Jul. 1968.

ICP and the Soviet Union. From 1975 onwards, the Ba'th sought rapprochement with western powers, most notably France. Furthermore, both domestically and internationally, the Ba'thi regime increasingly followed an independent line aiming at elevating Iraq to the level of major regional player.

Important developments had occurred in the Ba'thi movement since its last time in power in 1963. Ever since the decision of the 'historical leadership' ('Aflaq-Baytar) to disband the Syrian (Regional) Ba'th organisation in 1958 as a concession to Nasir upon formation of the UAR, a vehement opposition within its ranks had crystallised. Members of this opposition became known as *al-qutriyyun* ('regionalists'), whereas pan-Arabists remaining loyal to 'Aflaq where called *al-qawmiyyun* ('nationalists'). Most *qutriyyun* stemmed from Syria's minorities. Generally more disenfranchised than the majority Sunni group, which constituted the bulk of the *qawmiyyun*, the *qutriyyun* were in the main more interested in social issues and had joined the Ba'th because of its secularism.[2] On 23 February 1966, Syrian *qutriyyun* officers led by Salah Jadid and Hafez al-Asad took over the Syrian Ba'th, ousted the Baytar government and expelled the Old Guard from the party. Underlining their commitment to 'scientific socialism', class struggle, relations with the Soviet Union and continued nationalisation, the new group undoubtedly seemed like a 'leftwing' to outside observers.

In Iraq, the Ba'th had undergone a thorough reorganisation following the 1963 debacle. With no intact regional leadership, 'Aflaq in his capacity as Secretary-General of the Ba'th Party as a whole had stepped in and appointed Saddam Husayn (at that point still known as al-Tikriti) Secretary of the Iraqi Regional Command (IRC) and Ahmad Hasan al-Bakr director of the military branch. Following the Syrian Jadid coup, Saddam and other senior Iraqi Ba'thists remained loyal to 'Aflaq's National Command, something that continued after their ascendency to power in 1968.[3] While formally ruled by the Revolution Command Council (RCC), real Ba'thi power was vested in the IRC. After ousting their non-Ba'thist partners of the 17 July coup, Generals 'Abd al-Rahman Ibrahim al-Daud and 'Abd al-Razzaq al-Na'if, the RCC was made up of six veteran Ba'thi

[2] Eberhard Kienle, *Ba'th v. Ba'th: The Conflict between Syria and Iraq 1968–1989*, London: I.B. Tauris, 1990, pp. 32–33.

[3] Ibid., pp. 34–35.

generals: Ahmad Hasan al-Bakr, Hardan al-Tikriti, Saleh Mahdi 'Ammash, 'Abd al-Ghaffar al-Tikriti, Sa'dun Ghaydan and Hammad Shihab.[4] Yet, behind the scenes, Saddam, the IRC leader, was quietly busy plotting. At the Iraqi Ba'th's Seventh Congress, held on 24 November 1968, Dr. 'Izzat Mustafa, one of Saddam's staunchest opponents, was ousted from the IRC.[5] A year later, in November 1969, all IRC members and all Iraqis within the National Command collectively joined the RCC—in total ten new members. At the same time, Saddam became deputy RCC chairman. From his strengthened position he rooted out more opponents, thus despite the injection of a large quantity of new elements, RCC membership figures continuously dwindled until 1977 when they stabilised at five. At the Eighth Congress in 1974, another nine new IRC members, five of which were Saddam supporters, were incorporated, making the total of pro-Saddam members eight out of thirteen. In January 1977, another ten (six pro-Saddam) members were added, and thus by March 1977, Saddam had the support of fourteen out of twenty-one IRC members.[6] Finally, in July 1979 Saddam ousted his last remaining rivals and took over as President of Iraq.

Along with these internal developments, a series of political events occurred over the period that ultimately strengthened Ba'thi rule. One of the most important was the Ba'th's subduing of the Kurds. Following its takeover in 1968, the new regime put out feelers to the radical, but organisationally eclipsed, KDP-faction led by Ibrahim Ahmad and Jalal Talabani. On the face of it, they seemed the perfect partners of the Ba'th with their eclectic mix of socialist principles and nationalist sentiments. Mulla Mustafa Barzani, for his part, initially took a cautious stand towards the new regime. Cooperation, he insisted, was conditional on the Ba'thi regime suspending its patronage of the Ahmad-Talabani faction, which had received a stipend from the government and a licence to publish its paper, *al-Nur*. Despite initial attempts at reconciliation, such as the provision of Kurdish language teaching in all schools in Iraqi Kurdistan, relations soon became frosty between the KDP and the Ba'th and in March

[4] Amatzia Baram, 'The Ruling Political Elite in Bathi Iraq, 1968–1986: The Changing Features of a Collective Profile', *International Journal of Middle East Studies* 21, no. 4, Nov. 1989, pp. 450–1.

[5] Ibid., p. 451.

[6] Ibid., pp. 451–3.

1969, Mulla Mustafa's guerrilla fighters started to attack government troops in northern Iraq.[7]

Intimidated by the KDP's increased military strength after the Kirkuk oil fields had sustained shelling by its Iranian-provided artillery, the Ba'th Party was eventually forced into negotiations with Mulla Mustafa. Official deliberations began in December 1969, with Barzani now holding the trump card by virtue of his Iranian connection. The regime was thus forced to suspend its patronage of the Ahmad-Talabani faction and its government sponsored force of mercenaries—*Fursan Salah al-Din* ('The Knights of Saladin'). Despite serious disagreements, especially over the status of oil-rich Kirkuk, the two sides nevertheless signed a historical agreement on 11 March 1970, seemingly ending strife between the two parties. In short, the major points of this agreement provided for Kurdish to be used as an official language, Kurdish representation in government, that officials should be Kurdish-speaking in Kurdish majority areas, restoration of Kurds who had been uprooted in previous fighting, implementation of Agrarian Reform, inclusion in the Iraqi constitution of the term 'the Kurdish nationality', surrendering of a Kurdish broadcasting station and arms to the government, the provision that a Kurd should be vice-president, share of legislative power and unification of Kurdish majority areas as a self-governing unit.[8]

Relations between the two sides soon worsened again, however, and when in April 1972 the Ba'thi regime signed its Friendship Treaty with the Soviet Union, the KDP moved even closer to the Shah of Iran and, by extension, the US and Israel. In July, armed clashes ensued. Throughout 1972 and the first months of 1973, an uneasy truce followed. However, due to Mulla Mustafa's ever-closer relations with the 'imperialist' enemies of the regime, limited fighting eventually broke out again in late June. Between January and March 1974, a last attempt at reconciliation was made, but again Kirkuk proved the principal stumbling block. To it, 70 per cent of Iraqi oil production was attached, and with the nationalisation of the oil industry two years before, stakes were now enormous. Mulla Mustafa claimed Kirkuk as his capital but the Ba'th had no intentions of granting such a concession to the KDP as it would have made Iraqi Kurdistan more or less economically independent. As deliberations

[7] McDowall, *History of the Kurds*, pp. 325–326.

[8] Ibid., pp. 326–328.

ground to a halt, the regime unilaterally announced its Autonomy Law on 11 March 1974. Though the new law went further than any previous Iraqi legislation in granting Kurdish autonomy, it was still a long way from meeting Mulla Mustafa's demands.[9]

Following the broken-down negotiations all-out war erupted between Barzani and the Ba'thi regime in April 1974.[10] Mulla Mustafa's inferior force of some 50,000 tribal *peshmergahs* now stood against ca. 90,000 well-trained and well-equipped government forces. The Iraqi army swiftly moved in with full force and pushed the insurgents back. Had it not been for Iran providing logistical support over its borders, the rebellion would quickly have been crushed. Instead, the Kurdish guerrilla fighters held out until winter, but by February 1975, their situation was desperate.[11] However, when Saddam Husayn at the OPEC Conference in Algiers on 6 March, reached an agreement with Mohammad Reza Pahlavi, Shah of Iran, settling outstanding disputes between the two countries and ending Iranian support for the Kurds, the uprising was doomed.[12] The Iraqi regime, in accordance with the agreement, offered Mulla Mustafa a cease-fire from 13 March to 1 April, allowing him and his forces either to retreat into Iran or surrender. Distraught the KDP leadership decided to end the fighting and soon more than 100,000 Kurds—*peshmergahs* and relatives—made their way into Iran and the rebellion was finished.[13]

The regime swiftly moved in to fill the vacuum left by the KDP, and, anxious to convey the idea that it was 'progressive', soon began development works on an unprecedented scale. Some 336 million Iraqi Dinars

[9] Ibid., pp. 335–336.

[10] 'Civil War Returns to Kurdistan', *The Times*, 16 Mar. 1974.

[11] McDowall, *History of the Kurds*, pp. 330–338.

[12] The Algiers accord, later incorporated into a formal agreement in June, was undoubtedly an Iraqi concession in the short run, but proved to be strategically beneficial as it opened up the possibility of permanently settling one of the Ba'thi regime's endemic problems—the Kurdish question. Thus, in exchange for a cessation of Iranian support of the KDP and closure and increased supervision of the Iran-Iraq border that before had provided vital supply routes for the Kurdish rebels, Saddam had to yield to Iranian demands on the delineation of the territorial waters of the Shatt al-'Arab, thus recognising Iranian supremacy in the Persian/Arab Gulf, Kienle, Ba'th v. Ba'th, p. 87; Smolansky and Smolansky, *USSR and Iraq*, pp. 162–3; Penrose and Penrose, *Iraq*, pp. 372–373. See also 'Iran Closes Its Borders to Kurdish Nationalists', *The Times*, 7 Mar. 1975.

[13] McDowall, *History of the Kurds*, p. 338.

were spent on developing the region. Militarily, the Ba'thi regime aimed at eradicating the continuous threat of the KDP by establishing a security belt along the Iranian and Turkish borders, on the Israeli pattern. At first, this belt was 5 km wide but over time, it widened to 30 km in places. Initially, some 500 villages were razed to implement the scheme, a figure that might have risen to 1,400 by 1978. In the name of progress, people were removed from their villages and deported to modern *mujama'at* ('collectives'). The regime also tried to settle the demographic issue, which had been the main sticking point in the negotiations with the KDP in 1970 and 1974. According to Kurdish sources, some 1 million people were moved from the disputed areas of Kirkuk, Khanaqin, Mandali, Shaykhan, Zakho and Sinjar to other areas of the country and were replaced by Arab workers.[14]

For the ICP, the main preoccupation of the period was negotiations with the Ba'th to establish political cooperation between the two parties. Thus, the first half of the period was characterised by politico-ideological struggle over the nature of the front to be set up, and the second half by a frantic activity to safeguard the 'national front' once it had been established. Following lengthy deliberations, the alliance was finally agreed upon on 17 July 1973, the anniversary of the 1968 'revolution', under the name *al-Jabhah al-Wataniyyah wa l-Qawmiyyah al-Taqaddumiyyah* ('The Progressive National-Patriotic Front'). The joint signing of its charter by Ahmad Hasan al-Bakr and 'Aziz Muhammad was overseen by Sharif Rashidov, alternate member of the CPSU Politburo and First Secretary of the Communist Party of Uzbekistan, who visited Iraq on 13–20 July. The key concession the ICP had been able to wrest from the Ba'thi leadership during the negotiations was a guarantee for ideological, political and organisational independence, which had been absent from the original front charter published by the Ba'th in 1971.[15] Yet, the front was far from equal in setup. It was led by a Higher Committee with a Ba'thi chairman and sixteen seats; eight of these were allocated to the Ba'th, three to the ICP, three to the KDP (which refused to take them up), and one each to the Progressive Nationalists and the Independent Democrats. On 25 September, Na'im Haddad, member of the senior Ba'thi leader-

[14] Ibid., pp. 339–340.

[15] Haim Shemesh, *Soviet-Iraqi Relations, 1968–1988: In the Shadow of the Iraq-Iran Conflict*, London: Lynne Rienner, 1992, pp. 93–94.

ship, was appointed its Secretary-General. The front was not intended as a power sharing mechanism by the Ba'th who retained real power with the RCC. Instead, it was described as a voluntary organisation providing a discussion forum.[16]

The establishment of the front proved to be the undoing of the ICP. Once set up, it constrained communist action and confined the party to playing a secondary role to the Ba'thists for the remainder of the period. In the end, the party's fate was sealed in 1978–79 when Saddam Husayn, who throughout the period had pulled the strings from behind the scene but who had been restricted to second place in the Ba'thi hierarchy under Ahmad Hasan al-Bakr, now ascended to the position of Iraqi leader. Jockeying for power, he saw off his rivals in an internal Ba'thi purge. That spelt the end of the ICP-Ba'th alliance and any other attempt at political plurality in Iraq, as the Saddam-Ba'thi version of politics was firmly set on corporatism, one-party rule and brutal suppression of dissidence.

The Ba'th Party and the Theory of 'Revolutionary Democracy'

Concurrent with the Ba'thi takeover of power in 1968, developments also occurred in the communist 'revolutionary democracy' theory. The previously positive analysis of this category, which in the communist ideational realm was construed as being represented by the radical regimes in Egypt, Syria and Algeria, was severely dented by the outcome of the 1967 Six-Day War. The failure of these regimes to put their radical rhetoric into practice and their humiliating defeat by Israel, coupled with the dwindling fortunes of Nasir and his variety of Arab Socialism, all contributed to the formulation of a much more cautious and negative view on the political potential of the so-called 'revolutionary democrats'. Instead focus on the radicalisation of the 'masses', which was said to occur as a result of the polarisation that had been caused by the failure of these regimes, was now the central idea. Initially, as the ICP was targeted by Ba'thi repression, the Iraqi Ba'th was included in the negative assessment. Yet despite the originally pessimistic appraisal, the Iraqi communists refused to venture for power themselves because ideologically they still adhered

[16] Smolansky & Smolansky, *USSR and Iraq*, p. 117; Shemesh, *Soviet-Iraqi Relations*, p. 94. Note that Ismael claims the ICP received four seats on the Higher Committee, Ismael, *Rise and Fall*, p. 173.

to the overarching tenet that dictated the necessity of passing through the 'national-democratic' revolution before reaching the socialist stage.

The Iraqi communists argued that the June 1967 War marked a watershed in the social progression of the Arab world. The old 'radical' regimes, epitomised by Egypt, Syria and Algeria, had been de-legitimised and a new revolutionary mood among the masses was now said to be discernable. According to the ICP, the most prominent feature of this new 'consciousness' was the masses' 'increased resolve' to overthrow 'reactionary regimes' and the increased 'opposition to dictatorial and totalitarian regimes' and their 'bourgeois programmes and ideologies'. To the party, 'the masses' were 'tangibly turning to the left and to socialism'. Although the 'Aref regime had been overthrown by a small group of army officers in liaison with the Ba'th Party, the ICP nevertheless argued that the July 1968 coups were 'not isolated from this influence'.[17]

According to the Iraqi communists, the increased polarisation between the old regimes and the 'masses' had accelerated the 'class struggle'. In their view, this had been achieved as a result of the ICP's and other communists' 'persevering struggle' to spread 'Scientific Socialist thought', something that had given the 'Arab liberation movement' a 'radical and progressive' content and had propelled it 'to a new stage of struggle'.[18] A wave of revolutionary mass criticism had thence forced 'the petty bourgeois nationalist parties' to come to terms with 'the incorrectness' of their ways and thus, while keeping in 'pace with the movement of history', they 'corrected some of their former stands' and 'started to declare their adherence to certain scientific conceptions'.[19] This development, as we have seen in the previous chapter, was conceptualised by the communist theory of 'petty bourgeois revolutionary democrats', saliently represented by Nasir's Egypt. But after the debacle of the 1967 Six-Day War and especially following the end of Nasirism with Nasir's death in 1970, a more negative view on the potential of these 'revolutionary democratic' regimes crystallised. It was thus explained how these regimes were unable to 'assimilate the teachings and principles of Marxism-Leninism' because they adhered to 'nationalist socialism'. As a result, they resorted to 'defam-

[17] *Report of the Central Committee to the Second National Congress of the Iraqi Communist Party* (*n.p.*: Iraqi Communist Party: *n.d.*), pp. 28–29.

[18] Ibid., p. 31.

[19] Ibid., pp. 27–28.

ing the Arab communist parties and the Soviet Union and displayed sterile and harmful tendencies to present themselves as substitutes for the communist parties' and thus 'a new stage in the ideological struggle between nationalist socialism and Marxism-Leninism' had opened up.[20]

While still arguing that 'under the impact of the revolutionary movement and the increasing influence of ideas of socialism and progress', these regimes followed 'an anti-imperialist *watani* policy' that had 'brought about progressive changes in the economic construction', the ICP once again shifted its emphasis to their anti-democratic nature, which, it argued, was 'bound together with the manner of rule'.[21] This 'democratic dimension', as may be recalled from the discussion on Nasir's 'socialist' system in 1964–65, had previously been dropped in favour of a positive interpretation of that system as representing a workers' and peasants' democracy.[22] Now, however, it was argued that the 'autocratic bureaucratic character' of these regimes and their disregard for the national front, together with their combating of political parties and repression of democracy had produced 'dangerous cracks' in their 'foundation', which had caused their setbacks, and these cracks, according to the communists, were related to the wavering 'class nature of the petty bourgeoisie'.[23]

The newfound scepticism towards 'petty bourgeois' regimes and their superficial attachment to 'scientific socialism' was also initially reflected in the ICP's position on the Ba'th Party and its claims for socialist credentials. 'We do not exactly know what the Ba'th wants with "socialist transformation"', the party wrote in *Tariq al-Sha'b* in 1970, 'and "socialism" in the Ba'thi view continues till this day to be an unscientific ambiguous notion'. Socialism, in the communist view, was not 'mere economic implementations'. Judging from Ba'thi policy, the ICP thought it clear that the Ba'th Party did not desire 'a transformation of the ownership of the fundamental means of production to social ownership and the abolition of all phenomena of exploitation'. Such a transformation, at any rate, could not 'be brought about other than as part of a complete transformation of the socio-political system of the country', and in the light of that,

[20] Ibid., p. 28.

[21] 'al-Taqrir al-Siyasi al-ladhi Aqarrahu al-Mu'tamar al-Watani al-Thani li l-Hizb al-Shuyu'i al-'Iraqi', *Tariq al-Sha'b* 27, no. 9, Oct. 1970.

[22] See ch. 4.

[23] 'Taqrir Siyasi... Mu'tamar Thani'.

the Ba'thi slogan of socialist transformation had clearly been presented 'prematurely'.[24]

Nevertheless, while unmistakably refuting Ba'thi socialist credentials, the ICP leadership at the same time rejected the option of venturing for power itself to implement the desired changes. On the surface there was nothing to suggest that the Ba'th Party, which in 1970 still was far weaker than the ICP organisationally and politically and perhaps on an equal par in terms of support from the army, to say nothing of its somewhat vacuous exclusivist and chauvinist nationalist ideology, would be better suited to carry the country closer to 'socialism'. After all, to the communists, the ultimate warrant for the success of such a venture and the safeguarding of the country from 'imperialist plots' was a benign relationship with the Soviet Union.

Despite the ICP leadership's ideological reluctance to pursue such an 'adventurist' line, which was tantamount to contradicting the 'laws' of the 'national-democratic' stage, ICP First Secretary 'Aziz Muhammad nevertheless inadvertently conceded the possibility of such a development. 'In the early years after World War II', he wrote in *Problems of Peace and Socialism*,

> the struggle of Asian and African peoples for progressive social ideals and genuine liberation assumed vast proportions and *was particularly effective in countries where Communists were at the head of a mass liberation movement*—witness the historic victories of the Vietnamese (August 1945), Korean and Chinese revolutions. With due regard to the situation in their countries, the Communists led them along the road of people's democracy, which was a special form of transition to socialism and whose substance was the dictatorship of the proletariat.[25]

Why, given such historical precedents, did the Iraqi communists insist on sitting back, despite lacking Ba'thi commitment to 'socialism' and despite its continuous repression of the communists? The answer, indubitably, is ideological. The absolute necessity of passing through the stage of 'national-democratic revolution' was a core tenet the Iraqi communists would not discard. 'Our Communist Party', they argued to this effect, 'despite it being the fiercest struggler in terms of steadfastness for the sake

[24] 'Min Ajli Jabhah Wataniyyah Muwahhadah Haqiqiyyah', *Tariq al-Sha'b* 27, no. 7, Aug. 1970, Special Issue.

[25] Aziz Mohammed, 'Key Trends of the Liberation Process', *World Marxist Review* 20, no. 2, Feb. 1977, p. 6 (added emphasis).

of the country's progression towards socialism, does not believe in the theory of "burning stages" [*harq al-marahil*]'.[26]

'Struggle and Solidarity' with the Ba'th Party, 1968–71

Following its erstwhile pernicious encounter with the Ba'thists in 1963, the ICP's initial position towards the Iraqi Ba'th was, unsurprisingly, cautious. Nevertheless, after the Ba'thi 'self-criticism' expressed at its Sixth National Conference in late 1963, a more dichotomous communist view that distinguished between a Ba'thi 'rightwing' and 'leftwing' had arisen.[27] The semblance of a deep-seated ideological rift within the Ba'thi movement had then been further imprinted on the minds of the communists commensurate with developments on the ground throughout the 1960s.

The Third ICP Conference, held in late 1967, had analysed the 'new' Ba'th at length. It expressed caution about the 'worrying petty bourgeois nature' of the party and its 'crimes' during the 8 February coup, but it also took into consideration 'the self-criticism' of its Sixth Congress. Building on this, the congress decided to cooperate with the 'leftwing' of the Ba'th while staying away from the 'rightwing' led by al-Bakr and Saddam.[28] The comparatively 'peaceful' nature of the 17–30 July coups and public Ba'thi vows not to spill blood in order to move Iraq forward from its sanguinary past,[29] did however raise the ICP's esteem of the al-Bakr/Husayn 'rightwing' that had pulled the coups. Thus, despite avowedly intending to

[26] 'Min Ajli Jabhah Wataniyyah'.

[27] In reality, the self-criticism amounted to little. While acknowledging that the 'National Guard' programme had involved 'shortcomings' and 'mistakes', the congress nevertheless maintained that it was 'a safeguard of the revolution' and as such should be 'expanded and developed'. Indirectly, however, it warned that in Syria and Iraq, where the Ba'th held power at the time of the congress, there was a risk of 'infiltration of the party by opportunists' or that party members might succumb to 'the temptations of power'—Ba'thi euphemisms for the terror experienced in parts of Iraq during 1963 and the infighting that ended the first Ba'thi period in power, see Arab Ba'th Socialist Party, 'Decisions of the Sixth National Convention of the Arab Ba'th Socialist Party, 1963', in Abu Jaber, *Arab Ba'th*, pp. 159; 162.

[28] Khayri, *Dhakirat*, p. 287.

[29] The Ba'th Party later referred to the July coups as 'the White Revolution', during which 'bloodletting' consciously had been avoided as such action 'would spoil the image and divert the course of the Revolution', Arab Ba'th Socialist Party, *The 1968 Revolution in Iraq: Experience and Prospects*, London: Ithaca Press, 1979, pp. 30–31.

shun it, the Communist Party, through its representative Mukarram al-Talabani, did meet with Ahmad Hasan al-Bakr less than a month after the 17 July 1968 coup. At the meeting, al-Bakr spoke of 'the necessity of closing the negative pages of the past'. Instead, al-Bakr explained, the Ba'th sought cooperation.[30] According to Zaki Khayri, the ICP had also in advance of the coups been approached by Siddiq Shanshal, who, representing the Ba'th, wanted to 'feel the pulse' of the communists and see if they would be interested in supporting a prospective Ba'thi government. Khayri told Shanshal that the ICP was prepared to take part in a 'coalition government on a democratic basis' but that it was 'not prepared to play the role of the Unknown Soldier'.[31]

The ICP later characterised the period 1968–1971 as a period of 'struggle and solidarity' on the 'basis of opposition and criticism to everything negative and wrong in the Ba'th's path, especially its enmity towards communism and its oppression of the national parties'.[32] Its first reaction following the 17 July coup was to issue a statement demanding democracy, a stop to repression, the granting of liberties, an elected parliament, Kurdish autonomy, and establishment of friendly relations with the Soviet Union.[33] However, despite the Ba'th Party's previously poor record of delivering on any of those demands, the ICP nevertheless decided to give the new Ba'thi leaders the benefit of the doubt. Thus, the report of its Second National Congress, which was convened in 1970, conveyed the following conciliatory message:

> Our party is conscious of the deep consequences of the anti-democratic, anti-communist policy and the policy of persecution against our party, to which the former regimes resorted and especially in the period of the first Baath rule after the 8th February coup d'état. [...] Inspite of all this, our party did not base itself on the past negative experiences.[34]

30 Ibrahim, *Mudhakkirat*, p. 149.

31 Khayri, *Dhakirat*, pp. 292–293. Ismael, who clearly favours the Central Command, presents a different version. According to him, the ICP was 'very interested' in taking part and asked for time to think it over, although in the end deciding not to join the coup, Ismael, *Rise and Fall*, p. 161.

32 *Taqyim Tajribat Hizbina al-Nidaliyyah li l-Sanawat 1968–1979*, affirmed by the Fourth National Congress of the Iraqi Communist Party, 10–15 Nov. 1985 (*n.p.*; Iraqi Communist Party, *n.d.*), p. 22.

33 Statement of ICP Central Committee, 29 Jul. 1968, quoted in *Report Second Congress*, pp. 5–6.

34 *Report Second Congress*, p. 6.

From the outset the Ba'thi strategy was clear; using a stick and carrot approach, they hoped to terrorise the ICP into political submission.[35] While seemingly extending their hand, the Ba'thists made it clear that any form of cooperation would be strictly on their terms; al-Bakr personally told the ICP leadership that he would be willing to form a front, initiate dialogue and release communist prisoners, providing it accepted the Ba'thi terms. When the party in reply demanded democratisation, the Ba'th cleverly countered that the true meaning of democracy was not 'bourgeois democracy' but freedom from class oppression and that socialist states long since had rejected the bourgeois meaning of democracy,[36] thereby appropriating the communists' own rhetoric. In September, the ICP leadership sent a memo to al-Bakr demanding the establishment of a 'national-democratic coalition government' (*al-hukm al-watani al-dimuqrati al-i'tilafi*), whose 'minimum prerequisites' were outlined by the ICP Central Committee in October. The meeting made the following public statement:

> The most important principle which our Party adheres to in the case of a coalition with any other party or parties is the principle of our Party's class independence [*istaqlaliyyat hizbina al-tabaqiyyah*] and sticking to its strategic slogan. There would remain no meaning of a coalition with any party that does not recognise our Party's right to participate in a coalition government and to carry out overt political work and its freedom to publish newspapers with annulment of all exceptional situations and the anti-democratic associations and laws, and working to solve the Kurdish issue on the basis of recognition of the national [*qawmi*] rights of the Kurdish people, and especially its right to autonomy within the framework of the Iraqi Republic.[37]

The Ba'th Party's past and its ongoing military encounter with the 'Central Command' faction, nevertheless meant that the ICP leadership

[35] This policy became known as *al-tarhib wa l-targhib* ('intimidation and attraction') among Iraqis, Amatzia Baram, *Culture, History & Ideology in the Formation of Ba'thist Iraq, 1968–89*, New York: St. Martin's Press, 1991, p. 18.

[36] *al-Thawrah*, 17 Nov. 1968 and 29 Jan. 1969; *al-Jumhuriyyah*, 15 and 16 Aug. 1968, as quoted in Shemesh, *Soviet-Iraqi Relations*, p. 20.

[37] Quoted in 'Ma Huwa Wajh 'al-Ta'jiz' fi Shurut al-Hizb al-Shuyu'i al-'Iraqi li-Iqamat al-Jabhah al-Muwahhadah bayna Kafat al-Ahzab al-Siyasiyyah al-Wataniyyah wa al-Taqaddumiyyah?', *Tariq al-Sha'b* 26, no. 5, Jul. 1969; al-Kharsan, *Safahat min Ta'rikh*, pp. 134–135; For an alternative English translation, see quote in *Report Second Congress*, p. 7

wanted to proceed slowly in its relations with Iraq's new rulers. The party leaders grew increasingly worried as they watched how elements that to them were anything but 'progressive' and 'patriotic' made their way into the upper echelons of the Ba'thi regime. Observing these developments from the outside, two approaches to dealing with the Ba'th soon crystallised within the ICP leadership; one wanted to actively encourage the Ba'thists to stick to their announced intentions, while the other preached caution. In other words, opinions differed between active and passive support of the new regime.[38] Within the Central Committee, the cautious approach had the support of the majority. This was clearly reflected in the statement of the October Plenary Meeting. 'The regime that the Ba'th Party proposes to the country', it read, 'is in reality an undemocratic regime, and in essence a regime erected on exception [*al-istithna'*] and supremacy [*al-tasallut*].'[39]

As if to prove the communists right, the Ba'th launched a series of attacks on the ICP and its supporters from November onwards. It clamped down violently on a strike at a vegetable oil factory in Baghdad on 5 November and the security apparatus assassinated a number of known communist activists. The main Ba'thi repressive activity was naturally still directed against the Central Command, but by February 1969 when most of its senior figures were behind bars, focus was again firmly locked on the main ICP. Despite indirect dialogue between the ICP and Ba'th leaderships, the security apparatus pursued and arrested scores of communists, including, on 26 June 1969, Central Committee member Sattar Khudayr.[40]

[38] This divaricated view was echoed within the Ba'th Party. According to 'Abd al-Khaliq al-Samarra'i, who perhaps was the most ideologically committed Ba'thist and who as a rival to Saddam Husayn paid the ultimate price when he was executed following Saddam's ascent to power in 1979, most Ba'thists were genuinely interested in accommodating the ICP. Thus, one group desired cooperation to utilise the ICP's experience and another headed by al-Bakr and Saddam was convinced the ICP needed to be brought under control. Within the second trend, two factions developed. One wanted to 'neutralise' the ICP and render it an appendage of the Ba'th, while the second was bent on seeing the communists 'destroyed', Interview by Ismael with al-Samarra'i, as quoted in Ismael, *Rise and Fall*, p. 168.

[39] 'Hawla Abraz al-Masa'il al-Malhah fi l-Wad' al-Siyasi', quoted in al-Kharsan, *Safahat min Ta'rikh*, p. 135.

[40] al-Kharsan, *Safahat min Ta'rikh*, pp. 135–136.

This harsh reality was reflected in the ICP leadership's analysis of the Ba'th Party. But whereas in practical terms it preached caution and adopted a wait-and-see policy, in ideological terms it was ever so more accommodating. The Ba'th Party, it asserted, was 'a petty-bourgeois nationalist party', and the regime 'an anti-imperialist anti-feudal regime'. To get around the problem of Ba'thi repression, the ICP nevertheless had to concede that the regime still represented 'a dictatorial anti-democratic power'.[41] The ambivalence caused by the party's ideological support of the Ba'th while in pragmatic opposition to it was plain to see. Though the ICP leadership, somewhat self-deludingly, referred to its stand as a 'principled and flexible policy', the ambiguity of the situation was apparent as the communists explained that theirs was 'an opposition policy, criticizing every negative and erroneous aspect' of the regime while vowing to support its anti-imperialism.[42]

But Ba'thi heavy-handedness continued. Despite a temporary easing of repression during spring 1969, mainly a result of Ba'thi desire to gain Soviet sympathy in its ongoing conflict with Iran and also designed to break up ICP-KDP cooperation, nothing much changed in the Ba'thi attitude. Nevertheless, rapprochement with the Soviets led to the signing of an Iraqi-Soviet agreement for oil exploitation in August, which the ICP thought was 'a point of great transformation in the political, economic and social future of Iraq'.[43] The Soviets went even further, declaring in *Pravda* that the Ba'thi regime was implementing 'progressive measures meeting the interests of the workers and peasants'.[44] While to the ICP leaders these measures represented proof of the correctness of their earlier assessment of the regime as 'anti-imperialist', on the ground the problem of Ba'thi repression was still unresolved. 'Many of the country's urgent problems remain without a solution', *Tariq al-Sha'b* wrote in November,

> despite the passing of more than one year of the Ba'th Party in power. Among the most distinctive of these problems and at the fore of them, is the problem of

[41] *Report Second Congress*, p. 5.

[42] Ibid., pp. 19–20.

[43] 'al-Ittifaqiyyah al-'Iraqiyyah-al-Sufiyatiyyah li Istithmar al-Naft Khatwah Kabirah Nahw al-Istiqlal al-Iqtisadi', *Tariq al-Sha'b* 26, no. 6, Aug. 1969.

[44] E. Primakov, *Pravda*, 18 Sept. 1969, quoted in Shemesh, *Soviet-Iraqi Relations*, p. 36.

political democracy and democratic rule, which we consider to be the central task among all the other tasks that the country faces.[45]

The Ba'thi regime's 11 March 1970 agreement with the KDP enabled it to intensify its campaign against the ICP. Nevertheless, links with the Soviets continued to deepen and the CPSU took the controversial step of establishing party level relations with the Ba'th, an honour bestowed to few non-communist parties. On 27 July, a delegation headed by Saddam Husayn and invited to the Soviet Union by the CPSU Central Committee, met with senior Soviet officials, including Soviet Premier Alexei Kosygin.[46] At the request of the Soviets, the Ba'th also put out lukewarm feelers to the ICP—without easing its repression. The deliberations between the Ba'th Party and the ICP centred on a series of demands, which the Ba'thists had put forward as preconditions for cooperation. As these demands severely circumscribed the Iraqi communists' ideological and political independence, they decided to publicly reject them.

In a highly polemical article, published by *Tariq al-Sha'b* in August 1970, the ICP went through the Ba'thi demands one by one. The first condition, which amounted to recognition of the Ba'th as 'a revolutionary, unitarian, socialist and democratic party', the communists thought was not 'reasonable'. On the second demand, publicly appraising the '17 July Revolution', they were more forthcoming, albeit arguing there was no real disagreement in essence. 'With the nature of the situation', the article read,

the Ba'th has the right to appraise events in any form it likes, and others can maintain their right to make an appraisal in accordance with how they see it. Before, we have assessed the existing regime as an anti-imperialist and anti-reactionary power and that it is a patriotic regime [*hukm watani*] and we work together with it on this basis. We support every positive step it takes and criticise every step that is not in keeping with the interests of the people.... [...] For that reason, the question of appraising "17 July" and the regime of 17 July cannot be an obstacle unless the Ba'th wanted to create an obstacle out of it, as is clear from its presentation of the question.

Thirdly, on the issue of recognising the Ba'th Party's leading role in government and the future front the party was more polemical, as this

[45] 'al-Dimuqratiyyah—Hiya al-'Uqdah al-Ra'isiyyah fi al-Wad' al-Siyasi al-Rahin', *Tariq al-Sha'b* 26, no. 8, Nov. 1969.

[46] Shemesh, *Soviet-Iraqi Relations*, pp. 37–38.

was clearly the central point. 'Is it in any way in the national interest to open the pages of the records of the past?', the article asked rhetorically, while arguing that the issue only created 'an inimical spirit that the reactionaries and the agents of imperialism who are overcome with longing for these kinds of atmospheres applaud'. What the Ba'th demanded, according to the Communist Party, was to be recognised as 'the autocratic leadership'. The fourth and fifth conditions demanded that the ICP would not establish relations with any group hostile to the government or with 'the scattered remnants of the army' opposed to it. While pointing out that this apparently did not apply to the Ba'th Party itself, the party said, as regarding the Iraqi Ba'th Party's rival organisation in Syria, that it had, and would 'continue to call for strengthening of solidarity' with Syria 'regardless of all the existing differences between the ruling persons in the two countries', thereby 'serving the cause of joint struggle against imperialism'. On the topic of political activity in the army, the sixth condition, the ICP claimed that it had not 'and will never call for a division of the military centres on the side of the national front', meaning that should a front come into effect, it would regard the army as a 'national army'. Instead, the party called for the army to 'arm itself with a revolutionary patriotic consciousness alongside its arming with the most modern weapons and materiel'. The seventh condition demanded that parties of internationalist extraction would bring its 'internationalist extension' into the Ba'thi alliance, but such a condition the ICP would not agree to, arguing that there was 'no cause' for it and that it was impracticable. The eighth and ninth conditions, involving the Palestine question and Arab unity respectively, the party had no objections to.[47]

To the ICP, Soviet ideological sanctioning of the Ba'th Party along with its own generally favourable analysis of the Ba'th as an anti-imperialist 'petty bourgeois' organisation, put it in a difficult position. From an ideological point of view, the Ba'th Party constituted an organisation that in the communist view was important to support. Yet, on the level of everyday politics, the communists were forced into opposition due to Ba'thi repression. However, owing to their ideological accommodation of the regime, they could do little in terms of practical opposition other than to throw toothless tirades against it. 'The anti-communist and anti-democratic policy of the present regime', the party consequently argued, 'does

[47] 'Min Ajli Jabhah Wataniyyah'.

not put it in a better position than other newly liberated countries, where governments have been overthrown because of this same contradictory policy; the struggle on two fronts, against imperialism on the one side and against the revolutionary forces on the other.'[48]

Having rescinded their own oppositional weapons in order to please the regime, however, the ICP leadership could do little but fall back on the idea of the 'power of the masses' and that in the long run the Ba'th Party was weakening its own position by continuing its repression. 'The persistence of this policy', it wrote,

> put the present regime in a fatal isolation from the people. Consequently, it puts it under the mercy of imperialism and reaction whether it likes it or not. […] While our party does not underestimate the great possibilities at the disposal of the ruling party, i.e. the state and its resources, and the possibility of initiative that it enjoys thanks to this important position, we are not in the least of the opinion that the Baath Party has the decisive word in determining the destinies of the country.[49]

While in the long perspective such an assessment might have been true in the Mannian sense that a powerful regime built on 'despotic' force and coercion might be argued to be 'infrastructurally weak',[50] in the actual reality in which the ICP acted during this period it surely was not as in a very physical sense the repression decimated and demoralised the Communist Party.

Contrary to communist belief, the Ba'thi policy was not as arbitrary or haphazard as it appeared, but rather a strategy based on its Arab nationalist ideological beliefs and its desire to establish itself as an all-encompassing national party in Iraq. Although the Iraqi Ba'th had no programme and in the words of one commentator 'indulged in complete ideological vagueness',[51] in actual fact the two main tenets of its ideology, as spelt out by its Sixth Congress in 1963, was 'revolutionism' and 'pragmatism'.[52] While these concepts may appear to be rhetorical platitudes, they somewhat epitomise the Ba'thi strategical approach, especially in Iraq during

[48] *Report Second Congress*, pp. 17–18.

[49] Ibid., p. 18.

[50] See Michael Mann, *States, War and Capitalism: Studies in Political Sociology*, Oxford: Blackwell, 1988.

[51] Kienle, *Ba'th v. Ba'th*, p. 45.

[52] Ba'th Party, 'Sixth National Convention', p. 160.

the 1970s. Ideological principles, e.g. 'struggle against imperialism', 'socialism', 'land redistribution', and even its very raison d'être—'Arab unity', were frequently sidelined in the Ba'thi approach, and 'pragmatism' with a view to strengthen its regional position was at all times the primary focus. 'We aim at rendering our country its actual importance', Saddam Husayn later explained, giving evidence to the pompous megalomaniacal strategy of the Ba'thi regime under his leadership, 'estimating that Iraq is as great as China, as great as the Soviet Union and as great as the United States.'[53]

Despite the ICP's argument that Ba'thi repression ultimately meant that it undermined and weakened its own position, the Ba'thist leadership was unperturbed. Persecution continued and as a later Central Committee statement published in *Tariq al-Sha'b* reported, during October-November 1970 alone, a hundred ICP members and supporters in Basra, sixty in al-'Amarah, eighty in al-Nasiriyyah, eighty-three in the Babil *Muhafazah* and sixty-seven in al-Diwaniyyah had been arrested.[54] In mid-January 1971, a joint meeting of the Jordanian, Syrian, Iraqi and Lebanese communist parties came to the ICP's aid and condemned the Ba'thi repression.[55] The Iraqi communists for their part replied to the repression by stepping up its opposition, but as this was not aimed at overthrowing the regime, the party confined itself to restricting blows to its organisation and publicly trying to put across its views on the front.[56] But such pacifist methods could do little to curb the Ba'thi campaign, and in January 1971 *Tariq al-Sha'b* reported that ICP leaders Kazem al-Jasem, 'Aziz Hamid and 'Abd al-Amir Sa'id along with 'patriotic officers' Majid al-'Abbaychi and Mashkur Matrud had been killed under torture in the notorious Qasr al-Nihayah detention centre. Infuriated, *Tariq al-Sha'b* wrote the following:

> The perseverance of a policy of bloody terror, bodily liquidation and the clinging to methods of torture, murder and the elimination of fighters politically under

[53] *Alif Ba'*, 2 Jan. 1980, quoted in Kienle, *Ba'th v. Ba'th*, p. 94.

[54] 'Balagh Sadir 'an al-Ijtima' al-I'tiyadi al-Kamil li l-Lajnah al-Markaziyyah li l-Hizb al-Shuyu'i al-'Iraqi fi Adhar 1971', *Tariq al-Sha'b* 28, no. 3, Apr. 1971.

[55] 'Bayan al-Ahzab al-Shuyu'iyyah fi Suriya wa Lubnan wa l-Urdunn wa l-'Iraq 'an A'mal al-Qam' al-Muwajjahah Didd al-Shuyu'iyyin wa l-Dimuqratiyyin fi l-'Iraq', *Tariq al-Sha'b* 28, no. 2, Feb. 1971.

[56] al-Kharsan, *Safahat min Ta'rikh*, p. 136.

the penalty of death by torture, and also the maintaining of a torture apparatus and of the Qasr al-Nihayah and its secret annexes cannot serve anyone but imperialism and reaction, and the planners of this policy and those who hold on to it will never yield anything but loss. Any pretext put forth to justify this policy, or to cover these crimes, cannot relieve anyone of those responsible in government and the Ba'th Party from the heavy burden of historical responsibility....[57]

At the same time, however, the ICP continued to praise the 'progress' of the Ba'thi regime in the economic and foreign policy spheres, the 'blow' it had struck to 'imperialist espionage' networks, its progress in social reforms, its reconsidering of the old Agrarian Reform Law, and the 11 March agreement, but maintained the anti-imperialist/anti-democratic dichotomy. It criticised the regime for not having consulted 'the people' in its legislative measures, which had concentrated 'the supreme power' in RCC hands, while having preserved 'all the reactionary laws' and promulgated new ones. The regime had maintained the 'repressive institutions' and had 'invented' others, such as 'National Security', which was controlled directly by the Ba'th leadership and which had 'extended and deepened the terrorist policy of the regime'. The ICP also severely criticised the Ba'th Party for having 'Ba'thified' the state apparatus and the armed forces, which had meant the 'accommodating' of 'reactionary careerists'. Finally, it lamented the fact that the Ba'th Party had a 'tendency to monopolise power', and that it had resorted to 'fascist torture means' in Qasr al-Nihayah.[58]

The Communist Party thus put ideological analysis of the regime above operational considerations, for on the ground the policy followed by the al-Bakr–Husayn Ba'th Party after 1968 differed little in principle from that of the 1963 Ba'thist organisation. The post-1968 Ba'th still utilised 'fascist torture means' according to the ICP, it still followed a path of 'terror', and it had a 'tendency to monopolise power'. Yet, by ideologically sanctioning the Ba'th and its 'progressive measures', and by convincing itself and the public that the regime was following the 'non-capitalist' road, the Iraqi communists thus considerably strengthened the regime in terms of popular legitimacy. The real problem, as before, was the ICP's

[57] 'al-Majd li l-Shuhada'. Dahaya al-Irhab al-Ghashim Kazem al-Jasem, 'Aziz Hamid, 'Abd al-Amir Sa'id, Majed al-'Abbaychi, wa Mashkur Matrud', *Tariq al-Sha'b* 28, no. 1, Jan. 1971.

[58] *Report Second Congress*, pp. 8–15.

ideological denial of independent Ba'thist agency. While conceding that there were different wills in the party—a 'left' and a 'right'—it nevertheless interpreted any expression of 'irrational behaviour', i.e. actions falling outside its ideological framework, as instigated by outside or alien forces ('imperialism' or 'reaction'). The party thus only had two basic positions in its class-based analysis, either the side of the people, a position in which 'deviations' were interpreted as emanating from 'petty bourgeois class origins', or the side of counter-revolution in which all attempts at sensible analysis were thrown overboard and political actors were branded 'fascists' or 'agents'.

By summer-autumn 1971, repression gradually dropped in intensity due to further thawing of Soviet-Ba'thi relations. In June, Iraq was visited by a Soviet delegation that demanded an end to Ba'thist repression. As the Ba'thists granted its wish a clear shift in the Soviet view of the regime became noticeable, and in July *Pravda* wrote that the Ba'th Party aspired to 'rebuilding society on a socialist basis', albeit with the caveat that within 'strata of the army which have influence' on the regime, there were still 'vestiges of anti-communism'.[59] On 15 November, the Ba'th Party published its 'National Action Charter', which, it claimed, was the basis for any cooperation with the ICP. The charter underlined the Ba'thi regime's struggle against 'imperialism' and 'Israeli aggression', while at the same time adopting the communists' language by talking about the necessity of a national front comprising all the 'progressive forces', and to sweeten the prospective deal further, it even promised that the regime would adopt a permanent Iraqi constitution guaranteeing 'democratic freedoms' for the 'progressive' parties.[60] Added to this, there was also a further drop in anti-communist persecution.

Ba'thi-Soviet relations were further strengthened throughout 1972. On 10–17 February, an Iraqi delegation headed by Saddam Husayn visited the Soviet Union on invitation by the CPSU Central Committee. This time the Soviet delegation was led by Premier Kosygin and included Foreign Minister Andrei Gromyko—an indication of Iraq's growing importance to the Soviets. Saddam's intentions was to upgrade Iraq's relations with the Soviet Union to a 'strategic alliance', but while the Soviets were not yet ready for such a commitment, considering their relations

[59] R. Petrov, *Pravda*, 14 Jul. 1971, quoted in Shemesh, *Soviet-Iraqi Relations*, p. 66.
[60] Smolansky and Smolansky, *USSR and Iraq*, p. 111.

with Iran, the meeting communiqué nevertheless stated that the level of the two countries' relations would be raised. In April, Kosygin returned the favour and visited Iraq—the highest-ranking Soviet delegation ever to visit the country. On 9 April, Iraq and the Soviet Union signed a 'Treaty of Friendship and Cooperation'.[61] The day before, Kosygin had held talks with ICP First Secretary 'Aziz Muhammad, Politburo member Zaki Khayri and Central Committee-member 'Amer 'Abdallah at the Soviet Embassy, discussing the formation of a front between the ICP and the Ba'th. Further Soviet-Ba'thi deliberations led to the announcement on 14 May that two ICP members—Mukarram al-Talabani and 'Amer 'Abdallah—would be given seats in the Iraqi government.[62]

'Scientific Socialism' and Establishment of the National Front, 1971–73

The period 1971–73 saw a transformation of the communist position on the Ba'th Party and its regime. The culmination of this transformation was the establishment of the national front in 1973. The increasingly positive analysis of the regime along with 'progressive' Ba'thi measures such as its 1972 oil nationalisation and vital Soviet support made the ICP enter political cooperation with the regime. Crucially, the decision was primarily ideological and not pragmatic. Once established, the national front emerged as the *sine qua non* for the communists who continuously glorified it and their new Ba'thi allies. On the ideological level, the 'revolutionary democracy' theory was now re-used to describe the Ba'thists and make them fit the theoretical blueprint. Whereas before the 'petty bourgeois' and anti-democratic nature of the Ba'th had been stressed in communist analyses, now Ba'thi 'progressiveness' and its moving close to so-called 'scientific socialism' was emphasised. Rapid socio-economic transformations brought about by Ba'thi oil nationalisation and Soviet aid convinced the ICP leaders that Iraq once again was developing along the 'non-capitalist path' towards socialism.

The Ba'thi rapprochement with the Soviet Union, coupled with its nationalisation of the Iraqi oil industry on 1 June 1972 were, according to the ICP, the main factors for its entering negotiations to set up the

[61] Shemesh, *Soviet-Iraqi Relations*, pp. 70–74. See also 'Iraq Pact Strengthens Place of Russia in Arab World', *The Times*, 10 Apr. 1972.

[62] Shemesh, *Soviet-Iraqi Relations*, pp. 76–78.

front. These begun in earnest after the publication of the Ba'thi 'National Action Charter' in November 1971 and eventually led to the mutual signing of the front charter in July 1973.[63] Ismael, on the other hand, argues that oil nationalisation *led to* the strengthened Ba'thi-Soviet relations and not the other way around. However, such a revisionist position rather misses the point that rapprochement had been ongoing since 1969 and had deepened during the first half of 1972, i.e. before the June 1972 oil nationalisation. Like other commentators before him, Ismael also attempts to deny any Ba'thi ideological agency and thus argues that the Ba'thi decision to nationalise the oil industry was a result of economic mismanagement rather than a consistent Ba'thi policy, without providing any proof to back up the claim.[64]

It is clear, however, that the essentially positive analysis of the regime as anti-imperialist, coupled with the safeguarding of the party's fundamental independence and the material developments in the country, were the decisive factors in the ICP leadership's decision to enter into an alliance with the Ba'th Party. In other words, the ideological tenet claiming that the front was indispensable shaped the positive assessment of the Ba'th Party, which was further accentuated following the Soviet-Ba'thi rapprochement. While seemingly opportunistic, the ICP was in fact excessively ideological in its reading of the regime. Again, Ismael offers a completely different interpretation. He argues that since the 1968 Ba'thi takeover the ICP had been trying 'to reappear on the Iraqi political scene' by pursuing negotiations.[65] However, as we have seen, it is clear that during the period 1968–71 it was the Ba'th Party, *not* the Communist Party, that most actively sought cooperation.

The establishment of the front did entail some real material benefits for the ICP. First and foremost was the advantage of knowing that party organisations and members now were safe from persecution, allowing the party to emerge from clandestinity for the first time since the Qasim years. Secondly, its main organ, *Tariq al-Sha'b*, was legalised and transformed from a poorly equipped monthly paper printed on a stencilling

[63] 'Report of the Central Committee to the 3rd National Congress of the Iraqi Communist Party', in *The 3rd National Congress of the Iraqi Communist Party*, 4–6 May 1976, Special Issue of *Iraqi Letter*, no. 4.5, *n.p.*: Iraqi Communist Party: 1976, p. 51.

[64] See Ismael, *Rise and Fall*, pp. 167–168.

[65] Ismael, *Rise and Fall*, pp. 162–163.

machine to a professional-looking daily broadsheet. The paper was given a grand building in central Baghdad from which it could operate.[66] Various front committees were also set up throughout the country and abroad.[67] While these measures were welcome to the communists, it was clear the matters that really counted, such as power sharing, had not been granted. Though some ICP leaders, for example 'Amer 'Abdallah, who became minister without portfolio in the government, might have favoured the alliance for personal reasons, it is very unlikely that these 'perks', which in essence were symbolic, were decisive in the decision to enter the alliance. True, the party had been exposed to intimidation campaigns in the period leading up to the formation of the front and some might have been desperate for respite from persecution. But this was nothing new in ICP history. In fact, previous instances like these had only strengthened the communist resolve. The key to comprehending the communists' decision to join the front is to regard it from their ideological perspective, to grasp the front's perceived role in the development of Iraq and the strengthening of its 'non-capitalist' path to socialism—an idea that by now was unchallenged in the party.

While the Ba'thists may have entered the front out of a calculated self-interest in order to control the ICP and thus strengthen its own position, to the communists the front represented 'a great historical event in Iraq's political life and its revolutionary course'.[68] For them, it was the epitome of what they had been struggling for, albeit with defects. Once the unity of the 'national forces' had been secured in the front, it seemed the major obstacle in the progression towards socialism was overcome. 'With the announcement of the National Progressive Front', the party thus maintained,

> great possibilities in our country were made possible, capable to be used with revolutionary determination to carry out the democratic tasks. Wide horizons opened up in front of the subsequent development of the country, and the infliction of defeat on the imperialist and reactionary conspiracy.[69]

[66] In 1975, *Tariq al-Sha'b* reached an annual circulation of 6,712,140 copies—a truly astonishing amount compared to its previous clandestine distribution figures, Ismael, *Rise and Fall*, p. 169.

[67] al-Kharsan, *Safahat min Ta'rikh*, p. 146.

[68] 'al-Quwa al-Thawriyyah Tatatala' ila Mubadarat, H. D. K. lil-Indimam ila al-Jabhah'. *Tariq al-Sha'b*, no. 12, 28 Sept. 1973.

[69] 'al-Ta'bi'ah li l-Jamahir Mahammah Malhah', *Tariq al-Sha'b*, no. 15, 2 Oct. 1973.

In communist thinking, the main danger confronting Iraq at any time was 'imperialist' conspiracies using 'reactionary agents' or direct intervention. Thus, bringing on board the Ba'th Party into their progressive anti-imperialist alliance, would, with additional Soviet support, constitute a 'struggling tool to safeguard the national independence and to attain the victory in [the] difficult struggle against imperialism, Zionism and reaction'.[70] Despite the Ba'th Party's proven violent nature and its less than dialogue-seeking mode of conducting politics, the ICP nevertheless contemplated the front as 'the peaceful framework that is capable of realising the tasks lying before our national movement'. As such, the party had 'a responsibility' before the people 'to safeguard this achievement and develop and transform it into a real tool in the battle against the manifestations of backwardness and the imperialist and reactionary forces'.[71] To the party, the establishment of the front was almost an end in itself. After having convinced itself ideologically for many years of the absolute necessity of the front during the stage of national-democratic revolution, the mantra of the front had turned into a self-fulfilling prophecy whose very utterance equalled success and progress. 'The masses of the people', the ICP thus proclaimed following this logic,

> and its political vanguards have been convinced during the experiences and passing relapses which Iraq has lived through since the July Revolution that there is no assurance, no means, and no possibility to achieve the tasks of this national-democratic revolution, other than by establishing a united fighting front between the parties of the people and its national forces.[72]

This self-reassuring praise of the front was also accompanied by an uncritical glorification of the Ba'th Party, despite its past record. Ba'thi leaders, such as Ahmad Hasan al-Bakr and Saddam Husayn were referred to using the designation 'comrade' (*rafiq*), something that otherwise was restricted to members of the communist party.[73] This practice was also

[70] 'Quwa al-Thawriyyah'.

[71] 'Khatawat Daruriyyah 'ala Tariq Tarsikh al-Jabhah al-Wataniyyah', *Tariq al-Sha'b*, no. 17, 4 Oct. 1973.

[72] *Tariq al-Sha'b*, no. 194, 9 May, 1974.

[73] See for instance ICP First Secretary 'Aziz Muhammad congratulating 'comrades' al-Bakr and Husayn on their re-election as leader and deputy leader respectively at the Eighth Iraqi Ba'th Congress, held in Baghdad 8–12 Jan. 1974, 'Fi Barqiyyat al-Rafiq 'Aziz Muhammad li l-Ra'is al-Bakr: Hizbina Sayabdhul kull al-Juhud

followed on lower levels.[74] A deliberate policy could also be discerned among the communist leadership to avoid contentious topics in public dealings with their new allies. For instance, in April 1974 when the Ba'th Party celebrated its twenty-seventh anniversary, Karim Ahmad, who gave a speech on behalf of the ICP Central Committee, spoke about the history of joint struggle existing between the two parties. While talking at length about the alliance of 1956–7 and how the ICP and the Ba'th had overthrown the monarchy together in 1958, he then, tactically, moved on to the present situation without touching on the events of 1963.[75]

The new Ba'thist attitude was appreciated in Moscow. A statement following the Soviet-Ba'thi cooperation agreement, reached on 30 November 1973, expressed the Soviet approval of Iraq's 'progressive' policy under the Ba'th Party which, it maintained, was aimed at realising 'socialist transformations'.[76] The Iraqi communists' willingness to compromise with the Ba'th was also awarded by the Soviets; on 8 November 1973, ICP First Secretary 'Aziz Muhammad was granted an audience with Soviet leader Leonid Brezhnev, and in June 1974 he was awarded the 'Order of Friendship Among Peoples' on his fiftieth birthday by the Presidium of the Supreme Soviet.[77]

In the statement of the ICP Central Committee-meeting on 27 July 1973, ten days after the signing of the front charter, the party had declared that along with the Ba'thists they were now heading 'together to the building of socialism'.[78] The ideological notion allowing the communists to accommodate the Ba'thists in this manner was the old idea of the transformation of 'petty bourgeois' parties into 'revolutionary democratic' ones.

ma'akum li Muwasalat Masiratina al-Thawriyyah' and 'al-Rafiq 'Aziz Muhammad Yuhanni' al-Rafiq Saddam Husayn bi Munasabat Tajdid Intikhabihi', *Tariq al-Sha'b*, no. 100, 14 Jan. 1974.

74 See the report of an ICP organisation opening a new headquarter in al-Hillah, which was attended by 'comrades' of the local Ba'th organisation, 'Munazzamat al-Hizb al-Shuyu'i fi Babil Taftah Maqaran laha fi l-Hillah', *Tariq al-Sha'b*, no. 84, 23 Dec. 1973.

75 See 'Ihtifal Jamahiri Kabir fi al-Dhikra al-Sabi'ah wa l-'Ishrin li Ta'sis Hizb al-Ba'th al-'Arabi al-Ishtiraki', *Tariq al-Sha'b*, no. 168, 8 Apr. 1974.

76 *Pravda*, 3 Dec. 1973; *al-Thawrah*, 3 Dec. 1973, quoted in Shemesh, *Soviet-Iraqi Relations*, p. 128.

77 Shemesh, *Soviet-Iraqi Relations*, p. 128.

78 Resolution of Emergency Meeting of ICP, 27 Jul. 1973, quoted in *Report 3rd Congress*, p. 53.

While challenged by the deterioration of Nasirism since the late 1960s, the core of the theory had remained intact. Thus, following the establishment of the front, the theory was reapplied on the Ba'thists.

Although the Ba'th Party was a ruling party, and as such created around it a growing class of Ba'thist bureaucrats, functionaries and administrators,[79] the ICP nevertheless maintained that the 'class interests' it represented were those of the 'petty' rather than the 'national' bourgeoisie. 'The national-democratic parties', the ICP explained, 'give expression to the interest of the semi-proletarian masses, the masses of the petty bourgeoisie. But these parties are not homogenous when it comes to their ideology: some of them stand close to scientific socialism and others far away from it.' Although no such 'national-democratic' party could be said to have existed in the Iraq of 1973, what is significant is the communists' insistence that it would be 'possible for some of these parties to become revolutionary', which in fact 'happens during the transition from the stage of general democratic transformations to the stage of socialist transformations.'[80] To the communists, these 'revolutionary democrats' represented a qualitative leap in the 'progressive struggle' as they would go beyond the anti-feudal, liberationist slogans of the old national liberation movement and increasingly take on anti-capitalist notions. 'As the social content of the liberation movement grows deeper', 'Aziz Muhammad correspondingly argued, 'the slogan of national freedom acquires not only an anti-imperialist, but also an anti-capitalist complexion, reflected in the politico-ideological platform of the revolutionary democrats.'[81] As time wore on, the significance of this grouping became so immense (and inhibiting) in the minds of the communists that Muhammad did not hesitate to declare that 'development' in Asia and Africa was 'today unthinkable without the revolutionary democrats'.[82]

The main ideological tenet allowing communist-Ba'thi rapprochement, however, was the notion of 'scientific socialism', a term used by commu-

[79] Thus, for instance, out of 662,656 government employees in 1978, 151,301, or 22.8 per cent, worked in the bureaucracy of the Interior Ministry, Farouk-Sluglett and Sluglett, *Iraq Since 1958*, pp. 248–249.

[80] 'Harakat al-Taharrur al-Watani: Mahammuha. Quwaha al-Ra'isiyyah wa Afaquha', *Tariq al-Sha'b*, no. 13, 30 Sept. 1973.

[81] Aziz Mohammed, 'The Socialist Community is Our Dependable Ally', *World Marxist Review* 18, no. 1, Jan. 1975, p. 17.

[82] Mohammed, 'Liberation Process', p. 6.

nists to refer to the phenomenon of non-communist groups adopting certain Marxist-Leninist concepts. Without critically questioning the attachment of these groups to Marxist-Leninist ideology, the communists argued, echoing their earlier assessment of 'Arab Socialism', that any diffusion of 'scientific socialist' ideas was 'objectively' propitious as it raised the political consciousness of 'the masses'. 'We are living in the epoch of transition from capitalism to socialism on a world scale', 'Aziz Muhammad thus argued,

> in a period when the socialist system is becoming the decisive factor of social development.... The ideas of scientific socialism have an increasing impact, not only on the working class and other working people, but on new social and political forces, or revolutionary democrats. The latter no longer limit themselves to anti-imperialist and anti-feudal struggles but resist capitalist development more and more often. By studying the ideas and conclusions of scientific socialism, revolutionary democrats become more aware of their importance and effectiveness in the struggle for the victory of the national-democratic revolution and the establishment of a society free from exploitation. The spread of socialist ideas among large sections of the population is an objective factor contributing to Iraq's advance along a non-capitalist road. Our relations with the socialist community play a notable role in this.[83]

But despite this unreservedly positive view of the proselytising of 'scientific socialism' there was a fear among ICP leaders that the Communist Party might ultimately be ideologically subsumed and rendered obsolete. It was therefore argued at its Third Congress in 1976 that the Arab Communist parties needed support 'in preserving their ideological, organisational and political independence' and in 'defending their history and legacy'.[84]

The economic and political changes brought about by the Ba'th Party—the 1972 oil nationalisation and the increasing importance of the Soviet relationship—made the communists accept Ba'thi claims to socialism, which they had rejected only a few years earlier. Thus, at the apex of Ba'thi-Soviet cooperation in 1975, economic transformations, which previously had seemed insufficient for ICP ideologues as socialist credentials, were now re-appraised. The strengthening of the economy and the rela-

[83] Aziz Mohammed, 'Tasks of the Revolutionary Forces of Iraq', *World Marxist Review* 19, no. 9, Sept. 1976, p. 4.

[84] *Report 3rd Congress*, p. 32.

tionship with the Soviet Union, the party argued, paved way for further growth of the 'proletariat' and the other social forces that would be 'ultimately decisive in the choice of social evolution'.[85] In other words, in the party's analysis, it was first at this point—after oil nationalisation carried out by Ba'thi 'revolutionary democrats' and rapid industrialisation fuelled by dramatically increasing oil revenues as a result of the oil boycott following the 1973 October/Yom Kippur War,[86] and the influx of Soviet aid—that the 'proletariat', and hence the Communist Party as its representative, would come into its own and fulfil its historical role.

In accordance with the communists' rigid, historically determinist, worldview, the progression along the 'non-capitalist' path towards socialism was not restricted to Iraq alone but occurred in many countries in Asia and Africa, and as such was 'a reflection of the objective and historical determinateness that Lenin has analysed'.[87] Having grown wiser from earlier extreme expositions of historical determinism during the heyday of the August Line, when members of the ICP leadership argued for dissolution of the communist party on grounds of the inevitable triumph of the 'non-capitalist' path to socialism, however, the communists were now careful to point out that although the 'non-capitalist' theory was a historical 'law', it would not work in an 'automatic' way. 'The essential difference between the laws of history and the laws of nature', it was thus argued, 'is that the laws of history are realised through the actions of man.'[88]

Nevertheless, the ICP did make a theoretical distinction between the 'non-capitalist' path and socialism. 'The non-capitalist road', 'Aziz Muhammad argued, 'is not identical with the period of transition to socialism. The latter has its own laws.' He also warned that with a 'growing new bourgeoisie in the state sector', there was still the danger of 'reactionary forces ... trying to pull the country back to capitalism'; a development that could be stopped provided 'the revolution is steadily pressed forward.'[89] This newfound misgiving was clearly a reflection of

[85] Mohammed, 'Socialist Community', p. 17.

[86] Iraqi national income increased from ca. 1.41 billion Iraqi Dinars in 1973 to approximately 3 billion in 1974 and more than 10.5 billion in 1979, Farouk-Sluglett and Sluglett, *Iraq since 1958*, p. 232.

[87] 'Harakat al-Taharrur al-Watani'.

[88] 'al-Darurah al-Ta'rikhiyyah wa l-Nashat al-Insani', *Tariq al-Sha'b*, no. 162, 1 Apr. 1974.

[89] Mohammed, 'Tasks', p. 4.

geopolitical developments occurring since the establishment of the Front in July 1973. Once having secured ICP and Soviet cooperation, the Ba'th Party cautiously moved towards diversification of its international relations and began putting out feelers to western states. This move was sanctioned by the Eighth Iraqi Ba'th Congress, held in Baghdad 8–12 January 1974, although Iraq's 'strategic alliance' with the Soviets was to be kept. Due to this new orientation, and following the increase of oil revenues in 1974, Iraqi trade with the 'socialist camp' dwindled. In addition, the needs of the vast oil-fuelled Ba'thi development programmes could not be covered by Soviet aid, further necessitating rapprochement with the west.[90] 'There is no overlooking the changes in the social basis', Muhammad commented on this phenomenon, 'that have occurred in the region in recent years. In the past, imperialist influence was promoted mainly by Arab reaction. Nowadays, however, this role is also claimed by right-wing currents in the liberation movement that expresses the interests of new groups of the rural and urban bourgeoisie and pro-bourgeois elements in the state apparatus.'[91]

This kind of sentiment was also a reflection of the development that had occurred in Egypt since the death of Jamal 'Abd al-Nasir in 1970, with Anwar al-Sadat's economic *infitah* towards the west.[92] 'The domestic politics of Egypt', *Tariq al-Sha'b* argued, 'is witnessing an increased change towards the right. And so in the domestic politics it is adopting measures in order to enable the bourgeoisie to return to an important position within the national economy and the state administration and to strengthen the private sector at the expense of the public sector.'[93] This tied in well with the communist theory of 'non-capitalist' development as it allowed the ICP to make what would seem like an ideological volte-

[90] The share of the 'socialist camp' in Iraqi imports shrunk from 21 per cent in 1973 to a mere 13 per cent in 1974, Shemesh, *Soviet-Iraqi Relations*, pp. 111–113.

[91] Mohammed, 'Liberation Process', p. 7.

[92] Upon his death, the ICP called Nasir 'the distinguished leader of the Egyptian people's struggle'—an indication of the ideological length the party had travelled since Qasim's days, 'Ta'azi al-Hizb al-Shuyu'i al-'Iraqi bi Wafat al-Ra'is 'Abd al-Nasir', *Tariq al-Sha'b* 27, no. 9, Oct. 1970.

[93] 'al-'Ummal fi Misr Yudafi'un 'an Makasibihum', *Tariq al-Sha'b*, no. 140, 4 Mar. 1974; see also similar articles: 'al-Nizam al-Misri… ila Ayn?', *Tariq al-Sha'b*, no. 157, 25 Mar. 1974; and 'Burjuwaziyyat Misr fi Khidmat al-Ihtikarat', *Tariq al-Sha'b*, no. 172, 12 Apr. 1974.

face, but which to the communists was a logical function of the 'non-capitalist' path having been turned into a 'capitalist' one, despite the fact that they had indefatigably been dinning into the idea of Egypt passing through 'socialist transition' for the past decade or so. As the alliance with the Ba'th broke down, and Saddam increasingly began to assert an independent regional Iraqi foreign policy and an incipient *infitah* of his own, the same kind of reasoning was applied by the communists to explain these developments in Iraq, despite the previous communist alliance with the Ba'th in 'constructing socialism'.

The Kurdish Question: From National Liberation to Obstacle to Progress

The decade following the Ba'thi takeover of power in 1968 witnessed dramatic developments in the Kurdish areas of Iraq as well as in the country as a whole. These events reverberated in the ICP's ideological understanding of the Kurdish question. Prior to the formation of the national front in 1973, the party assumed a cautiously positive position towards Mulla Mustafa Barzani and the KDP. Yet, ideologically the Kurdish issue was undoubtedly still ambiguous to the communists by virtue of its *qawmi* nature. The problem was partly circumvented by construing Kurdish *qawmiyyah* as 'anti-imperialist' and Arab-Kurdish unity as one of Arab and Kurdish workers.

Nevertheless, following the 1973 formation of the front between the ICP and the Ba'th, relations between the communists and the Kurdish nationalists deteriorated rapidly. In contradistinction to the circumstances of the 1960s when the ICP had found itself in a subordinated position vis-à-vis Barzani, however, the communists were now in a stronger position due to their alliance with the ruling Ba'th Party. Ideologically, the party thus toughened its position on the KDP and Barzani, making a distinction between the 'just nationalism' of the Kurds in general and that of the KDP. The 1974 Autonomy Law marked the final breakdown of relations between the KDP and the ICP. Because the front to the communists was the ideological solution to all problems facing Iraq, including the Kurdish issue, the KDP were derided as imperialist stooges for not joining it. Accordingly, the stress on the KDP leadership's 'feudalist' aspects was now re-actualised in ICP analyses. This way, the communist leadership ideologically justified supporting the Ba'thi regime's fierce suppression of the Kurdish rebellion of 1974–75 and its 'progressive' measures implemented in Iraqi Kurdistan.

Initially, however, the relatively benign relations that had existed between the ICP and Mulla Mustafa's KDP since the 1958 revolution continued after the 1968 Ba'thi coup and until the establishment of the National Front in 1973. During the period of Ba'thi repression of the ICP and the KDP, the communists raised the general slogan of 'democracy for Iraq and autonomy for Kurdistan'. In a seminal article entitled 'What does Autonomy Mean for Iraqi Kurdistan?', published in *Tariq al-Sha'b* in February 1969, the party treated its position on the Kurdish problem at length. Just as before, it maintained that the right to self-determination was an 'indisputable principle' of all peoples, which in 'a multi-ethnic society' comprised 'the right to autonomy within a unified state or a federal union of two unionist states'. But what was more interesting was the notion that, at least theoretically, all peoples also had the right to 'separation and the creation of an independent state'. The article made haste to add, though, that the self-determination right would 'not necessarily require separation', but that its provisioning would bring peoples together. A people would usually not exercise its right to separation, the article explained, unless under 'unbearable oppression in which peaceful co-existence with the majority ethnicity is impossible' and unless there were no 'conditions for economic and political development'.[94] Of course, in reality the ICP never advocated this solution and in fact did everything in its power to contravene it.

To the ICP the Kurdish question, as indeed any national question, was especially awkward. The difficulty was epitomised by the old notions of *qawmiyyah* and *wataniyyah*. As we have seen, during the late 1950s and throughout the 1960s, the Communist Party, in keeping with the language of Arab nationalism, employed the term *al-Watan al-'Arabi* to denote the 'Arab homeland', that is, an undefined imagined area which 'Arabs' once controlled and to which they had a historical claim. Similarly, the party used the term *al-Watan al-Kurdi* to designate an equally indefinable entity for which 'the Kurds' had a right to strive.[95] To complicate matters further, Iraq itself, although a creation of 'imperialism', was also

[94] 'Madha Ya'ni al-Hukm al-Dhati li Kurdistan al-'Iraq?', *Tariq al-Sha'b* 26, no. 2 (mid-Feb. 1969).

[95] See Chapters 3 and 4.

a *watan* in the minds of the communists. The propagation of an Iraqi *watan* was clearly inclusivist in intention, designed to bring the Kurdish nationalist movement under the umbrella of 'Iraqi' anti-imperialist struggle by focusing on the *watani* aspect of Kurdish nationalism rather than its more onerous *qawmi* essence. This policy was equalled by the Ba'thi regime in its dealings with the Kurdish nationalists until the outbreak of the 1975 Kurdish revolt, following which such considerations were dropped in favour of an 'Arab' notion of a common Shi'i-Sunni Iraqi *watan*.[96] However, while the ICP usually referred to Arab nationalists, especially of the Iraqist inclination, as *wataniyyun*, Kurdish nationalists, for the most part represented by the KDP, were exclusively termed *qawmiyyun* although never publicly advocating separation from the Iraqi *watan*.

In an article published in 1978 in the party's cultural organ, *al-Fikr al-Jadid*, former First Secretary Karim Ahmad al-Daud, who himself was a Kurd, explicated the ICP's position on the complicated 'national question':

> Our Party has always distinguished between the notion of right to self-determination for a people succumbing under the yoke of imperialism on the one hand and a nationality [*qawmiyyah*] living within the framework of a state comprising more than one ethnicity in the colonised or dependent countries or that have gained its independence and liberated itself from the yoke of imperialism on the other hand.[97]

The peoples of the first category, Ahmad argued, would have the right 'to wrest their complete independence and set up an independent *watani* state', whereas the peoples in 'a multi-ethnic state' would have to follow the route of 'a voluntary union between the nationalities' to be 'set up on complete equality'.[98] In other words, once a *watan* had been established, the right to fight a separatist struggle more or less ceased. Of course, in the rather one-dimensional worldview of the communists, mostly consist-

[96] Amatzia Baram, 'A Case of Imported Identity: The Modernizing Secular Ruling Elites of Iraq and the Concept of Mesopotamian-Inspired Territorial Nationalism, 1922–1992', *Poetics Today* 15, no. 2, 1994, p. 304.

[97] Karim Ahmad, 'al-Qadiyyah al-Qawmiyyah al-Kurdiyyah: Juz' min Qadiyyat Sha'bina al-'Iraqi fi l-Taharrur wa l-Taqaddum al-Ijtima'i wa l-Dimuqratiyyah', *al-Fikr al-Jadid*, no. 297, 24 Jun. 1978.

[98] Ibid.

ing of a clear-cut dichotomy between 'imperialism' and 'oppressed nations', there was no provision for the eventuality of a 'nation' oppressed by imperialism (in this case the Iraqi Arabs led by the Ba'th Party) in turn oppressing another 'nation' (the Iraqi Kurds).

To the communists, *qawmi* nationalism—whether Arab or Kurdish—was intrinsically fallacious, but having continuously instilled it with a positive connotation in the form of 'anti-imperialism', they eventually found themselves in the quagmire of philosophical sophistry. While to most outside observers Kurdish *qawmi* nationalism would have seemed detrimental to the interests of the Iraqi *watan*, al-Daud argued that the Kurds' fight for *qawmi* rights in fact 'forms one of the fundamental struggling forces in our Iraqi people's *watani* liberation struggle as a whole' and that it was 'a natural ally [*halif tabi'i*]' of the Iraqi working class.[99] This kind of reasoning is testimony to the difficult ideational position the Iraqi communists had put themselves in, because if, as al-Daud argued, there was an Iraqi *watan*, would not the Kurds already form part of it by nature of its definition as 'Iraqi' rather than 'Arab'?

The national issue was thus a complicated matter, to say the least. Accordingly, the communists would argue on the one hand that the 'recognition of autonomy for the Kurdistan region on an ethnic basis is the only way to solve the Kurdish question democratically far from the dangers of bourgeois chauvinist views'. However, at the same time, they also argued the complete opposite, claiming that they were 'against the separation of the working class of the two peoples'. Instead, the ICP maintained that because the interests of Kurdish and Arab workers were 'approximately the same' especially when it came to 'the joint struggle for the sake of *qawmi* liberation, democracy and social progress', the Kurdish workers would adopt 'the voluntary union with their Arab brothers within a single state'.[100] Thus, although the very notion of ethnic 'nationalism' (*qawmiyyah*) to the communists was a 'bourgeois' idea promoting the bourgeoisie's desire for a separate socio-economic entity in which it could maximise its profits and exploit its 'own' workers and peasants, they contradictory claimed it was also in the interest of the Kurdish and Arab *workers* to struggle for *qawmi* liberation.

This idea of a 'voluntary union' of Kurdish and Arab workers coupled with the ICP's relatively benign relations with Mulla Mustafa Barzani,

[99] Ibid.
[100] 'Hukm al-Dhati'.

the KDP leader, meant that during the period from the Ba'thi takeover of power in 1968 until the communists themselves became allies of the Ba'th Party in 1973, they usually tried to mitigate the situation whenever contradictions between KDP and the Ba'th flared up. 'Our Iraqi Communist Party is firmly convinced that there are wide possibilities', the ICP leadership thus argued in October 1969,

> if the two sides, especially the government, show a real understanding of the conditions that our country and the Arab nation face. If they do not understand, then the scheming imperialist, Zionist and reactionary plans deepen not only against our *watani* independence and the Arab liberation movement, but also against the *qawmi* democratic movement of the Kurdish people itself...[101]

Even during times of strife, the party went to great lengths to mend fences with the Ba'th and the KDP. Thus, when the Ba'th Party reached its historical 11 March 1970 agreement on Kurdish autonomy with KDP, the ICP leaders claimed credit for it, arguing that it had been 'brought about by urging the government continuously and patiently by us.'[102]

When during 1971–73 the ICP moved closer to the Ba'th and eventually entered an alliance with it, this led to a sharp deterioration in its relations with the KDP. Though the communists did their best to persuade the Kurds to enter the national front, through the dispatching of high-ranking ICP delegations to deliberate with Mulla Mustafa at his headquarters in the north, the KDP would have none of it. Mulla Mustafa's position was clear: he would only enter a front between the KDP and the Ba'th—the forces that in his opinion represented the two main ethnicities.[103]

In June 1973 (before the establishment of the Front), the antagonism between the KDP and the ICP descended into armed confrontation. The

101 'Ta'azzum al-Wad' fi Kurdistan Yastalzam Nuhud Jami' al-Ahzab wa l-Quwa al-Wataniyyah wa l-Dimuqratiyyah bi Mas'uliyyatiha li Iqaf al-Qital Fawran wa Tahqiq al-Hall al-Salmi al-Dimuqrati li l-Mas'alah al-Kurdiyyah', *Tariq al-Sha'b* 26, no. 7, Oct. 1969.

102 *Report Second Congress*, p. 20; See also the ICP's expression of general support for the agreement: 'Hizbuna al-Shuyu'i al-'Iraqi Yad'am Ittifaq 11 Adhar 1970' and 'Ila Ra'is al-Hizb al-Dimuqrati al-Kurdistani wa Qa'id al-Harakah al-Qawmiyyah al-Kurdiyyah Mustafa al-Barzani al-Muhtaram', *Tariq al-Sha'b* 27, no. 3, Mar. 1970.

103 al-Kharsan, *Safahat min Ta'rikh*, p. 147.

military conflict, which was initiated by the KDP, further escalated throughout the autumn and winter of 1973–1974. Armed attacks by KDP *Peshmergahs* on ICP fighters and kidnappings, such as the 'disappearance' of ten communists in Zakho in August, became commonplace.[104] Throughout this period, a fierce propaganda war was fought on the leading pages of the ICP's *Tariq al-Sha'b* and the KDP's *al-Ta'akhi*. On 3 October, the ICP leadership tried to convince the KDP about its Leninist understanding of the national question, which, it argued, could only be solved 'in the current of revolutionary struggle against imperialism'. Throughout the newly independent countries of Asia and Africa with 'multiple nationalities' and 'tribes', it asserted, 'neo-colonialism is working towards inciting national and tribal strife with a view to weaken the positions of the anti-imperialist forces'.[105] Although earlier arguing that the 'national question' could be solved theoretically through separation if the minority ethnicity was suffering oppression, the ICP leadership now averred that separatism would objectively only serve the interests of imperialism.

Thus, instead of fighting back when clashes further intensified in November 1973 (which might have been detrimental anyway considering the ICP's inferior armed forces in Iraqi Kurdistan), the party leadership implored the 'brothers' in the KDP leadership 'in the interest of the Kurdish people and the Iraqi people in its entirety' to 'desist' from the 'dangerous road' and 'to be alert to the machinations and conspiracies of the imperialist, reactionary and Zionist circles'.[106] Meanwhile, the KDP leadership denied that it had launched a persecution campaign against the ICP and claimed that the communists had started it. At this point, the Soviets, who otherwise tried to steer away from direct interference in internal Iraqi political problems as they sought friendly relations with all three major parties, saw fit to intervene. On 14 November, a Kurdish delegation to the Soviet Union that included senior KDP-leader Saleh Yusufi was received by Boris Ponomarev, the chief of the International Department of the CPSU Central Committee. Four days later, *al-Ta'akhi* announced it would unilaterally cease its propaganda campaign, and on

[104] Ibid.

[105] 'Hawla l-Hall al-Ishtiraki li l-Mas'alah al-Qawmiyyah', *Tariq al-Sha'b*, no. 16, 3 Oct. 1973.

[106] 'Nahj Khatar. Nadu' ila al-Kaff 'anhu', *Tariq al-Sha'b*, no. 48, 12 Nov. 1973.

19–20 November, ICP and KDP representatives held talks that brought about an end to the hostilities for the time being.[107]

But new tensions soon flared up again. During the winter of 1973–1974 armed clashes between the two parties erupted once more. This time, the ICP leadership went 'back to basics' in order to fully spell out its position on the KDP and leave no room for misinterpretation or misconstruing by the KDP leaders. 'Our Iraqi Communist Party considered the founding of the Kurdistan Democratic Party at the end of the Second World War an objectively positive phenomenon', it explained in an article in *Tariq al-Sha'b* in January 1974,

> which the concrete historical and national circumstances in the Kurdish society and the development and growth of the social classes with their own distinct interests in this society had dictated. On the basis of this scientific view our Iraqi Communist Party defined its position on the occurrence of the KDP in the arena of the national political movement in Kurdistan, with regard to the fact that it was a patriotic [*watani*] and bourgeois nationalist [*qawmi*] party opposed to colonialism, reaction and national oppression. And starting from this position our Party found that there were important convergence points and common political goals between it and the Kurdistan Democratic Party. And in the light of that, it sketched the policy of cooperation and front alliance with it.[108]

Whereas during the period of the 'Arefs in the 1960s, the ICP had yielded to Mulla Mustafa's omnipotent position within the KDP and throughout Iraqi Kurdistan in general, now by virtue of its newly established alliance with the Ba'th Party it could allow itself to assume a much harder line towards Barzani. The changing attitude was no doubt also sped up by Mulla Mustafa's own ill-advised 'foreign policy' statements, such as when he in June 1973, weeks before the establishment of the National Front, declared that should he receive 'sufficient support' from the US he would 'be able to control the Kirkuk oilfields and confer exploitation rights on an American company'[109]—a statement that undoubtedly rendered him enemies in most parts of Iraq.

[107] Shemesh, *Soviet-Iraqi Relations*, pp. 117–118.

[108] 'Min Jadid Hawl Dawafi' wa Marami Hamlat al-Fi'at al-Yaminiyyah fi al-Hizb al-Dimuqrati al-Kurdistani 'ala al-Shuyu'iyyin wa Sa'ir al-Taqaddumiyyin fi Kurdistan: Mawqifuna min al-Hizb al-Dimuqrati al-Kurdistani', Part 3, *Tariq al-Sha'b*, no. 104, 18 Jan. 1974.

[109] As quoted in McDowall, *History of the Kurds*, p. 333.

In the communist view, Kurdish infighting and ideological disagreements was a logical consequence of the eclectic mix of people that had rallied around Barzani. Following its own rather narrow class-based analysis, these ideological frictions were explained as 'aspects of the class struggle' that was ongoing in Kurdish society, which, it was said, 'flares up whenever the country is on the road to more profound progress'.[110] Thus to the communists, the KDP's reluctance to join the National Front was a display of its 'fear of progress', which was a natural result of its 'bourgeois' class position. To further underline this point, the ICP insisted the Kurdish national movement as a whole did not equate the KDP, and that the party distinguished between its 'principled position' on the Kurdish people with its 'just nationalism' (*al-qawmiyyah al-'adilah*) and the KDP 'which has its own special solutions and its own defined role in the arena of the Kurdish issue, all in accordance with its ideological departure points and the class interests that it gives expression to.'[111] While such a stand might have appeared somewhat unrealistic given the sheer dominance of the KDP on the Kurdish political scene, it was nevertheless a clear signal to its leadership that the ICP did not regard it as indispensable and that it indeed had its own policy on the Kurdish issue.

The KDP, for its part, charged the ICP leadership with complicity in a pronounced Ba'thi policy of 'Arabisation' in Iraqi Kurdistan.[112] The accusation hit a nerve, as this phenomenon was much harder to explain with the usual rhetoric about Ba'thi 'progressiveness'. 'There is no doubt', *Tariq al-Sha'b* thus wrote, 'that in a state of multiple nationalities the attempt to change the national character of the regions in which the national minorities or the oppressed nationalities live, creates a glaring and distasteful phenomenon of the politics of national oppression which the bourgeoisie of the big nationalities pursues against the other nationalities.'[113] The party took pains, however, to point out that this matter was nothing new, but had in fact been going on 'since the days of the destroyed monarchical-

[110] 'Min Jadid…: al-Yamin La Yamthul al-Wajh al-Mushrifah li l-Harakah al-Taharruriyyah al-Kurdiyyah', Part 2, *Tariq al-Sha'b*, no. 103, 17 Jan. 1974.

[111] 'Min Jadid', Part 3.

[112] These allegations were expressed in a KDP memo, quoted by *Tariq al-Sha'b*, no. 109, 24 Jan. 1974.

[113] 'Min Jadid…: Mawqif Hizbina al-Shuyu'i min Mas'alat Taghyir al-Tarkib al-Qawmi fi Kurdistan', Part 7, *Tariq al-Sha'b*, no. 109, 24 Jan. 1974.

feudal age' and was part of 'the politics of national-historic repression' of Iraqi Kurdistan which aimed at 'erasing the national traits of the Kurdish people or narrowing the area known as Iraqi Kurdistan'. The party also pointed out that it had always had a 'clear and resolute' position against any 'Arabisation' attempts occurring in the past, but since 'at the present no Arabisation operations' were ongoing, to the ICP leadership there was no problem to discuss.[114] The KDP, for its part, insisted on this issue and brought up the forced emigration of Iraqi Fayli Kurds to Iran in mid-1971.[115] While the ICP did not deny that their now firm Ba'thist allies indeed had carried out this atrocity, it is testimony to its strange self-image when replying that since the incident occurred in 1971 it 'did not possess any means to communicate its voice' because not until later did 'relationships of positive cooperation' with the Ba'th materialise.[116]

The final chapter of the breakdown of KDP-ICP relations was written as the regime presented its plans for a new 'autonomy law' (*qanun al-hukm al-dhati*) during January-March 1974. The law, which was an offshoot of the 11 March 1970 Agreement, was backed by the ICP who cooperated with the Ba'th in its preparation. The party saw the new law as the practical implementation of the 1970 agreement and warned the KDP, who rejected its terms, that carrying out the agreement was 'a joint national responsibility that no national section can exempt itself from' and that it was connected with 'the safeguarding of the existing revolutionary system and the deepening of its content'.[117] To the ICP leadership, its alliance with the Ba'th in the National Front constituted an even better opportunity for the KDP to gain its rights in negotiation with the regime. To them, the KDP leadership's position was untenable because it had

[114] Ibid.

[115] The Fayli Kurds, a Shi'i minority in the overwhelmingly Sunni Kurdish community, had lived in Iraq since Ottoman times but had been refused Iraqi citizenship since the creation of the Iraqi state. As a vulnerable minority, they were caught up in the demographic struggle between the regime and the KDP. Arguing that they were Iranians, the Ba'thi government expelled some 50,000 of them during 1971, McDowall, *History of the Kurds*, pp. 329–330.

[116] 'Min Jadid...: Mawqif Hizbina al-Shuyu'i min Mushkilat al-Akrad al-Fayliyyin', Part 8, *Tariq al-Sha'b*, no. 111, 28 Jan. 1974.

[117] 'Min Jadid...: Bi Sadr Asbab al-Khilafat bayna Hizbina al-Shuyu'i wa l-Jinah al-Yamini fi l-Hizb al-Dimuqrati al-Kurdistani', Part 5, *Tariq al-Sha'b*, no. 106, 21 Jan. 1974.

accepted the terms four years earlier, and as Iraq now was more 'progressed', logically there was even more cause for the KDP to cooperate at this point.[118] The new Autonomy Law was finally presented on 11 March 1974—four years after the original agreement. Following its announcement, 'comrade' Saddam issued an ultimatum to the KDP granting it another five months to decide whether to join the front.[119] The ICP, for its part, claimed the new law was 'a means with which the poor of the city and the countryside can realise their demands for land, work, wages, social inclusion and a better life'.[120]

Following the inauguration of the Autonomy Law and the complete breakdown of relations with the KDP due to its continued refusal to join the front or accept the new law, ICP propaganda switched focus, now instead trying to eradicate KDP's role in the Kurdish nationalist movement. The communists argued that 'the existence of a progressive Arab nationalist party in the leadership of the regime', which had 'adopted the Kurdish question from a more progressive position than all the parties and Arab nationalist forces that have obtained power in Iraq', had created 'a new opportunity to solve the national question peacefully and democratically'. As for the KDP leadership, they were 'following the road of cooperation with imperialism, Iranian reaction and Israel'—a road that could only lead 'in the end to destruction'.[121] The reason the KDP had taken this road was once again explained in class terms. As during previous periods of antagonistic relations between the KDP and the ICP in the 1960s, the main class characteristic of the KDP leadership changed from 'bourgeois nationalist' to 'feudalist' in communist assessments. It was thus said to be made up of the 'Kurdish feudalist', who,

[118] 'Min Jadid…: Man al-ladhi Bada'a Yatakhala Fa'lan 'an Qadiyat al-Sha'b al-Kurdi wa Maslahatiha?' Part 6, *Tariq al-Sha'b*, no. 107, 22 Jan. 1974.

[119] 'al-Rafiq Saddam Husayn: Sayabqi al-Bab Maftuhan Amam Mumathili al-Hizb al-Dimuqrati al-Kurdistani li l-Indimam ila al-Jabhah al-Wataniyyah', *Tariq al-Sha'b*, no. 148, 13 Mar. 1974.

[120] 'Min Ajli Tatbiq wa Tatwir Qanun al-Hukm al-Dhati', *Tariq al-Sha'b*, no. 150, 15 Mar. 1974; see also ICP's reporting on how 'the people' received the news about the new law, especially one man who was reported as saying: 'My joy over the autonomy is the joy of every Kurdish citizen', 'al-Sha'b. 'an al-Hukm al-Dhati', *Tariq al-Sha'b*, no. 152, 18 Mar. 1974.

[121] 'al-Jinah al-Yamini fi H.D.K. Yaqud al-Harakah al-Qawmiyyah al-Kurdiyyah ila Mazaliq Khatirah', *Tariq al-Sha'b*, no. 182, 24 Apr. 1974.

dreams… that the elimination of national oppression and the realisation of nationalist slogans, including autonomy, will lead to the creation of a Kurdish feudal emirate which he himself and the sons of his class will rule unrestricted, and transform the peasants, or [let them] remain as they are, slaves who build palaces for them and who produce honey and butter for them.[122]

The Kurdish *qawmi* nationalist movement in Iraq, the party argued, was still part of the *watani* movement of the Iraqi people as a whole, but because it consisted of 'different social classes and groups' who did not have 'a unified understanding' of national rights, it was 'not strange that contradictions show between them'. Nationalism, the communists explained, could be used either to further 'progressive' interests or as 'a tool that sanctifies the control of the big capitalists and the big landowners'.[123]

Despite the draconian measures used by the Ba'thi regime to suppress the Kurdish rebellion and 'Arabise' Iraqi Kurdistan, the ICP leadership invariably put the blame for the Kurdish nationalist movement's perishment on the 'rightwing' KDP leadership. Although in reality little had changed in its composition since the days of close ICP-KDP cooperation, ICP First Secretary 'Aziz Muhammad argued that the 'right wing of the Kurdish movement' was 'hostile to the progressive political line of the national authority, resist social changes, especially the agrarian reform, and are openly anti-communist'.[124] At its Third National Congress in 1976, when the Kurdish rebellion had been crushed, the ICP outlined the reasons for its break-up with the KDP. The party maintained that the 'rightwing' KDP leadership had disregarded the 'social content' of its Kurdish national movement and insisted on 'the narrow national course' emanating from 'selfish class interests' and 'backward tribal behaviour'. This, it argued, could be seen in the period from 1970 to 1975 when, as a result of the 1970 Agreement, the KDP exercised limited autonomy in certain areas of the northern region. That autonomy had provided 'the opportunity for the reactionary rightist elements to assume the leading posts' in the KDP, it had led them to 'opposing communism' and to

122 'Waqfah Mas'ulah ma'a al-Jinah al-Yamini fi Qiyadat al-Harakah al-Qawmiyyah al-Kurdiyyah: Hawla Tabi'at al-Sira' wa Dawafi'uhu bayna Atraf al-Harakah al-Qawmiyyah al-Kurdiyyah', Part 2, *Tariq al-Sha'b*, no. 186, 29 Apr. 1974.

123 'Li Madha Yata'awan al-Yaminiyyun fi l-Harakah al-Qawmiyyah al-Kurdiyyah ma'a A'da' al-Sha'b al-Kurdi wa Harakatihi al-Taharruriyyah?', *Tariq al-Sha'b*, no. 191, 6 May 1974.

124 Mohammed, 'Socialist Community', p. 17.

adopt 'bourgeois and liberal points of view' in the socio-economic field, to drift away from the Soviets and move closer to 'the reactionary forces at home and in the region and to the imperialist and Zionist forces'; it had also led them to reject agrarian reform and to ally with the *aghas*, but most important, in the minds of the communists, was the KDP's rejection of the national front.[125] Accordingly, the main achievement of that front was said to have been 'the liquidation of the reactionary rightist rebellion'.[126]

The same line was essentially kept until the end of Ba'thi-ICP relations in 1979, despite the cracks appearing in the veneer of that cooperation. Thus, 'Adel Haba, alternate member of the ICP Politburo, would argue in 1977 that the Kurdish rebellion, due to it having been taken over by 'reactionary feudal elements' was essentially 'an armed uprising against the autonomy of Iraqi Kurdistan'. Following previous class-based analysis, Haba maintained that the rebellion occurred because the KDP leadership 'refused to have autonomy under a progressive regime'.[127] Astonishingly, he also claimed that the Autonomy Law, which was implemented with the ICP's assistance, 'helped to put an end to the bloodshed and opened up fresh vistas for the working people of Iraqi Kurdistan'.[128] Similarly, Karim Ahmad al-Daud argued that it was only 'natural' that the party 'took a stand against an armed revolt propped up by imperialism and reaction',[129] which, incidentally, was precisely how the ICP had described the Ba'thi coup in 1963.

In the end, it was the ICP's ideological understanding of the Iraqi political situation in the 1970s that prompted it to join forces with the Ba'th Party against its erstwhile ally, the KDP. Its socio-economic composition and role on the Iraqi political scene had changed little since Mulla Mustafa Barzani's ascendency to the top position in 1964. Ideologically, the KDP under his leadership, not very dissimilar from the Ba'th Party, had been guided by relentless pragmatism with the ultimate goal of extending its influence and position within the Iraqi polity. Barzani's flirtations with the 'mortal enemies' of the Iraqi Republic, such as

125 *Report 3rd Congress*, pp. 65–66.

126 Ibid., p. 55.

127 Adel Haba and Sarada Mitra, 'We Saw the Brotherhood of Nations', *World Marxist Review* 20, no. 6, Jun. 1977, p. 21.

128 Ibid., p. 16.

129 Ahmad, 'Qadiyyah al-Qawmiyyah'.

his pronounced willingness in 1973 to cede oil concessions to the Americans in exchange for military support, while obviously a thorn in the side to both the Ba'th Party and the ICP, was nothing new. Already in 1966, when the ICP had characterised him as a 'patriotic and national leader',[130] he was receiving substantial support from both Iran and Israel.[131] But while the ICP at that point had been in the political wilderness, it could now allow itself to sharpen the 'class struggle' against the KDP's and Mulla Mustafa's 'reactionary' aspects. The ideological accommodation of the Ba'th Party, and, in particular, the reification of the National Front, were thus the decisive factors in shaping the ICP's shifting policy vis-à-vis the KDP and Barzani. On the ground, this policy travelled great lengths from almost unquestioning support of the KDP in the mid-1960s to outright condemnation and active participation in its suppression a decade later. On the ideological level, however, it had only needed a minor shift from contemplating the KDP leadership as 'feudal-tribal' leading a just 'national cause' to seeing it as a 'rightist reactionary' leadership promoting 'chauvinist', 'narrow-minded' and 'egotistical' class interests.

Interestingly, a similar U-turn on nationalism occurred in the social sciences following the end of the Cold War. Whereas at the height of the 'progressivist' domination during the 1970s political scientists tended to view nationalism through the prism of 'cultural autonomy', 'freedom' and 'sovereignty', in the 1990s it was usually regarded as an expression of 'chauvinism' and 'expansionism'.[132] However, with the increasing political fortunes of the Kurdish nationalist movement following the 2003 Anglo-American invasion of Iraq, this negative conceptualisation seems once again to have swung back to the understanding of the 1970s.

Zionism, the October War and the Palestine Question

Since the early days of the ICP, the communists had been concerned with the issue of Zionist nationalism and its impact on the region. In the

[130] See ch. 4.

[131] McDowall, *History of the Kurds*, p. 320.

[132] See Michael Barnett, 'Sovereignty, nationalism, and regional order in the Arab states system', in *State sovereignty as social construct*, Thomas J. Biersteker and Cynthia Weber (eds), Cambridge: Cambridge University Press, 1996.

1940s, their large-scale mass organisation the League Against Zionism attracted many Jews to the party. After the Soviet Union's complicity in the creation of the Israeli state in 1947–48, however, the issue somehow dwindled in importance. But with the disastrous outcome of the Six-Day War of 1967 and the prospect of a powerful Israeli state propped up by US 'imperialism' on their doorstep, the issue once again moved to the fore.

In ideological terms, Zionism had initially seemed unambiguous to the international communist movement. As the Zionist movement gathered pace in the 1920s and 1930s, it was unceremoniously condemned as the 'colonialist project' of the 'Jewish bourgeoisie'. Increasingly, however, Jewish Labour Zionists on the ground were able to transform the idea of the *Yishuv* (the Jewish community in Palestine) from one of 'oppressor' to that of 'oppressed', and by the end of World War II they had managed to gather enough international support for the idea of a Labour Zionist state as a 'progressive' force in the Middle East to secure Soviet endorsement.[133] Although the international communist movement, including the Iraqi communists, collectively made a corresponding ideological volte-face to accommodate the new Soviet foreign policy, this was a short phase, and with the deterioration of Soviet-Israeli relations in the 1950s the ideological pendulum soon swung back again.

In a sense there was little new in the Iraqi communists' view on Zionism; following the 1967 war, they still argued that Zionism was 'an expression of a reactionary ideology belonging to the Jewish bourgeoisie'.[134] In their minds, Zionism was of the same make as Nazism because both were fundamentally bent on destroying communism. 'It is natural', *Tariq al-Sha'b* thus wrote, 'that the racist Zionists are of the opinion, just as was the case with the fascist Nazis in their time, that the existence of the Soviet Union in itself is a danger to their [own] existence.' But both the Nazis and the Zionists were in essence tools of imperialism without much agency of their own. 'Of course', the same article thus argued,

> also before the Second World War the Zionist agents were utilised for the sake of destroying the world Communist movement. But during the first decades

[133] See Johan Franzén, 'Communism versus Zionism: The Comintern, Yishuvism, and the Palestine Communist Party', *Journal of Palestine Studies* 36, no. 2, 2007.

[134] 'al-Sahyuniyyah wa l-Ihtikarat: Sani'u al-Mawt Yad'amun Isra'il', *Tariq al-Sha'b*, no. 149, 14 Mar. 1974.

of the twentieth century, imperialism was relying in a fundamental manner on fascism in the fight against the socialist state. Zionism, which indeed did not have a state apparatus and did not represent the power of an influential organisation, if anything, then stood out as a reserve with which to counteract Communism.[135]

Following the Six-Day War, however, the Israeli role had developed and, while still not granting the Zionist movement any agency of its own, the communists argued that the 'fundamental intention of the Israeli aggression' since the 1967 war had been 'to finish off the progressive gains of the Arab liberation movement and put an end to the spreading of the revolutionary mass movement ... in order to pave the way for better circumstances for the continued outflow of Arab resources to the vaults of the imperialist states'.[136]

Given this stern and rigid understanding of Zionism and the Israeli state, it is not strange that as the Ba'thi regimes in Syria and Iraq along with the Egyptian regime became increasingly rhetorically vociferous in the wake of the Six-Day War, the Arab communists moved closer to these regimes for the sake of combating what they saw as the overriding danger. But by allowing themselves to be dragged into the Palestine issue from a thoroughly nationalist angle, the Iraqi communists simultaneously undermined their own cause when they ideologically accommodated seemingly incongruent nationalist tenets with their own purportedly internationalist outlook. The ICP thus found itself fanning primordial 'national' sentiments among the Arabs to counter the 'Israeli aggression', while simultaneously trying to put the lid on the same type of feelings among the Kurds as regards their fight against the Iraqi Ba'th. Entangled in this web of *qawmi/watani* propaganda, the ICP had before the establishment of the National Front in 1973 tried to ideologically link the Kurdish problem with the Palestinian question in order to gather all the forces of the 'Arab liberation movement' in the Arab *watani* struggle against Israel. Nevertheless, the party argued that 'the liquidation of Israeli aggression and then solution of the Palestinian question requires the mobilisation of the defensive capabilities of the Arabs, whether the

[135] 'Takhrib Sahyuni didd al-Buldan al-Ishtirakiyyah', *Tariq al-Sha'b*, no. 164, 3 Apr. 1974.

[136] 'Daf' al-Ma'rakah ila Ib'adiha al-Haqiqiyyah Yastalzam Tasfiyyat al-Masalih al-Imbiriyaliyyah', *Tariq al-Sha'b*, no. 21, 9 Oct. 1973.

solution is possible with political means or not, and whether the solution is possible through war or peace'.[137]

Given this militarist line, it was no surprise that the communists hailed the 1973 October War at its outbreak. The war, which according to the ICP broke out 'as a response to aggression', was by 'nature' a 'just national liberation war'. The war was a vindication of their endorsement of the Ba'thi regime as 'revolutionary democratic' since it proved the regime's 'progressiveness'. 'The October national war', *Tariq al-Sha'b* thus solemnly declared,

> made clear the important and fundamental role of the progressive Arab regimes and their regime armies. These regimes, despite there being in some of them worrying gaps and orientations, raced along in the fight against the aggression and the occupation, and aimed with their defiance side by side with the current national and progressive Arab forces, including the Palestinian resistance, at striking a crushing blow to the concentrated psychological war that the Arab peoples were subjected to, especially since the June aggression, with the aim of paralysing their liberational struggle, and to show that there is no other way before them than to surrender to the administration of the colonialists and the Zionists.[138]

Additionally, the 'liberational battles of October' were another opportunity to 'expose the imperialist role that American imperialism plays against the Arab liberation movement'.[139]

The war also prompted a changing view of the Iraqi army within the party. Although traditionally Marxism-Leninism teaches that the army is the tool of the ruling class, it was clear that the ICP leadership by now, in line with its newfound militarist outlook, began to perceive the armed forces as a 'people's army'. One of the most important results of the war, the ICP consequently argued, was that it had 'strengthened the belief of the soldiers and the officers in themselves and in their weaponry'.[140] This,

137 'Hall al-Mas'alah al-Kurdiyyah min Ula Mustalzimat Musahamat al-'Iraq fi Ma'rakat al-'Arab al-Taharruriyyah', *Tariq al-Sha'b* 26, no. 9, Dec. 1969.

138 'Bayan Hamm 'an Ijtima' al-Ahzab al-Shuyu'iyyah fi l-Buldan al-'Arabiyyah: La Yumkin al-Tanazzul 'an Haqq al-Sha'b al-Filastini wa la Yumkin Qabul Wasayat 'alayhi Tawtid al-Anzimah al-Taqaddumiyyah wa Iqamat wa Ta'ziz al-Jabhat al-Wataniyyah Mahmah Ta'rikhiyyah Hasimah', *Tariq al-Sha'b*, no. 57, 21 Nov. 1973.

139 'La-Tatawahhad Quwa Harakat al-Taharrur al-'Arabiyyah li Ihbat al-Mukhatatat al-Imbiriyaliyyah al-Amrikiyyah', *Tariq al-Sha'b*, no. 55, 19 Nov. 1973.

140 'Bayan Hamm'.

of course, was a line the Iraqi communists had followed for some years. Already at the party's Second Congress in 1970, it had argued for strengthening Arab armies and their patriotic education in loyalty, stressing that unless 'in the hands of a well trained human element, impregnated with a patriotic and revolutionary doctrine and a spirit of sacrifice', weapons alone could not be 'a means of victory'.[141] Thus, the outcome of the October War, although quite detrimental to the cause of 'Arab liberation' in the territorial sense, was construed as a moral victory. 'The army's joining of the side of the popular movement', *Tariq al-Sha'b* later described it, 'has been … a real and important action in the completion of the struggle for the benefit of the national movement and the victory of the will of the people'.[142]

The *problématique* of the politics of nationalism, as ever, continued to cause the ICP serious ideological challenges. As with Kurdish and Arab nationalism, the Palestinian national movement was caught in the dichotomy of *qawmiyyah* and *wataniyyah*. Although the party argued that 'the Palestinian Arab people' had taken up '*watani* resistance' against 'the Zionist aggression', which had started 'under the auspices of the British mandate as part of an imperialist plan', they hastened to add that this Palestinian *wataniyyah* had 'an organic link to the Arab liberation movement and the anti-imperialist international revolutionary movement', and so the Palestinian people's battle for liberation and self-determination was 'at the same time the battle of the Arab people against Zionism'.[143] Thus, while conceding the existence of a Palestinian 'people' struggling for its own *watan*, somehow this people was 'organically' linked to the Arabs as a whole, presumably, although unmentioned in the text, as a result of imagined ethnic and linguistic ties.

Senior ICP leader 'Adel Haba later explained how the 'national feelings of the Arabs' had been 'hurt' by the defeat in the Six-Day War, and how such sentiments had been instrumental in 'rallying' them to fight during the October/Yom Kippur War of 1973, arguing that those 'national feelings are totally legitimate and natural'.[144] Haba thus implicitly argued

141 *Report Second Congress*, p. 34.

142 'Fi 'Id al-Jaysh. al-Tadammun al-Kifahi bayna l-Jaysh wa l-Sha'b', *Tariq al-Sha'b*, no. 93, 6 Jan. 1974.

143 'Taqrir Siyasi… Mu'tamar Thani'.

144 Naim Ashhab, Mahgoub Osman and Adel Haba, 'The Arab Front in the Middle East Conflict', *World Marxist Review* 17, no. 1, Jan. 1974, p. 35.

that the Palestine question was an Arab *qawmi* problem as it evoked such 'legitimate' sentiments. This, concisely, was the communist dilemma. Given the socio-political landscape of the Middle East and the dominance of Arab nationalist thought among its population (and, arguably, among the communists themselves) propaganda that took its starting point in primordial sentiments of imagined common Arab interests were ultimately more likely to receive a willing audience than a class-based internationalist approach stressing commonality of interests among Jewish and Arab workers. But while thus complicit in stirring up primordial sentiments, the ICP simultaneously undermined its own position as it conceded important ideological ground in the battle of ideas waged against the nationalist parties.

Caught in the maelstrom of Arab nationalism, the ICP desperately tried to imbue *qawmi* nationalism with a social content, transforming it into progressive *watani* nationalism. However, by so doing, the communists unavoidably played into the hands of the *qawmiyyun*, be they 'Arab', 'Kurd' or 'Palestinian'. Thus, while doing their best to assert the *watani* aspect of the Palestinian resistance movement, they simultaneously argued for 'the just *qawmi* aspirations of the Palestinian Arab people' which included the right to self-determination on 'its' land.[145] The logically inconsequent reasoning whereby the 'Palestinians' had 'just' claims to constitute a *qawm* and had the right to self-determination seemingly contradicted the argument that their struggle was 'organically' linked with the Arabs' *watani* struggle. It did, however, provide the ideational justification for a situation essentially brought about by imperialism and the Zionist movement, and as such was a clear sign of ideological pragmatism. To complicate matters even further, at its Second National Congress in 1970 the party had argued that 'the Palestinian people' had 'legitimate' *watani* rights and that its *watani* 'liberation movement' which sought self-determination 'on the ground of' its *watan* actually took place 'within the historical course' of the Arab *qawmi* 'liberation movement'.[146] Thus, the ICP ostensibly conceded the existence of not only 'Palestinian' and 'Arab' *qawms*, but also, enigmatically, of 'Palestinian' and 'Arab' *watans*.

On balance, however, the ICP could have done little to withstand the nationalist onslaught of the times. It could have ill afforded to go against

145 'Balagh Sadir 'an Ijtima'Adhar 1971'.

146 'Taqrir Siyasi... Mu'tamar Thani'.

the Arab nationalist movement on this issue, especially as the Iraqi Ba'th Party had made the Palestinian question one of its most prominent rhetorical features. Following the 1970 takeover of Hafez al-Asad in Syria, the struggle between the Syrian and Iraqi Ba'th Parties, though improving as compared to the ill-tempered relations during the previous Salah Jadid regime, continued to be infected. Ba'thi Iraq under Saddam and al-Bakr utilised the country's geographic remoteness from Israel to step up its radicalism on the Palestine issue to put pressure on its regional (Syria) and domestic (ICP) rivals. The Iraqi regime thus continuously rejected negotiations with Israel, repeatedly calling for a military solution to the problem, while denouncing Syria as 'defeatist' when it agreed to cease-fire following the 1973 October/Yom Kippur War.[147] The Iraqi regime also continuously rejected UN resolutions 242 and 338.[148] To further put ideological pressure on the ICP, the Ba'thist regime also supported George Habash's radical Palestinian nationalist/Marxist-Leninist organisation, the Popular Front for the Liberation of Palestine (*al-Jabhah al-Sha'biyyah li Tahrir Filastin*).[149]

The ICP thus ideologically had its back against the wall. Yet, the ideological twists and turns of the Iraqi communists on the Palestine issue nevertheless illustrates with painstaking clarity the difficulties of pursuing pragmatic policies based on nationalist ideological foundations that are in apparent contradiction to fundamental internationalist principles.

Demise of the Front and Ideological Plasticity, 1975–79

With the crushing of the Kurdish nationalist movement and the successful nationalisation of the Iraqi oil industry, the Ba'th Party emerged as a more powerful force in the mid-1970s. Although having established a 'strategic alliance' with the Soviet Union, which had helped lure the communists into the National Front, on Saddam Husayn's initiative the Ba'thists now began moving towards a diversification of its international relations. Links with western European states, China, and, remarkably, the United States were thus established from 1975 onwards.[150]

[147] Kienle, *Ba'th v. Ba'th*, p. 54.
[148] Ibid., p. 63.
[149] Penrose and Penrose, *Iraq*, p. 368.
[150] In Sept. 1975, France started building a nuclear reactor in Iraq, 'France-Iraq

From their strengthened position, the Ba'thist leaders began asserting pressure on the ICP. Desperately trying to keep the front intact, the Iraqi communist leaders replied with concessions; from 1975 onwards, they started to dissolve their mass organisations, such as the General Union of Students, the League of Iraqi Women and the Democratic Union of Iraqi Youth. The party also withdrew its representatives on international bodies like the World Peace Council (WPC) and the Asian and African Peoples' Solidarity Organisation (AAPSO), which instead were replaced by Ba'thi representatives. Ba'thist propagandists also directly targeted low-ranking ICP members instructing them to join the Ba'th Party, and with the help of the security services they were able to penetrate communist mass organisations and spread disinformation on various levels. The Ba'thists also used the ICP's *Iqlim* organisation in Iraqi Kurdistan where, for logical reasons, the Ba'th Party previously held no influence, to gain ground and force Kurdish citizens to join the Ba'th.[151] But despite the worsening Ba'thi attitude towards political pluralism, the ICP leadership kept insisting that the alliance met the requirements of the 'national-democratic stage'. Thus, in 1976 First Secretary 'Aziz Muhammad explained that the party's 'guiding idea was a class and political alliance meeting the exigencies of the given stage of the liberation struggle, a stage at which the tasks of the national-democratic revolution must be accomplished and the prerequisites of the transition to socialism created in co-operation with the Baathists.'[152]

There were of course still tangible benefits to be had from the Front, such as when the party was able to convene its Third National Congress on 4–6 May 1976 at the party headquarters in Baghdad. Because of its legality, the ICP could amass no less than 318 delegates representing all

---

Nuclear Accord Announced', *The Times*, 9 Sept. 1975. Later, in 1977, following the visit of the French Premier, a deal delivering French fighter planes was struck. But negotiations with the French had been ongoing since the nationalisation of the Iraqi Petroleum Company (IPC) in 1972, in which the French had considerable assets. In addition, during 1977 US Under-Secretary of State, Philip Habib, also visited Iraq, the highest US official to do so since diplomatic relations had been cut in 1967, Shemesh, *Soviet-Iraqi Relations*, pp. 147–148; Penrose and Penrose, *Iraq*, pp. 434–436. See also David Styan, *France and Iraq: Oil, Arms and French Policy Making in the Middle East*, London: I. B. Tauris, 2005.

[151] al-Kharsan, *Safahat min Ta'rikh*, pp. 162–163.

[152] Mohammed, 'Tasks', p. 3.

of its organisations—a staggering amount when compared to earlier party congresses and conferences.[153] As the congress was held openly under the watchful eyes of the Ba'thi *mukhabarat*, however, it had the negative effect of essentially revealing the complete party leadership structure to the Ba'thists, which would later prove most detrimental. But despite the open nature of the congress, and its full 'democratic' representation of party members, those elected to the highest positions in the Politburo were all familiar names.[154] Furthermore, since the political report of the congress had been thoroughly studied throughout the party organisations prior to the congress and any eventual dissent had been weeded out, no real opposition was voiced at the actual congress, although some members criticised the alliance with the Ba'th. The new Politburo consisted of 'Aziz Muhammad, who was re-elected as First Secretary, Zaki Khayri, Baqer Ibrahim al-Musawi, 'Abd al-Razzaq al-Safi, 'Umar 'Ali al-Shaykh, Thabit Habib al-'Ani and Karim Ahmad al-Daud.[155]

The congress report claimed that the four years of cooperation with the Ba'th Party had rendered 'a positive outcome not only for our Party, but also for the entire joint action and the revolutionary experiment waged by our country.'[156] To repudiate further the possibility of cancelling the alliance, the report explained it as 'a new experience' due to it being not 'an opposition Front' but 'a Front of construction'. As such, it had adopted 'a revolutionary programme which basically covers the aims of the stage of the national democratic revolution, and has a strategical perspective to carry on the alliance until the building of socialism.'[157] Thus, unlike the previous 'Aref period when the party leadership had been prepared ideologically to accommodate the regime as 'progressive' but had been forced into opposition by the party base due to the 'undemocratic nature' of those regimes, that caveat had now been removed with the establishment of the front. Thence, to the communists, the Ba'thists were the materialisation of their 'revolutionary democrats' and the National Front the instrument with which to attain socialism. Thus, in the name of the

[153] al-Kharsan, *Safahat min Ta'rikh*, p. 149

[154] Interviews with attendees of the congress carried out by Ismael have also confirmed that elections to the leadership were a mere formality, Ismael, *Rise and Fall*, pp. 180–181.

[155] al-Kharsan, *Safahat min Ta'rikh*, pp. 149–151.

[156] *Report 3rd Congress*, p. 54.

[157] Ibid., pp. 55–56.

higher good, they were prepared to endure whatever the Ba'thists threw at them for the sake of 'building socialism'. In fact, such was the glorification of the front that 'Aziz Muhammad argued, 'our liberation movement owed all its gains to the existence, in one form or another, of a bloc of national forces' and that the emergence of the front in 1973 had been 'a result of the deepening revolutionary process in Iraq'.[158] In that sense, the alliance was a clear case of the Communist Party forcing theory on practice, rather than abstracting theory from reality.[159]

The front theory, which might have corresponded fairly well to the conditions of the 1940s and 1950s when an all-embracing front could be achieved on the basis of anti-imperialism, was now hampering the development of the party's own political function. Having ideologically disclaimed any role for themselves, the communists could therefore do little but keep clinging to the front as, in their view, its turning into 'an active political force' was 'a vital necessity and indispensable condition for Iraq's advance to socialism'.[160] Therefore, although it appeared as if the Ba'thists had a strategy to liquidate the ICP—at least ideologically—with Saddam Husayn declaring in February 1976 that the regime's intention was 'to make all Iraqis in this country Ba'thists in membership and in belief or in the latter only',[161] the ICP persisted in maintaining that 'great achievements' containing 'progressive and deep democratic content' had been materialised in their alliance with the Ba'th.[162]

The close alliance with the Ba'th Party and the communist belief that this relationship was leading Iraq towards socialism made the ICP leadership regard the Ba'thists as 'class allies', which, as we have seen, had led

[158] Mohammed, 'Tasks', p. 3.

[159] That this was the case was inadvertently acknowledged by senior ICP leader Rahim 'Ajinah. In his memoirs he wrote that despite the ICP's Second National Congress in 1970 having defined the Ba'th as an 'enemy of democracy' and denouncing its tendency to monopolise power, there was still 'an internal inclination controlling us, that the Front had to remain and be victorious.', 'Ajinah, *Ikhtiyar al-Mutajaddad*, p. 129.

[160] Baqir Ibrahim, 'Essential Condition for Progress: United Action by the Patriotic Forces and International Solidarity', *World Marxist Review* 20, no. 6, Jun. 1977, p. 110.

[161] As quoted in Shemesh, *Soviet-Iraqi Relations*, p. 165.

[162] 'Tajribat al-Tahalluf al-Jabhawi wa l-Afaq al-Rahbah', interview with Dr. Mahdi al-Hafez, member of the Secretariat of the National Front, *al-Fikr al-Jadid*, no. 249, 16 Jul. 1977.

them to take the regime's side against the KDP. It was thus not strange that when an Islamist challenge against the state arose during the 1970s, the ICP once again chose the side of the Ba'th Party. In the shadow of secular politics, religiously inspired political movements had inconspicuously been working in the background since the 1958 Revolution. Foremost among these groups was Muhammad Baqir al-Sadr's Da'wah Party (*Hizb al-Da'wah*), which had been set up on a clandestine basis shortly after the revolution. From its inception, the party's main guiding thought had been anti-communism and a burning desire to counter the ever-increasing secularisation of Iraqi society. During the Qasim period it had been allowed to publish its monthly journal *al-Adwa'*.[163] The party supported the Ba'thi-'Aref crackdown on the communists following the overthrow of Qasim, and throughout the period of the 'Arefs it enjoyed relative freedom and was able to increase its membership. But, following the 1968 Ba'thi takeover its position became more perilous as the new regime cracked down on it, with a wave of arrests in 1972 and 1973.[164]

Although religion had always been a contentious issue for the ICP, with a virtual ban on its discussion in public, from the position of formal ally of the Ba'th Party the ICP leadership now felt the time had come to denounce the 'reactionary' character of religious politics. Since 1970 the Ba'thi regime had tried to prohibit the yearly commemoration of Imam Husayn, the so-called *Marad al-Ras* procession from al-Najaf to Karbala'. In February 1977, it imposed an outright ban on the procession, which sparked riots involving some 30,000 demonstrators in al-Najaf. Fearing a large-scale Shi'i uprising in the South, the Ba'thi regime enlisted the service of Ayatollah Muhammad Baqir al-Hakim, a moderate Shi'i cleric who would later form the Supreme Council for the Islamic Revolution in Iraq (SCIRI) whilst in exile in Iran. He tried to act as mediator, but negotiations with the demonstrators soon broke down. Instead, the regime dispatched a whole army brigade, complete with tanks, helicopters and fighter planes, to curb the protesters.[165] The riots, which were later remembered as *Intifadat Safar*, were thus quelled. A number of Shi'i pil-

[163] T. M. Aziz, 'The Role of Muhammad Baqir al-Sadr in Shii Political Activism in Iraq from 1958 to 1980', *International Journal of Middle East Studies* 25, no. 2, May 1993, pp. 208–209.

[164] Ibid., pp. 211–212.

[165] Ibid., pp. 213–214.

grims were killed and some 2,000 people arrested, including Muhammad Baqir al-Hakim.[166] Seven people were sentenced to death and fifteen to life imprisonment, including al-Hakim. The Ba'thi regime suspected that the Da'wah Party and Muhammad Baqir al-Sadr were behind the uprising and therefore arrested him. However, due to popular protests he was eventually released. Even so, following the Iranian Revolution in 1978–79, the regime's fear of the Islamist movement once again heightened and on 31 March 1980 the RCC issued a law making membership of the Da'wah Party punishable by death, and so on 5 April, al-Sadr and his sister, Bint al-Huda, were arrested and eventually executed.[167]

The ICP, for its part, fully supported its Ba'thi allies during the *Intifadah*. In an internal party directive, it blamed 'imperialism' and 'reactionary circles' for the 'exploitation of religious and sectarian sentiments'. The party leadership further called upon its members to liaise with the Ba'thists to undertake 'joint action' against 'the plot'. Later, the ICP Central Committee justified the violent Ba'thi suppression of the revolt, claiming the 'assumption of stern measures against the conspiratorial activity is one of the revolution's rights, and a principle that defines the duties of the revolutionary forces in the safeguarding of its achievements.'[168]

But despite rendered services, the ICP soon found itself on the receiving end of the 'revolutionary forces'. From autumn 1977 to spring 1978, Saddam instigated numerous reshuffles within the top echelons of the Ba'thi regime thus significantly consolidating power in his own hands. With the strengthening of his grip a noteworthy change in the Ba'thi attitude to the communists could be discerned. A Ba'thi campaign against the ICP in Iraqi Kurdistan eventually spread also to the central and southern parts of the country. This forced the ICP leadership to call an extended meeting on 2 March 1978. The report of the meeting, which was published in *Tariq al-Sha'b* on 4 March, alarmed the party base and raised many questions as to whether the front with the Ba'thists had any future. In May, the Ba'thists countered the report in an anti-communist

166 Farouk-Sluglett and Sluglett, *Iraq Since 1958*, p. 198. For more a more detailed account of the uprising, see Ra'ad al-Musawi, *Intifadat Safar al-Islamiyyah fi l-'Iraq*, Qom: Amir al-Mu'minin, 1983.

167 Aziz, 'Baqir al-Sadr', pp. 214–217.

168 Internal Directive of the Politburo of the ICP, 8 Feb. 1977, as quoted in al-Kharsan, *Safahat min Ta'rikh*, pp. 159–160.

article appearing in the journal *al-Rasid*.[169] Later the same month, twenty-one communists were executed for allegedly having formed cells in the army.[170] In November, a further thirty-one army officers accused of being part of a communist conspiracy were arrested and executed.[171] Meanwhile, the regime was 'deviating' from the communist position on major international issues. As a later ICP assessment makes clear, within the party there was much resentment of how the Ba'th had 'ruined the unity of the PLO', opposed the Ethiopian and Afghan 'revolutions', supported Somalia against Ethiopia and finally because it was against the Islamic revolution in Iran and supported the Shah's regime until the end.[172]

Although the party at this point slowly began to implement some organisational safeguarding measures, whole party organisations were nabbed by Ba'thi security forces—a legacy of the trust awarded the Ba'thists and the party's abandonment of clandestinity. At the Central Committee meeting in June 1978, the leadership raised the slogan of 'Stop the Decline' (*Waqf al-Tadahwur*), and at the end of the month it instructed party members to step up party security a further notch, but to little avail. In November, the National Front's Higher Committee held its last meeting, and in January 1979, the last ever meeting between the Ba'thi and ICP leaderships was held, following which all official ties were cut and repression began in earnest.[173]

Despite the renewed Ba'thi terror and the increasingly independent course taken by the regime, the ICP leadership religiously stuck to the front to the bitter end. In December 1978, at the height of Ba'thi persecution, ICP Politburo member 'Abd al-Razzaq al-Safi wrote that the front was 'an instrument for building a progressive social system in Iraq' and that the communists therefore sought 'to make it play an even greater part in the country's political and social life, to become the foundation for revolutionary-patriotic rule.' Apologetically, he went on, desperately

[169] al-Kharsan, *Safahat min Ta'rikh*, pp. 163–164; Ismael, *Rise and Fall*, p. 182.

[170] Shemesh, *Soviet-Iraqi Relations*, p. 166; 'Communists "Executed" By Iraqi Baathists', *The Times*, 1 Jun. 1978.

[171] Ismael, *Rise and Fall*, p. 183.

[172] 'Taqyim Tajribat Hizbina', p. 53.

[173] Al-Kharsan, *Safahat min Ta'rikh*, pp. 165–167. 'Ajinah claims there were Ba'thi attempts in Feb. 1979 to renegotiate the terms of the front, which were rejected by the ICP, 'Ajinah, *Ikhtiyar al-Mutajaddad*, p. 137.

trying to rescue any communist role within the front by arguing that it was the 'deep conviction' of the Iraqi communists that 'positive, constructive criticism is a necessity, for it is an organic part of the revolutionary-democratic process as a whole'.[174] The party's intellectual collapse was thus plain to see, and so as to corroborate the notion of the power of ideological conviction or, some would say, self-deception, al-Safi pledged that the ICP would 'deepen' the alliance 'by means of which it is possible ... so that it becomes one of the instruments for building socialism in Iraq.'[175]

During spring 1979, the all-out crackdown on the ICP began. Although the campaign targeted ordinary members as well as leaders, most of the Politburo and Central Committee members managed to escape. But despite the ordering of an 'Organised Conscious Withdrawal', thousands of rank-and-file ICP members were arrested by the Ba'thi *mukhabarat* and were forced to inform on others, leave the party, and sometimes join Ba'thist organisations.[176] Yet, although the ICP-Ba'thi alliance was dead and buried, in March 1979 senior ICP leader Dr. Nazihah al-Dulaymi still insisted that the ICP was a member of the front and amazingly cautioned the Ba'thists that their actions were 'imperilling the gains of the revolutionary movement in Iraq and may play into the hands of the reactionaries.'[177]

Eventually, matters were brought to an end when on 16 July 1979 Saddam Husayn, following the resignation of Ahmad Hasan al-Bakr, took over as President of Iraq, Ba'th Party Secretary-General, RCC Chairman, head of the executive and Commander-in-Chief of the armed forces thus effectively concentrating all powers in his own hands to a degree no other Iraqi leader had been able to do. At the end of July, he purged the higher echelons of the regime and emerged as the autocrat of Iraq.[178] With Saddam's assumption of power the last vestiges of 'ideological politics' died, a process that had been continuously ongoing throughout his

[174] Abdul Razzak al-Safi, 'Responsibility to History: The Mass Media and the Struggle for Democratic and Revolutionary Transformations, for Socialism', *World Marxist Review* 21, no. 12, Dec. 1978, p. 91.

[175] Ibid.

[176] al-Kharsan, *Safahat min Ta'rikh*, pp. 167–168.

[177] Naziha Duleimi, 'Stop the Repressions and Persecution', *World Marxist Review* 22, no. 3, Mar. 1979, p. 86.

[178] Efraim Karsh and Inari Rautsi, *Saddam Hussein: A Political Biography*, New York: Grove Press, 1991, p. 110; Shemesh, *Soviet-Iraqi Relations*, p. 149.

Fig. 11. Life in exile. CC-member Saleh Mahdi Duglah in Beirut in 1979, following the end of the alliance with Ba'th Party.

ascendancy to supremacy. Remarkably, even when faced with this reality the communist leaders, who gathered the shattered Central Committee the same month, avoided advocating the regime's overthrowing, instead merely raising the slogan of 'End the Dictatorial Rule'—an indication that ideologically they were still convinced the regime could be brought back on track.

Years later, at the party's Fourth Congress in 1985, the ICP would adopt a different view of the period. While not abandoning their ideas about 'revolutionary democrats', the communists focused on the socio-economic changes that had occurred in Iraq from 1974–75. The 'new economic path' on the international level and the economic *infitah* ('opening up') to the capitalist world, they argued, had caused the transformation of the leading Ba'thi circles from 'petty bourgeois' to 'bureaucrat bourgeois' positions. They also claimed that the Ba'th Party had been intimidated by the ICP's capabilities after its Third Congress in 1976.[179]

[179] 'Taqyim Tajribat Hizbina', pp. 49–50.

Fig. 12. Fleeing the terror of Saddamist Iraq. Members of the party leadership in Iraqi Kurdistan in the early 1980s. From right to left: First Secretary 'Aziz Muhammad, candidate member of the Central Committee Yusuf Hanna, and members of the Politburo Baqer Ibrahim al-Musawi and Karim Ahmad al-Daud.

Still, they argued, the alliance with the Ba'th had been the first of its kind in history and they had entered it 'with unshaken confidence'. The alliance, in hindsight, had been a 'class battle' that had taught the party a lot.[180] Characteristically, the ICP refused to think that its theory on 'revolutionary democrats' had been wrong. Instead, it was the Ba'th Party's fault for not having fitted the theoretical mould. In a revealing assessment they established that the Iraqi Ba'th Party:

[180] Ibid., p. 38.

was not one of those revolutionary democratic parties that are liberated from enmity towards democracy and Communism, which lead the political power and during the class struggle in the stage of national-democratic revolution refrains from its ideological positions that are linked to the special property of the means of production and the exploitation of power; [parties] influenced by the ideas and the role of the working class and its Marxist-Leninist party, and by the victories of international socialism; [parties that] embrace the characteristic of the age—i.e. the transition from capitalism to socialism in the international sphere. These groups abandon their origins and petty bourgeois positions and change their positions to those of the working class and adopt Marxism-Leninism and the international proletariat and progress with the national-democratic revolution to its end with the transition to the socialist revolution.[181]

It is thus clear that the original ideological assessment of the Ba'th Party, describing it as a 'revolutionary democratic' party, was what ultimately caused the disastrous demise of the ICP.

From this point onwards, the Iraqi Communist Party was forced to go underground and many party members had to flee abroad. This situation essentially remained unchanged until Saddam Husayn himself was forcibly removed by the 2003 Anglo-American invasion, following which the ICP managed to re-appear on the Iraqi political scene in a significantly weakened shape. Yet, as a political organisation capable of changing the course of Iraqi history its role had undoubtedly ended during those ominous days in 1979.

[181] Ibid., pp. 40–41.

CONCLUSION

The Iraqi Communist Party stands out as arguably the most important political organisation in the Middle East never to have attained state power. Its immense impact on the course of modern Iraqi and Middle Eastern history is beyond doubt. From its founding in 1934 until its organisational and ideological demise in the face of Ba'thi persecution in 1979, the ICP constituted one of the key political players in Iraq and influenced politics in a myriad of ways.

This period also essentially marked the rise and fall of ideological politics in Iraq. From the 1940s, the old politics based on patrimonialism and patron-client relations started to crumble. Now instead politics based on ideas became the common practice. Thus, not only the ICP but also other political groupings and constellations—Nasirists, Iraqists, Ba'thists, Istiqlalists, Free Officers, and so on—were guided in their political action by ideologies. During this period, these groups changed the course of Iraqi history through political conviction, thus giving evidence to the role of human agency and ideas in history.

The main change that brought about the rise of the communists and the other political actors, however, was undeniably of a structural nature. Changing patterns of ideology production had occurred with the introduction of modern secular education with its separation from the control of the religious classes (the *'ulama'*). This had allowed for the rise of a new socio-political group—the intelligentsia. Unattached to traditional loyalties, and increasingly relying on the state for livelihood rather than at the service of private interests, this group was exceptionally susceptible to new ideas, theories and ideologies promoting supra-sectarian loyalties to the state (Iraqism), the nation (pan-Arabism, pan-Kurdism) or the international proletariat (communism). In this manner, they became revolutionary intellectuals working for the radical transformation of society.

These intellectuals were equally instrumental in the formation of a new political culture during this period. Whilst an 'Iraqi' culture had been precariously constructed by the elites of the new state following the formation of the Iraqi mandate in 1920, its nature was tenuous and conflicting loyalties existed among Iraq's diverse constituent parts. With the rise of the new intelligentsia over the course of the 1940s and 1950s a new political culture emerged in the intersection of traditional culture and the syncretisation of communist, socialist and nationalist ideas with these intellectuals as cultural intermediaries. As bearers of both traditionalism and radicalism, they fused ideas of new and old and produced a distinctly different political culture.

The case of the ICP serves as a good example of how political ideas shape and are shaped by the culture in which they emerge and develop. Iraqi communism developing in these circumstances in the 1940s was as much 'Iraqi' as foreign, and had as much indigenous roots as Iraqist nationalism or Iraqi pan-Arabism. True, the 'foundational' ideas of this type of communism stemmed not from within Iraq but from nineteenth century Europe and early-twentieth century Russia, but the political milieu that allowed them to firmly take root in Iraqi soil and the communist intellectuals that made sure they did so were thoroughly 'Iraqi' in make-up and constitution. As with pan-Arabism, the originating ideas lay outside Iraq, but the driving forces were Iraqi, and the resulting fusion of ideas thus made for a uniquely local blend. In other words, communism or pan-Arabism as practiced in Iraq was not a mirror image of communism or pan-Arabism practised in Egypt or Syria or elsewhere. What is even more important, the type of communism or pan-Arabism that saw daylight in Iraq in the early parts of the twentieth century were not the same ideologies that later emerged out of the convergencies of these political belief systems over the course of the 1960s and 1970s. Thus, the Iraqi communists turned distinctively 'nationalist', accommodating pan-Arabist (*qawmi*), Iraqist nationalist (*watani*) as well as pan-Kurdist (*qawmi*) ideas, as their ideology developed into a fused 'communist nationalism', whereas the pan-Arabists took onboard large chunks of the communist political imagery as their ideology fused into 'Arab Socialism'.

The Iraqi Communist Party was also markedly different from the other political parties bourgeoning at the same time in that it was highly organised and institutionalised. From the mid-1940s, it emerged as an independent, self-sustaining political organisation with a clearly defined political ideology of its own. Not only were firm structures erected and organisational discipline implemented but also, importantly, the production of ideology became professionalised. Thus, over the course of the 1940s and 1950s, but above all following the 1958 Revolution, a small number of communist intellectuals developed into a group of professional revolutionaries sustained by and fully devoted to the Communist Party. These intellectuals were thus cut off from traditional society and acted from an independent platform, which allowed them to become more radical than any other group in Iraqi society. Yet, over time, this institutionalisation developed into caution and conservatism as dependency on the party meant they were reluctant to pursue policies that might jeopardise the safety of the party and thus their own positions, as clearly shown in Chapters 4 and 5.

In the end, it was the political and ideological *successes* of the Iraqi Communist Party that caused its ultimate downfall. The fact that it had a better political, social, economic and ideological organisation than any other party in Iraq and the fact that it drew support from all corners of Iraqi society—from Sunnis, Shi'is, Kurds, Arabs, Chaldeans, Turkmen, Assyrians, Faylis, workers, peasants, intellectuals, etc.—made it an organisation to fear and envy and to copy and emulate for other groups. Thus, the Free Officers that pulled the military coup which ended the monarchy in 1958 was modelled organisationally on the ICP. Copying communist practices, the Free Officers operated from the basis of small cells and were fiercely clandestine, something that undoubtedly provided the necessary element of surprise in its military operation on 14 July.

Similarly, the Iraqi Ba'th Party not only copied the organisational set-up of the ICP but also sought to emulate most other aspects of the successful approach of the communists. Thus, when first ascending to power through the bloody overthrow of Qasim in 1963, the Ba'thists seemingly tried to physically eradicate the ICP from the Iraqi political scene—an endeavour that ultimately failed. The second time around, however, the Ba'thist approach was different (and arguably more lethal). Now the Ba'thists aimed at luring the communists into a political alliance by virtue of assimilation of (parts of) its policies, something that eventually proved more successful. The national front that was established between the Ba'th Party and the ICP in 1973 proved to be the real undoing of the communists, because not only did it give Saddam Husayn and the other Ba'thist leaders an opportunity to unravel all the hitherto fiercely guarded communist party secrets but, importantly, it discredited the ICP in the eyes of the general public. Thus, when Saddam Husayn ultimately ended the alliance after having usurped all the powers of the state in 1979, the Iraqi Communist Party had effectively expended its role. At this point, there was no longer any room for manoeuvre in the political system that had gradually been implemented by Saddam—a system in which political ideology could no longer shape the course of politics.

BIBLIOGRAPHY

Archival Material

The National Archives (TNA): Public Records Office (PRO)
FO 624; FO 209; FO 371

Works in English

Abu Jaber, Kamel S., *The Arab Ba'th Socialist Party: History, Ideology, and Organization*, Syracuse, NY: Syracuse University Press, 1966.

Agwani, M.S., *Communism in the Arab East*. Bombay: Asia Publishing House, 1969.

Arab Ba'th Socialist Party, *The 1968 Revolution in Iraq: Experience and Prospects*. The Political Report of the Eight Congress of the Arab Ba'th Socialist Party in Iraq, January 1974. Translated by the Ministry of Information, Baghdad, Iraq. London: Ithaca Press, 1979.

———, 'Decisions of the Sixth National Convention of the Arab Ba'th Socialist Party, 1963'. Printed in *al-Nahar*, 29 Oct. 1963. Translated and reproduced in Kamel S. Abu Jaber. *The Arab Ba'th Socialist Party: History, Ideology, and Organization*, pp. 157–165. Syracuse, NY: Syracuse University Press, 1966.

Aziz, T. M., 'The Role of Muhammad Baqir al-Sadr in Shii Political Activism in Iraq from 1958 to 1980', *International Journal of Middle East Studies* 25, no. 2, May 1993, pp. 207–222.

Baram, Amatzia, *Culture, History & Ideology in the Formation of Ba'thist Iraq, 1968–89*, New York: St. Martin's Press, 1991.

———, 'A Case of Imported Identity: The Modernizing Secular Ruling Elites of Iraq and the Concept of Mesopotamian-Inspired Territorial Nationalism, 1922–1992', *Poetics Today* 15, no. 2, 1994, pp. 279–319.

———, 'The Ruling Political Elite in Bathi Iraq, 1968–1986: The Changing Features of a Collective Profile', *International Journal of Middle East Studies* 21, no. 4, Nov. 1989, pp. 447–493.

Barnett, Michael, 'Sovereignty, Nationalism, and Regional Order in the Arab states System', in *State Sovereignty as Social Construct*, Thomas J. Biersteker and Cynthia Weber (eds), Cambridge: Cambridge University Press, 1996, pp. 479–510.

Bashkin, Orit, *The Other Iraq: Pluralism and Culture in Hashemite Iraq*, Stanford, California: Stanford University Press, 2009.

Batatu, Hanna, *The Old Social Classes and the Revolutionary Movements of Iraq: A Study of Iraq's Old Landed and Commercial Classes and of its Communists, Ba'thists and Free Officers*, Princeton: Princeton University Press, 1978. Reprint, *n.p.*: Saqi Books, 2004.

Beeley, Brian W., 'The Turkish Village Coffeehouse as a Social Institution', *Geographical Review* 60, no. 4, Oct. 1970, pp. 475–493.

Beinin, Joel, *Was the Red Flag Flying There?: Marxist Politics and the Arab-Israeli Conflict in Egypt and Palestine, 1948–1965*, London: I.B. Tauris, 1990.

Bengio, Ofra, *Saddam's Word: Political Discourse in Iraq*, New York: Oxford University Press, 1998.

Brunner, Rainer and Werner Ende (eds), *The Twelver Shia in Modern Times: Religious Culture & Political History*, Leiden: Brill, 2001.

Caractacus (pseud.), *Revolution in Iraq: An Essay in Comparative Public Opinion*, London: Victor Gollancz, 1959.

Carrère d'Encausse, Hélène, *La Politique Soviétique au Moyen-Orient 1955–1975*, Paris: Presses de la Fondation nationale des sciences politiques, 1975.

Communist Party of China, *Long Live Leninism*. Originally published as an editorial in *Hongqi* [Red Flag] 8, 16 Apr. 1960, *n.p.*: Foreign Languages Press, 1960.

Confino, Michael and Shimon Shamir (eds), *The U.S.S.R. and the Middle East*, New Brunswick, NJ: Transaction, 1973.

Daniel, Norman, 'Contemporary Perceptions of the Revolution in Iraq on 14 July 1958', in *The Iraqi Revolution of 1958: The Old Social Classes Revisited*, Robert A. Fernea and Wm. Roger Louis (eds), London: I.B. Tauris, 1991, pp. 1–30.

Dann, Uriel, *Iraq under Qassem: A Political History, 1958–1963*, Praeger: Pall Mall, 1969.

Davis, Eric, *Memories of State: Politics, History, and Collective Identity in Modern Iraq*, Berkeley, CA: University of California Press, 2005.

Dawn, C. Ernest, 'From Ottomanism to Arabism: The Origin of an Ideology', in *From Ottomanism to Arabism: Essays on the Origins of Arab Nationalism*, Chicago: University of Illinois Press, 1973.

———, 'The Formation of Pan-Arab Ideology in the Interwar Years', *International Journal of Middle East Studies* 20, no. 1, Feb. 1988, pp. 67–91.

Dodge, Toby, *Inventing Iraq: The Failure of Nation Building and a History Denied*, London: C. Hurst & Co., 2003.

Eppel, Michael, *The Palestine Conflict in the History of Modern Iraq: The Dynamics of Involvement 1928–1948*, Ilford: Frank Cass, 1994.

———, 'The Elite, the Effendiyya, and the Growth of Nationalism and Pan-Arabism in Hashemite Iraq, 1921–1958', *International Journal of Middle East Studies* 30, no. 2, May 1998, pp. 227–250.

Eskander, Saad, 'Britain's Policy in Southern Kurdistan: The Formation and the Termination of the First Kurdish Government, 1918–1919', *British Journal of Middle Eastern Studies* 27, no. 2, Nov. 2000, pp. 139–163.

Farouk-Sluglett, Marion and Peter Sluglett. 'The Social Classes and the Origins of the Revolution', in *The Iraqi Revolution of 1958: The Old Social Classes Revisited*, ed. Robert A. Fernea and Wm. Roger Louis (eds), London: I.B. Tauris, 1991, pp. 118–141.

———, *Iraq since 1958: From Revolution to Dictatorship*, London: I.B. Tauris, 2001.

Fernea, Robert A. and Wm. Roger Louis (eds), *The Iraqi Revolution of 1958: The Old Social Classes Revisited*, London: I.B.Tauris, 1991.

Franzén, Johan, 'Communism versus Zionism: The Comintern, Yishuvism, and the Palestine Communist Party', *Journal of Palestine Studies* 36, no. 2, 2007, pp. 6–24.

———, 'Education and the Radicalization of Iraqi Politics: Britain, the Iraqi Communist Party, and the "Russian Link", 1941–1949', *International Journal of Contemporary Iraqi Studies* 2, no. 1, Jun. 2008, pp. 99–113.

———, 'Development vs. Reform: Attempts at Modernisation During the Twilight of British Influence in Iraq, 1946–58', *The Journal of Imperial and Commonwealth History* 37, no. 1, 2009, pp. 77–98.

———, 'Losing Hearts and Minds in Iraq: Britain, Cold War Propaganda and the Challenge of Communism, 1945-58', *Historical Research* 83, no. 222, Nov. 2010, pp. 747–762.

Gabbay, Rony, *Communism and Agrarian Reform in Iraq*, London: Croom Helm, 1978.

Gallman, Waldemar J., *Iraq under General Nuri: My Recollections of Nuri al-Said, 1954–1958*, Baltimore: Johns Hopkins University Press, 1964.

Haddad, Mahmoud, 'The Rise of Arab Nationalism Reconsidered', *International Journal of Middle East Studies* 26, no. 2, May 1994, pp. 201–222.

Haithcox, John Patrick, *Communism and Nationalism in India: M.N. Roy and Comintern Policy 1920–1939*, Bombay: Oxford University Press, 1971.

Haj, Samira, *The Making of Iraq, 1900–1963: Capital, Power, and Ideology*, Albany: State University of New York Press, 1997.

Hosseinzadeh, Esmail, *Soviet Non-Capitalist Development: The Case of Nasser's Egypt*, New York: Praeger, 1989.

Hourani, Albert, *Arabic Thought in the Liberal Age 1798–1939*, *n.p.*: Oxford University Press, 1962. Reissued, with a new preface, *n.p.*: Cambridge University Press, 1983. Reprint, 1998.

Ismael, Tareq Y., *The Communist Movement in the Arab World*, London: Routledge, 2005.

———, *The Rise and Fall of the Communist Party of Iraq*, Cambridge: Cambridge University Press, 2008.

Karsh, Efraim and Inari Rautsi, *Saddam Hussein: A Political Biography*, New York: Grove Press, 1991.

Kaylani, Nabil M., 'The Rise of the Syrian Ba'th, 1940–1958: Political Success, Party Failure', *International Journal of Middle East Studies* 3, no. 1, Jan. 1972, pp. 3–23.

Khadduri, Majid, *Independent Iraq 1932–1958: A Study in Iraqi Politics*, 2nd ed. London: Oxford University Press, 1960.

———, *Republican 'Iraq: A Study in 'Iraqi Politics since the Revolution of 1958*, London: Oxford University Press, 1969.

———, *Socialist Iraq: A Study in Iraqi Politics since 1968*, Washington DC: Middle East Institute, 1978.

Kienle, Eberhard, *Ba'th v. Ba'th: The Conflict between Syria and Iraq 1968–1989*, London: I.B. Tauris, 1990.

Laqueur, Walter, *Communism and Nationalism in the Middle East*, London: Routledge, 1956.

Lenin, Vladimir I., 'Left-Wing Communism: an Infantile Disorder', written Mar.-Apr. 1920, in *Collected Works* 31, Moscow: Progress Publishers, 1964, pp. 17–118.

———, 'The Right of Nations to Self-Determination', in *Selected Works* 1, Moscow: Progress Publishers, 1963, pp. 595–665.

———, 'Preliminary Draft Theses on the National and the Colonial Questions', written 28 Jul. 1920, in *Theses, Resolutions and Manifestos of the First Four Congresses of the Third International*, Alan Adler (ed), Alix Holt and Barbara Holland (trans.), 2nd ed., London: Pluto Press, 1983, pp. 76–81.

Louis, Wm. Roger, *The British Empire in the Middle East 1945–1951: Arab Nationalism, The United States, and Postwar Imperialism*, Oxford: Clarendon Press, 1984. Reprint, 1998.

———'Britain and the crisis of 1958' in *A Revolutionary Year: the Middle East in 1958*, Wm. Roger Louis and Roger Owen (eds), London & New York: I. B. Tauris, 2002, pp. 15–76.

Louis, Wm. Roger and Roger Owen (eds), *A Revolutionary Year: the Middle East in 1958*, Wm. Roger Louis and Roger Owen (eds), London & New York: I. B. Tauris, 2002.

Lovat, François-Xavier, *Kurdistan Democratic Party, n.p.*: G.I.D. Editions, 1999.

Mann, Michael, *States, War and Capitalism: Studies in Political Sociology*, Oxford: Blackwell, 1988.

Marr, Phebe, *The Modern History of Iraq*. 2nd ed. *n.p.*: Westview Press, 2004.

McDowall, David, *A Modern History of the Kurds*, 2nd ed., London: I.B. Tauris, 2000.

Naef, Silvia, 'Shi'i-Shuyu'i or: How to Become a Communist in a Holy City', in *The Twelver Shia in Modern Times: Religious Culture & Political History*, Rainer Brunner and Werner Ende (eds), Leiden: Brill, 2001, pp. 255–267.

Owen, Roger, 'Class and Class Politics in Iraq before 1958: The "Colonial and Post-Colonial State"', in *The Iraqi Revolution of 1958: The Old Social Classes Revisited*, Robert A. Fernea and Wm. Roger Louis (eds), London: I.B. Tauris, 1991, pp. 154–171.

Özoğlu, Hakan, '"Nationalism" and Kurdish Notables in the Late Ottoman-Early Republican Era', *International Journal of Middle East Studies* 33, no. 3, Aug. 2001, pp. 383–409.

Penrose, Edith and E. F. Penrose, *Iraq: International Relations and National Development*, London: Westview Press, 1978.

Pfaff, Richard F., 'The Function of Arab Nationalism', *Comparative Politics* 2, no. 2, Jan. 1970, pp. 147–167.

Podeh, Elie, *The Quest for Hegemony in the Arab World: the Struggle over the Baghdad Pact*, Leiden: Brill, 1995.

Pool, David, 'The Politics of Patronage: Elites and Social Structure in Iraq', Ph.D. diss., Princeton University, Ann Arbor: U.M.I. Dissertation Services, 1972.

———, 'From Elite to Class: The Transformation of Iraqi Political Leadership', in *The Integration of Modern Iraq*, Abbas Kelidar (ed), London: Croom Helm, 1979, pp. 63–87.

Porath, Yehoshua, *In Search of Arab Unity 1930–1945*, London: Frank Cass, 1986.

Radwan, Samir, *Agrarian Reform and Rural Poverty, Egypt, 1952–1975*, Geneva: International Labour Office, 1977.

Schoenberger, Erica and Stephanie Reich, 'Soviet Policy in the Middle East', *MERIP Reports*, no. 39, Jul. 1975, pp. 3–28.

Shawkat, Sami, 'The Profession of Death', in *Arab Nationalism: An Anthology*, Sylvia Haim (ed), Berkeley: University of California Press, 1962, pp. 97–99.

Shemesh, Haim, *Soviet-Iraqi Relations, 1968–1988: In the Shadow of the Iraq-Iran Conflict*, London: Lynne Rienner, 1992.

Simon, Reeva S., 'The Hashemite "Conspiracy": Hashemite Unity Attempts, 1921–1958', *International Journal of Middle East Studies* 5, no. 3, Jun. 1974, pp. 314–327

———, *Iraq Between the Two World Wars: The Militarist Origins of Tyranny*, 2nd ed., New York: Columbia University Press, 2004.

Sluglett, Peter, *Britain in Iraq, 1914–1932*, London: Ithaca Press for the Middle East Centre, St Antony's College, Oxford, 1976.

———, 'From the Politics of Notables to the Politics of Parliamentary Government: Iraq 1918–1932', Paper presented at the Sixth Mediterranean Social and Political Research Meeting of the Mediterranean Programme of the Robert Schuman Centre for Advanced Studies at the European University Institute, Montecatini Terme, Mar. 2005.

Smith, Charles D., *Palestine and the Arab-Israeli Conflict*, 4th ed. Boston: Bedford/St. Martin's, 2001.

Smolansky, Oles M., *The Soviet Union and the Arab East under Khrushchev*, Lewisburg, PA: Bucknell University Press, 1974.

Smolansky, Oles M. and Bettie M. Smolansky, *The USSR and Iraq: the Soviet Quest for Influence*, Durham, NC: Duke University Press, 1991.

Stork, Joe, 'The Soviet Union, the Great Powers and Iraq', in *The Iraqi Revolution of 1958: The Old Social Classes Revisited*, Robert A. Fernea and Wm. Roger Louis (eds), London: I.B. Tauris, 1991, pp. 95–105.

Styan, David, *France and Iraq: Oil, Arms and French Policy Making in the Middle East*, London: I. B. Tauris, 2005.

Swanson, John R., 'The Soviet Union and the Arab World: Revolutionary Progress through Dependence on Local Elites', *The Western Political Quarterly* 27, no. 4, Dec. 1974, pp. 637–656.

Tarbush, Mohammad A., *The Role of the Military in Politics: A Case Study of Iraq to 1941*, London: KPI, 1982.

Trevelyan, Humprey, *The Middle East in Revolution*, London: Macmillan, 1970.

Tripp, Charles, *A History of Iraq*, Cambridge: Cambridge University Press, 2000.

———, 'Iraq and the 1948 War: Mirror of Iraq's Disorder', in *The War for Palestine: Rewriting the History of 1948*, Eugene L. Rogan and Avi Shlaim (eds), Cambridge: Cambridge University Press, 2001, pp. 125–150.

Ulam, Adam B., *Expansion and Coexistence: Soviet Foreign Policy, 1917–73*, 2nd ed, New York: Praeger Publishers, 1974.

Vinogradov, Amal, 'The 1920 Revolt in Iraq Reconsidered: The Role of Tribes in National Politics', *International Journal of Middle East Studies* 3, no. 2, Apr. 1972, pp. 123–139.

Wien, Peter, 'The Youth and the Nation: Generational Conflict as a Trigger of National Consciousness in Iraq during the 1930s', paper presented at the Sixth Mediterranean Social and Political Research Meeting of the Mediterranean Programme of the Robert Schuman Centre for Advanced Studies at the European University Institute, Montecatini Terme, Mar. 2005.

———, *Iraqi Arab Nationalism: Authoritarian, Totalitarian, and Pro-Fascist Inclinations, 1932–1941*, SOAS/Routledge Studies on the Middle East, London and New York: Routledge, 2006.

Yaqub, Salim, *Containing Arab Nationalism: the Eisenhower Doctrine and the Middle East*, Chapel Hill, N.C.: University of North Carolina Press, 2004.

Yousif, Abdul-Salaam, 'The Struggle for Cultural Hegemony during the Iraqi Revolution', in *The Iraqi Revolution of 1958: The Old Social Classes Revisited*,

Robert A Fernea and Wm. Roger Luis (eds), London: I.B. Tauris, 1991, pp. 172–196.

Zubaida, Sami, 'Community, Class and Minorities in Iraqi Politics', in *The Iraqi Revolution of 1958: The Old Social Classes Revisited*, Robert A Fernea and Wm. Roger Luis (eds), London: I.B. Tauris, 1991, pp. 197–210.

Works in Arabic

'Abd al-Karim, Samir, *Adwa' 'ala l-Harakah al-Shuyu'iyyah fi l-'Iraq* (Light on the communist movement in Iraq), 5 vols., Beirut: Dar al-Mirsad, *n.d.*

'Abd al-Nasir, Jamal, *Nahnu wa l-'Iraq wa l-Shuyu'iyyah* (We, Iraq and communism), Beirut: Dar al-Nashr al-'Arabiyyah, [1959].

———, 'Qasim al-'Iraq (The divider of Iraq)', speech given in Damascus on 11 Mar. 1959, in *Nahnu wa l-'Iraq wa l-Shuyu'iyyah*, Beirut: Dar al-Nashr al-'Arabiyyah, [1959], pp. 57–61.

———, 'Irhab al-Shuyu'iyyin (The communists' terror)', speech given at an anti-communist demonstration in Damascus on 12 Mar. 1959, in *Nahnu wa l-'Iraq wa l-Shuyu'iyyah*, Beirut: Dar al-Nashr al-'Arabiyyah, [1959], pp. 63–67.

———, 'al-Hiqd al-Aswad (Black hatred)', speech given in Damascus on 13 Mar. 1959, in *Nahnu wa l-'Iraq wa l-Shuyu'iyyah*, Beirut: Dar al-Nashr al-'Arabiyyah, [1959], pp. 69–80.

———, 'Sa-Naqdi 'Ala al-Diktaturiyyah al-Hamra'! (We will exterminate the red dictatorship!)', speech given at a military manoeuvre in Syria on 14 Mar. 1959, in *Nahnu wa l-'Iraq wa l-Shuyu'iyyah*, Beirut: Dar al-Nashr al-'Arabiyyah, [1959], pp. 81–86.

———, 'Dimuqratiyyat al-Irhab wa l-Mashaniq (The democracy of terror and of the gallows)', speech given at a rally in Syria on 15 Mar. 1959, in *Nahnu wa l-'Iraq wa l-Shuyu'iyyah*, Beirut: Dar al-Nashr al-'Arabiyyah, [1959], pp. 87–100.

———, 'Kunna Wahdana (We were alone)', speech given at a rally outside the presidential palace in Damascus on 16 Mar. 1959, in *Nahnu wa l-'Iraq wa l-Shuyu'iyyah*, Beirut: Dar al-Nashr al-'Arabiyyah, [1959], pp. 101–121.

'Aflaq, Michel, *Fi Sabil al-Ba'th* (On the path of resurrection), 12th printing, Beirut, 1959; Beirut: Dar al-Tali'ah li l-Taba'ah wa l-Nashr, 1974.

'Ajinah, Rahim, *al-Ikhtiyar al-Mutajaddad: Dhikriyat Shakhsiyyah wa Safahat min Masirat al-Hizb al-Shuyu'i al-'Iraqi* (The new selection: personal recollections and pages from the course of the Iraqi Communist Party), Beirut: Dar al-Kunuz al-Adabiyyah, 1998.

'Alaywi, Hadi Hasan, *al-Ittijahat al-Wahdawiyyah fi al-Fikr al-Qawmi al-'Arabi al-Mashriqi 1918–1952* (Unionist trends in eastern Arab nationalist thought 1918–1952), Silsilat Atruhat al-Dukturah (38), Beirut: Markaz Dirasat al-Wahdah al-'Arabiyyah, 2000.

'Ali, Muhammad Kazim, *al-'Iraq fi 'Ahd 'Abd al-Karim Qasim: Dirasah fi al-Quwa al-Siyasiyyah wa l-Sira' al-Aydiuluji 1958–1963* (Iraq in the age of 'Abd al-Karim Qasim: a study of the political forces and the ideological struggle 1958–1963), Baghdad: Maktabat al-Yaqzah al-'Arabiyyah, 1989.

'Aref, 'Abd al-Salam, *Mudhakkirat al-Ra'is al-Rahil 'Abd al-Salam 'Aref* (The memoirs of late president 'Abd al-Salam 'Aref, Baghdad: Sharikat al-Tab' wa l-Nashr al-Ahliyyah, 1967.

al-Badrani, Fadil Muhammad Husayn, *al-Fikr al-Qawmi lada l-Ahzab wa l-Harakat al-Siyasiyyah fi l-'Iraq 1945–1958* (Nationalist thought amongst the political movements and parties in Iraq, 1945–1958), Silsilat Atruhat al-Dukturah (54), Beirut: Markaz Dirasat al-Wahdah al-'Arabiyyah, 2005.

al-Basri, Salim Isma'il, *al-Sira': Min Mudhakkirat Shuyu'i 'Iraqi* (The struggle: from the memoirs of an Iraqi communist), Damascus: al-Mada, 2006.

al-Chadirchi, Kamel, *Mudhakkirat Kamel al-Chadirchi wa Ta'rikh al-Hizb al-Watani al-Dimuqrati* (The memoirs of Kamel al-Chadirchi and the history of the National Democratic Party), Cologne: Manshurat al-Jamal, 2002.

Duglah, Saleh Mahdi, *Min al-Dhakirah: 'Sirat Hayat'* (From the memory: 'history of a life'), Damascus: Dar al-Mada, 2000.

Habib, Kazem, 'Reply to Questionnaire sent by Author', unpublished manuscript, Jan. 2006.

al-Hajj, 'Aziz, *Dhakirat al-Nakhil: Safahat min Ta'rikh al-Harakah al-Shuyu'iyyah fi l-'Iraq* (The memory of the date palm: pages from the history of the communist movement in Iraq), Beirut: al-Mu'assasah al-'Arabiyyah li l-Dirasat wa l-Nashr, 1993.

———, *Ma'a al-A'wam: Safahat min Ta'rikh al-Harakah al-Shuyu'iyyah fi l-'Iraq bayna 1958–1967* (With the years: pages from the history of the communist movement in Iraq between 1958–1967), Beirut: al-Mu'assasah al-'Arabiyyah li l-Dirasat wa l-Nashr, 1994.

———, *Shahadah li l-Ta'rikh: Awraq fi l-Sirah al-Dhatiyyah al-Siyasiyyah* (Witness to history: papers on the personal political conduct), London: al-Rafid, 2001.

al-Halwa'i, Jasem, *Dhikriyat* (Memoirs), unpublished manuscript, 2006.

———, 'Reply to a Questionnaire sent by Author', unpublished manuscript, Feb. 2006.

al-Hasani, 'Abd al-Razzaq. *Ta'rikh al-Wizarat al-'Iraqiyyah fi l-'Ahd al-Maliki* (History of the Iraqi cabinets in the monarchical period), 10 vols., *n.p.*: Dar al-Shu'un al-Thaqafiyyah, *n.d.*

Husayn, Khalil Ibrahim, *al-Sira'at bayna 'Abd al-Karim Qasim wa l-Shuyu'iyyin wa Rif'at al-Hajj Sirri wa l-Qawmiyyin* (The struggles between 'Abd al-Karim Qasim, the communists, Rif'at al-Hajj Sirri and the nationalists), Mawsu'at 14

Tammuz 2: Thawrat al-Shawwaf fi l-Mawsil. Baghdad: Dar al-Hurriyyah li l-Taba'ah, 1988.

al-Husri, Sati', *Abhath Mukhtarah fi al-Qawmiyyah al-'Arabiyyah 1923–1963* (Selected studies on Arab nationalism 1923–1963), 2 vols, Beirut: Dar al-Quds, [1974].

———, "Awamil al-Qawmiyyah (The factors of nationalism)'. From a lecture given at Nadi al-Mu'allimin in Baghdad, 1928, in *Abhath Mukhtarah fi al-Qawmiyyah al-'Arabiyyah 1923–1963*, vol. 1, Beirut: Dar al-Quds, [1974], pp. 37–56.

———, 'al-Wataniyyah wa l-Qawmiyyah', from lectures given at the Dar al-Mu'allimin al-'Aliyyah in Baghdad, in *Abhath Mukhtarah fi al-Qawmiyyah al-'Arabiyyah 1923–1963*, vol. 1, Beirut: Dar al-Quds, [1974], pp. 27–36.

Ibrahim, Baqer, *Safahat min al-Nidal: 'ala Tariq al-Tashih wa l-Tajdid wa l-Wahdah* (Pages from the struggle: on the path of correction, renewal and unity), Beirut: Dar al-Kunuz al-Adabiyyah, 1997.

———, *Mudhakkirat Baqer Ibrahim* (The memoirs of Baqer Ibrahim), Beirut: Dar al-Tali'ah, 2002.

al-Ja'fari, Muhammad Hamdi, *Britaniya wa l-'Iraq: Hiqbah min al-Sira' 1914–1958* (Britain and Iraq: the age of struggle 1914–1958), Baghdad: Dar al-Shu'un al-Thaqafiyyah al-'Ammah, 2000.

Khayri, Zaki, *Sada al-Sinin fi Dhakirat Shuyu'i 'Iraqi Mukhadram* (Echo of the years in the memory of an old Iraqi communist), 2nd print, Gothenburg: Arabiska Bokstavscentret, 1996.

———, *Sada al-Sinin fi Kitabat Shuyu'i 'Iraqi Mukhadram* (Echo of the years in the writings of an old Iraqi communist), Stockholm: Ny Era, *n.d.*

Khaznadar, Shawkat, *Safar wa Mahattat: al-Hizb al-Shuyu'i al-'Iraqi… Ru'yah min al-Dakhil* (A journey and stopping places: the Iraqi Communist Party … a view from the inside), Beirut: Dar al-Kunuz al-Adabiyyah, 2005.

al-Kharsan, Salah, *Safahat min Ta'rikh al-'Iraq al-Siyasi al-Hadith: al-Harakat al-Marksiyyah 1920–1990* (Pages from the modern political history of Iraq: the Marxist movements 1920–1990), Beirut: Mu'assasat al-'Arif li l-Matbu'at, 2001.

Kojaman, Hesqil, *Thawrat 14 Tammuz 1958 fi l-'Iraq wa Siyasat al-Hizb al-Shuyu'i* (The 14 July 1958 revolution in Iraq and the policy of the Communist Party), Guildford, UK: Biddles, 1985.

———, *Dhikriyati fi Sujun al-'Iraq al-Siyasiyyah* (My memoirs in Iraq's political prisons), unpublished manuscript, 2002.

Kubbah, Muhammad Mahdi, *Mudhakkirati fi Samim al-Ahdath, 1918–1958* (My reminiscences at the heart of events, 1918–1958), Beirut: Dar al-Tali'ah, 1969.

Mahmud, Najm (pseud.), *al-Sira' fi l-Hizb al-Shuyu'i al-'Iraqi wa Qadaya l-Khilaf fi l-Harakah al-Shuyu'iyyah al-'Alamiyyah* (The struggle within the Iraqi Communist Party and the issues of disagreement within the world communist movement), Paris: *n.p.*, 1980.

al-Musawi, Ra'ad, *Intifadat Safar al-Islamiyyah fi l-'Iraq* (The Islamic Safar uprising in Iraq), Qom: Amir al-Mu'minin, 1983.

Nuri, Baha' al-Din, *Mudhakkirat Baha' al-Din Nuri: Sikritir al-Lajnah al-Markaziyyah li l-Hizb al-Shuyu'i al-'Iraqi* (The memoirs of Baha' al-Din Nuri: secretary of the Central Committee of the Iraqi Communist Party), London: Dar al-Hikmah, 2001.

Sa'id, 'Ali Karim, *al-'Iraq—al-Birriyyah al-Musallahah: Harakat Hasan Sari' wa Qitar al-Mawt 1963* (Iraq—the armed beret: the movement of Hasan Sari' and the death train 1963), Beirut: al-Furat, 2002.

al-Sa'id, Nuri, *Mudhakkirat Nuri al-Sa'id 'an al-Harakat al-'Askariyyah li l-Jaysh al-'Arabi fi al-Hijaz wa Suriya 1916–1918* (The reminiscences of Nuri al-Sa'id of the military movements of the Arab army in the Hejaz and Syria 1916–1918), Beirut: al-Dar al-'Arabiyyah li l-Mawsu'at, 1987.

Sbahi, 'Aziz, *'Uqud min Ta'rikh al-Hizb al-Shuyu'i al-'Iraqi* (Decades from the history of the Iraqi Communist Party), 3 vols., Damascus: Manshurat al-Thaqafah al-Jadidah, 2003.

al-Wakil, Fu'ad Husayn, *Jama'at al-Ahali fi l-'Iraq 1932–1937* (The Ahali group in Iraq 1932–1937), Baghdad: Dar al-Hurriyyah li l-Taba'ah, 1980.

Yusuf, Thaminah Naji and Nazzar Khaled, *Salam 'Adel: Sirat Munadil* (Salam 'Adel: biography of a fighter), 2 vols., Damascus: Dar al-Mada, 2001.

Newspapers, Organs and Magazines

al-Fikr al-Jadid. ICP weekly journal, published legally in Arabic and Kurdish 1972–79.

Hurriyat al-Watan. ICP journal aimed at political work in the Iraqi army, published illegally 1954–55.

Iraqi Review. English edition of ICP mouthpiece *Ittihad al-Sha'b*, published legally 1959–60.

Ittihad al-Sha'b. Principal ICP mouthpiece, published illegally 1956–1959, legally 1959–60.

al-Qa'idah. Principal ICP mouthpiece, published illegally 1943–56.

Risalat al-'Iraq. ICP political magazine, published in exile 1980–.

Tariq al-Sha'b. Principal ICP mouthpiece, published illegally 1961–71, legally 1973–79.

al-Thaqafah al-Jadidah. ICP cultural organ, published illegally in 1953, legally 1958–60 and illegally 1969–79.

World Marxist Review. English edition of *Problems of Peace and Socialism* (*Problemy Mira i Sotzializma*), international communist magazine published in various languages under the auspices of the Communist Party of the Soviet Union, published 1958–90.

Pamphlets, Reports and Manifestoes

'Adel, Salam (Husayn Ahmad al-Radi), *al-Burjuwaziyyah al-Wataniyyah fi l-'Iraq* (The national bourgeoisie in Iraq), in *Salam 'Adel: Sirat Munadil*, ed. Thaminah Naji Yusuf and Nazzar Khaled, vol. 1, Damascus: Dar al-Mada, 2001, pp. 305–337.

Fahad (Yusuf Salman Yusuf), *al-Batalah—Asbabuha wa 'Alajuha* (Unemployment—its causes and remedies), first printed in 1946, reprinted in 1954 and 1973, in *Kitabat al-Rafiq Fahad: Min Watha'iq al-Hizb al-Shuyu'i al-'Iraqi*, Beirut: Dar al-Farabi, 1976, pp. 185–216.

———, *Hizb Shuyu'i, La Ishtirakiyyah Dimuqratiyyah* (A communist party, not democratic socialism, in *Kitabat al-Rafiq Fahad: Min Watha'iq al-Hizb al-Shuyu'i al-'Iraqi*, Beirut: Dar al-Farabi, 1976, pp. 17–99.

———, 'al-Isti'mar al-Hadith (Modern imperialism)', first published on 6 Jun. 1946, in *Kitabat al-Rafiq Fahad: Min Watha'iq al-Hizb al-Shuyu'i al-'Iraqi*, Beirut: Dar al-Farabi, 1976, pp. 219–222.

———, 'al-Kifah al-Fikri (Ideological struggle)', first published on 6 Jun. 1946, in *Kitabat al-Rafiq Fahad: Min Watha'iq al-Hizb al-Shuyu'i al-'Iraqi*, Beirut: Dar al-Farabi, 1976, pp. 230–233.

———, *Kitabat al-Rafiq Fahad: Min Watha'iq al-Hizb al-Shuyu'i al-'Iraqi* (The writings of comrade Fahad: from the documents of the Iraqi Communist Party), Beirut: Dar al-Farabi, 1976.

———, 'Qadiyyatuna al-Wataniyyah: Taqrir Alqahu al-Rafiq Fahad Amam Mu'tamar (Kunfirans) al-Hizb al-Awwal 'Am 1944 (Our national cause: a report delivered by comrade Fahad before the party's first congress (conference) in 1944)', in *Kitabat al-Rafiq Fahad: Min Watha'iq al-Hizb al-Shuyu'i al-'Iraqi*, Beirut: Dar al-Farabi, 1976, pp. 101–132.

———, 'Taqrir al-Rafiq Fahad Hawla l-Wad' al-'Alami wa l-Dakhili: Alqahu fi l-Mu'tamar al-Watani al-Awwal li l-Hizb al-Shuyu'i al-'Iraqi (Comrade Fahad's report on the international and domestic situation: delivered at the First National Congress of the Iraqi Communist Party)', in *Kitabat al-Rafiq Fahad: Min Watha'iq al-Hizb al-Shuyu'i al-'Iraqi*, Beirut: Dar al-Farabi, 1976, pp. 141–150.

al-Hizb al-Shuyu'i al-'Iraqi (Iraqi Communist Party), *Fi Sabil al-Hurriyah al-Dimuqratiyyah, Fi Sabil al-Masalih al-Hayawiyyah li Jamahir al-Sha'b* (For the sake of democratic liberties, for the sake of the essential interests of the masses of the people), Jul. 1955.

———, *Fi Sabil Siyasah Wataniyyah 'Arabiyyah, Fi Sabil al-Hurriyat al-Dusturiyyah, Fi Sabil Inqadh Iqtisadina al-Watani wa Takhfif Mashakil al-Jamahir* (For the sake of a patriotic Arab policy, for the sake of constitutional liberties, for the sake of salvaging our national economy and easing the problems of the masses), in *al-Qa'idah* 12, no. 1, Nov. 1955.

———, *al-Hizb al-Shuyu'i al-'Iraqi wa l-Mas'alah al-Fallahiyyah: Min Watha'iq al-Hizb al-Shuyu'i al-'Iraqi* (The Iraqi Communist Party and the peasant question: from the documents of the Iraqi Communist Party), Baghdad: Manshurat al-Thaqafah al-Jadidah, 1974.

———, *Intifadat 1956 wa Mahammuna fi l-Waqt al-Rahin* (The 1956 uprising and our tasks at the present moment), May 1957.

———, *Jabhat al-Kifah al-Watani didd al-Isti'mar wa l-Harb* (The front of national struggle against imperialism and war), in *Salam 'Adel: Sirat Munadil*, Thaminah Naji Yusuf and Nazzar Khaled, vol. 1, Damascus: Dar al-Mada, 2001, pp. 57–62.

———, *Khittatuna al-Siyasiyyah fi Sabil al-Taharrur al-Watani wa l-Qawmi: Taqrir al-Lajnah al-Markaziyyah li l-Kunfirans al-Thani* (Our political plans for patriotic and national liberation: report of the Central Committee to the Second Conference), Baghdad: Sept. 1956.

———, *Min Ajli Jabhah Wataniyyah Muwahhadah Haqiqiyyah* (For a real united national front), in *Tariq al-Sha'b* 27, no. 7, Aug. 1970. Special Issue.

———, *Min Ajli Ta'ziz Wahdat al-Quwa al-Wataniyyah fi l-Difa' 'an al-Jumhuriyyah wa Makasib al-Thawrah* (For the sake of strengthening the unity of the national forces in the defence of the republic and the gains of the revolution). Report of the Central Committee of the Iraqi Communist Party, mid-July 1959, originally published in *Ittihad al-Sha'b*, 29 Aug. 1959, in *Salam 'Adel: Sirat Munadil*, Thaminah Naji Yusuf and Nazzar Khaled, vol. 2, Damascus: Dar al-Mada, 2001, pp. 505–553.

———, *al-Mithaq al-Watani li l-Hizb al-Shuyu'i al-'Iraqi* (The national charter of the Iraqi Communist Party), in *Kitabat al-Rafiq Fahad: Min Watha'iq al-Hizb al-Shuyu'i al-'Iraqi*, Beirut: Dar al-Farabi, 1976, pp. 133–37.

———, 'al-Nizam al-Dakhili li l-Hizb al-Shuyu'i al-'Iraqi (The internal system of the Iraqi Communist Party)', in *Kitabat al-Rafiq Fahad: Min Watha'iq al-Hizb al-Shuyu'i al-'Iraqi*, Beirut: Dar al-Farabi, 1976, pp. 151–183.

———, *Report of the Central Committee to the Second National Congress of the Iraqi Communist Party. n.p.*: Iraqi Communist Party: *n.d.*

———, 'Report of the Central Committee to the 3rd National Congress of the Iraqi Communist Party', in *The 3rd National Congress of the Iraqi Communist Party*, 4–6 May 1976, special Issue of *Iraqi Letter* 4.5, *n.p.*: Iraqi Communist Party: 1976, pp. 9–117.

———, *Shuhada' al-Hizb, Shuhada' al-Watan 1934–1963* (Martyrs of the party, martyrs of the homeland 1934–1963), Beirut: Dar al-Kunuz al-Adabiyyah, 2001.

———, 'al-Taqrir al-Siyasi al-ladhi Aqarrahu al-Mu'tamar al-Watani al-Thani li l-Hizb al-Shuyu'i al-'Iraqi (The political report that the second national congress of the Iraqi Communist Party affirmed)', in *Tariq al-Sha'b* 27, no. 9, Oct. 1970.

———, *Taqyim Tajribat Hizbina al-Nidaliyyah li l-Sanawat 1968–1979* (Appraisal of our party's struggle experience for the years 1968–1979), affirmed by the Fourth National Congress of the Iraqi Communist Party, 10–15 Nov. 1985, *n.p.*: Iraqi Communist Party: *n.d.*

———, 'The National Charter of the Iraqi Communist Party', in *Iraqi Review* 1, no. 22, 18 Jan. 1960.

———, *The 3rd National Congress of the Iraqi Communist Party*, 4–6 May 1976, Special Issue of *Iraqi Letter* 4.5, *n.p.*: Iraqi Communist Party: 1976.

al-Shabibi, Husayn Muhammad, Foreword to *Hizb Shuyu'i, La Ishtirakiyyah Dimuqratiyyah*, by Fahad, in *Kitabat al-Rafiq Fahad: Min Watha'iq al-Hizb al-Shuyu'i al-'Iraqi*, Beirut: Dar al-Farabi, 1976, pp. 17–30.

———, *al-Jabhah al-Wataniyyah al-Muwahhadah Tariquna wa Wajibuna al-Ta'rikhi* (The united national front is our historical path and duty), in *Kitabat al-Rafiq Husayn Muhammad al-Shabibi: Min Watha'iq al-Hizb al-Shuyu'i al-'Iraqi*, Baghdad: Matba'at al-Sha'b, 1974, pp. 1–70.

———, *Kitabat al-Rafiq Husayn Muhammad al-Shabibi: Min Watha'iq al-Hizb al-Shuyu'i al-'Iraqi* (The writings of comrade Husayn Muhammad al-Shabibi: from the documents of the Iraqi Communist Party), Baghdad: Matba'at al-Sha'b, 1974.

INDEX